KU-720-792

SCOTLAND

THE COMPLETE GUIDE

By

SHARMA KRAUSKOPF

The Globe Pequot Press

APPLETREE PRESS

First published in 1999 by The Appletree Press Ltd
The Old Potato Station, 14 Howard Street South,
Belfast BT7 1AP
Tel: +44 (0) 28 90 243074 Fax: +44 (0) 28 90 246756
E-mail: reception@appletree.ie
Web Site: www.appletree.ie

Text © The Appletree Press Ltd, 1999.
Photographs © The Still Moving Picture Company, 1999.

All rights reserved. Printed in China. No part of this publication may be
reproduced or transmitted in any form or by any means electronic or
mechanical, photocopying recording or in any information and retrieval
system, without prior permission in writing from the publishers.

The information given in this book is believed to be correct at the time of
printing. However, the publisher cannot accept responsibility for any loss,
injury or inconvenience sustained as a result of information contained in it.

Acknowledgements:
This book is dedicated to Robert, Margaret, Sarah and Jenny Macdonald who
taught the author to love and respect Scotland. The author thanks the Scottish
Tourist Board for their assistance with travel details, information onthe local
tourist boards and suggestions for the tours. The author also thanks the
web site Stone Pages (http://www.stonepages.com) for detailed information
on stone monuments in Scotland.

A catalogue record for this book is available from The British Library.

ISBN 0-86281-755-2

704006
MORAY COUNCIL
DEPARTMENT OF TECHNICAL
& LEISURE SERVICES
941.1

CONTENTS

INTRODUCTION

Scotland is a land of magnificent beauty with awe-inspiring coastlines, heather-cloaked Highlands, gleaming lochs, elegant castles, ancient ruins, picturesque villages, and impressive cities. With only five million people the country still echoes with the cries of its long, tormented, and complex history. Scotland has struggled to survive down the centuries: from the north came the Vikings, from the south stormed the English, and from inside its own borders proud clans fought each other for territory and power. A plaid-garbed Highlander running through the mist to slay the invading southerner is still a familiar cultural image - think of Rob Roy and Braveheart. Ancient ruins, some over 5,000 years old, speak to mysteries surrounding the people who created them.

Worldwide ties to Scotland are strong. Highland games and Burns Night Suppers are held in many countries, while Celtic music is popular everywhere. The people who hear the call of Scotland from around the world have what is known as a Celtic Soul. It is for you that this guide is written.

While much of Scotland's romance and beauty remain largely unaffected by modern developments, good roads and exceptional public transportation make it easy to reach the most spectacular sights. Places of historic interest are well signposted and local tourist boards are extremely helpful to visitors. Scotland's cities boast fine historic buildings, modern shopping facilities and gourmet restaurants. Modern Scotland is alive with a sense of opportunity, especially now as it own parliament meets for the first time since 1707.

This guidebook introduces you to the beauty and history of Scotland, but be sure to meet the people: although they may be descended from warriors, Scots are friendly, gentle, and kind. It is they who really make Scotland special.

HISTORY

Standing stones, brochs, cairns and burial chambers are evidence of Scotland's earliest inhabitants. When the Romans invaded in AD 82, they found a people whom they called the Picts or "Painted Ones." No matter how hard they tried, the Romans could not conquer the Picts, so they resorted to building Hadrian's Wall to keep them out of Roman territory.

The Dalriad Irish – called Scots – successfully attacked the Picts in AD 500

Facing page: Kinloch Castle, Isle of Rum
© Robert Lees/ The Still Moving Picture Company

> **Scotland is the country above all others that I have seen, in which a man of imagination may carve out his own pleasures; there are so many inhabited solitudes.**
>
> Dorothy Wordsworth
> Taken from
> *A Little Book of Scottish Quotations*
> published by Appletree Press

and settled the Argyll Peninsula. Intermarriage between the Scots and the Picts, together with the inward migration of Britons from the south and Norsemen from the north, created a new people. The mysterious nature-worshiping Druids were active at the time and many of their artefacts – among them, runic etchings and stone circles – still exist today. The mix of languages spoken by these peoples included Celtic, Norse, Low German and Saxon English.

St Columba came from Ireland to the Hebridean island of Iona in 563 to begin his missionary work. Along with St Ninian and St Mungo – who had introduced Christianity to Strathclyde – St Columba helped spread Christianity and establish the Scots as the dominant population in Scotland.

Bound together by the ties of Christianity and a mutual fear of their neighbours to the north and south, the Scots and Picts united under the leadership of Kenneth MacAlpin in 843 . Later, the Britons and Angles who lived in the south of Scotland also united with the Scots and Picts under Malcolm II (1005-34). Malcolm's son and heir was later murdered by Macbeth of Moray, a story made famous by Shakespeare in Macbeth.
Malcolm III further unified the people by marrying Margaret, an English princess. Margaret brought with her an English priest who reformed the church and replaced St Columba's Gaelic rites. She also brought her English language, the spread of which brought Scotland closer politically and culturally to England. Margaret was canonised a saint in 1251.

During feudal times Scotland was torn by clan warfare and border disputes with

England. David I (1081-1153) gave grants of land to many Anglo-Norman families who became Scotland's aristocracy, including the first Frasers, Setons and Lindsays. David built many famous buildings still standing today, such as the abbeys at Jedburgh, Kelso, Melrose and Dryburgh. At his death he also left Scotland heavily in debt.

After the Battle of Largs in 1266 the Western Isles were taken back from Norse control. The island people chose to join the Donald (or MacDonald) clan, making it one of the most powerful in Scotland for nearly a hundred years. With the title of Lord of the Isles their king ruled independently of the mainland.

The great ambition of Edward I of England (known as "Longshanks" and later the "Hammer of the Scots") was to rule Scotland, Wales and England. He placed John de Balliol on the Scottish throne as "vassal king" in order to appease the Scots. However, the stratagem failed and a series of Scottish heroes emerged: Sir William Wallace (1270-1305) drove the English out of Perth and Stirling; Sir James Douglas (known

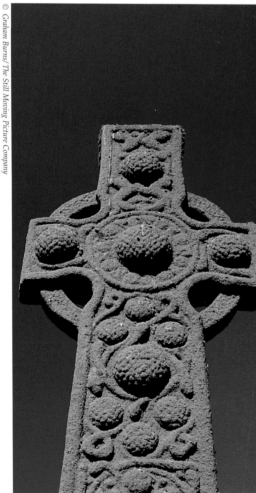

© Graham Burns/ The Still Moving Picture Company

St Martin's Cross, Iona

Sweetheart Abbey

© Pinhole Productions/The Still Moving Picture Company

as "Black Douglas") (1286-1330) constantly attacked the northern areas of England; and Robert the Bruce (1274-1329), who finally freed Scotland and became its king, Robert I. Robert defeated Edward II at the Battle of Bannockburn in 1314 and Scotland became independent under the Treaty of Northampton in 1328. The Orkney and Shetland Islands were made part of Scotland in 1468 as part of the dowry of Margaret, Princess of Denmark, to James III, King of Scotland.

The real powers in Scotland were still the clan chiefs. Jealous of their bloodlines and territory they were constantly at war among themselves and could only agree on their hatred for the English. To help them in their fight with the English the Scots aligned themselves with the French, which later brought the Stuarts (or Stewarts) to the Scottish throne.

At the time of the Reformation, John Knox was a disciple of the Genevan Protestant John Calvin. Knox hated the

Catholic and Anglican churches and was constantly in dispute with Mary Queen of Scots, who was a devoted Catholic. Knox helped shape the democratic form of Scottish government and many aspects of the Scottish church, including its rigid ethical stance, organisation, finances and its relationship with the state. After Knox died, Andrew Melville continued his work. Under Melville's leadership the Scottish Presbyterian Church became clearly established and Scottish universities emphasised classical studies and the study of the Bible. Today, the Scots still reflect this blend of spirituality, conservatism, rigid morality and intellectual independence.

Mary Stuart, Queen of Scots (1542-87), was the daughter of James V of Scotland and Mary of Guise of France. She became queen when she was only six days old and went on to marry the heir to the throne of France, returning to Scotland after his death. A devout Roman Catholic, she made enemies of John Knox and the

Calvinists, while in an attempt to make herself absolute monarch of Scotland she alienated the Scottish clan chiefs. One of Mary's greatest mistakes was to trust her cousin, Elizabeth I of England, who eventually had her beheaded. James VI of Scotland, Mary's son and Elizabeth's heir, became King of England as James I. He broke the power of the great Lords of Scotland and united England and Scotland, but he was unable to close the religious divide between the two countries. His promotion of a non-self ruling Church of Scotland governed by bishops so angered the Scots that in 1638 they signed the National Covenant, which restated the tenets of the Reformation and challenged the king's right to make law. The "Covenanters" believed Parliament should make the laws with only minimal involvement from the king. The Scots went on to support Charles I and his son, which led to Cromwell's invasion of Scotland in 1650. The Scots were defeated at Dunbar but religious conflict continued.

The Scots were upset when the English Parliament deposed the Catholic king, James II, and placed William and Mary, Protestants from Holland, on the throne. In 1715 the Jacobites (a name derived from the Latin form for James) attempted to place on the throne James Edward, James II's son and known as the Old Pretender. Unsuccessful, the Scots then supported his son, Charles Edward, known then as the Young Pretender and to the world now as Bonnie Prince Charlie. Charles Edward Stuart's return to Scotland sparked the 1745 uprising. Even though some of the Scottish clans put their religious differences aside to support the cause, the Scots were completely crushed at the Battle of Culloden by English forces led by the Duke of Cumberland. Many supporters of Bonnie Prince Charlie were killed, executed or fled. The English feared another uprising and completely suppressed the clan system (even Highland dress was illegal until 1782). The Young Pretender was smuggled out of the country with the assistance of Flora MacDonald, one of Scotland's best-known heroines.

In the 18th century the British government built roads and bridges throughout the country to speed military access from London in case of revolt. This construction became the backbone of a stronger Scottish economy by facilitating business and commerce. At the same time trade between Aberdeen, Glasgow and Leith and British overseas colonies expanded, with tobacco as a major commodity until the American Revolution. From 1750 to 1850 large landowners expelled small farmers and crofters from their homesteads to make way for sheep grazing. This infamous action – known as the Clearances – changed the demographic profile of Scotland forever. The "cleared" population emigrated to the United States, Canada, Australia, South Africa and New Zealand, taking their Scottish culture and customs with them. The Scottish traits of thrift, hard work, cunning, and conservatism brought rapid progress in all areas. Many of the inventions that transformed the developing world were either

© Angus G Johnston/The Still Moving Picture Company

FLORA MACDONALD

PRESERVER OF
PRINCE CHARLES EDWARD STUART

HER NAME
WILL BE MENTIONED IN HISTORY
AND IF COURAGE AND FIDELITY
BE VIRTUES
MENTIONED WITH HONOUR

Flora Macdonald's grave, Skye

invented or inaugurated by Scottish genius and industry.

The Depression, World War I and World War II took heavy tolls on Scotland. Manufacturing facilities became out of date, shipbuilding was no longer in demand and Scotland's automobile industry declined from the 1930s. After the discovery of oil in the North Sea in the 1970s the Scottish economy began to strengthen and thousands of jobs were created. In 1981 the largest oil terminal in Europe opened in the Shetland Islands. As part of the United Kingdom, Scotland joined the European Common Market in 1973. The country was restructured in 1974 and regions were renamed; Perth and Angus, for example, became Tayside.

Scientific and technological development continues in Scotland. Scientists in Roslin created the first cloned animal by cloning the udder cells of a mature sheep to create "Dolly." In 1997 "Polly" was created, a sheep with a human gene in every cell of its body. Some 13 per cent of Europe's personal computers, 45 per cent of Europe's workstations and 50 per cent of Europe's automatic banking machines are made in Scotland. Scotch whisky, woollen tweeds and knitwear are exported all over the world. Tourism is booming.

Many Scots are now thinking of a more independent Scotland. In September 1997 Scotland voted to establish a legislature of its own for the first time since 1707. The Stone of Scone, sometimes called the Stone of Destiny, was brought back to Scotland from Westminster Abbey in London, where it sat under the coronation chair: in Scotland the stone had been used for centuries in the coronation of Scottish monarchs.

Princes and lords are but the breath of kings: An honest man's the noblest work o'God.

Robert Burns 1754-96
Taken from *A Little Book of Scottish Sayings* published by Appletree Press

Edinburgh from Calton Hill

© S J Taylor/The Still Moving Picture Company

GEOGRAPHY

Scotland has a total area of 30,414 square miles (48,944 km). Most parts of the country are no more than 60 miles (96 km) from either the Atlantic Ocean or the North Sea, both of which cut deeply into the mainland. Scotland's population is approximately five million and about a third of its 787 islands are inhabited. Over 95 percent of Scotland is rural and the country divides naturally into three areas: the southern uplands, the central lowlands and the Highlands.

The southern uplands lie between the central plain and the English border and comprise rolling moorland broken with low crags and threaded with rivers and valleys. In the southwest corner of the country are the granite Galloway Hills. The tallest of these are the Merrick at 2,764 feet (842 m), Criffel at 1,886 feet (575 m) and Cairnsmore of Fleet at 2,331 feet (710 m). The sources of the Clyde and Tweed rivers are in the Lowther Hills. The Solway Firth receives the waters of the Nith, Annan and Esk rivers. The Southern Upland Fault forms the Moorfoot and Lammermuir Hills to the east. The Merse, a fertile farming area, lies in the south surrounded by the Cheviot Hills.

The central lowlands are where the three valleys and estuaries (firths) of the Clyde, Forth and Tay rivers form a fertile belt from the Atlantic across to the North Sea. The Highland Boundary Fault running from Stonehaven to Helensburgh, along with the Southern Upland Fault, form the boundaries of the central lowlands. Most of the area is more than 400 feet (122 m) above sea level, while the Campsie Fells, Kilpatrick Hills, Ochils and the Sidlaws rise even higher. Between the Firth of Forth, the sea at Dunbar, and the Pentland Hills near

Edinburgh are the Lothian plains. This area contains the cities of Stirling and Edinburgh.

The majority of the Highlands of Scotland are not that high – most of the area is less than 2,000 feet (609 m) above sea level. The granite Highlands include many lochs, glens, mountains and hundreds of islands. Great Glen Fault divides the Grampian Mountains from the northwest Highlands. Most of the Cairngorms are more than 3,500 feet (1,067 m) above sea level, while Cairn Gorm, Ben Macdhui and Braeriach reach over 4,000 feet (1,219 m). West of the Spey River are the Monadhliath Mountains and the high peaks of Ben Nevis at 4,406 feet (1,343 m) and Ben Lawers at 3,984 feet (1,214 m). In 1891 Sir Hugh Munro compiled a table of all Scottish peaks over 3,000 feet (914 m). There are some 280 of these peaks – known as "the Munros" – and "Munro-

bagging" has become the lifetime ambition of some climbers. Most of the Munros are in the Highlands. Also in the Highlands are Loch Fyne and Loch Long, two of the finest sea lochs in Scotland. The best known of the many freshwater lochs are Loch Lomond, Loch Katrine, Loch Awe and Loch Tay. The most prominent of Scotland's rivers (the Spey, Tay, Dee, and Don) make their way through the Highlands. The wildest and most isolated areas of Scotland are found north and west of the Great Glen, where some mountains rise well above 2,500 feet (762 m). The western coastline is dotted with major sea lochs and offshore are the Inner and Outer Hebrides.

The eastern coastline of Scotland is smoother and straighter than the west, which is deeply indented and rocky. There are major heads and cliffs on both coasts. Sea stacks are quite common and good examples are at Hoy in the Orkney Islands, Cape Wrath, Duncansby Head and St Abbs. Scattered about are magnificent sandy beaches, some with white sand and some with black.

Of the 787 Scottish islands the largest group is the Hebrides, the 500 islands of which are off the west coast. The Inner Hebrides include such beautiful places as Skye, Mull, Iona, Jura and Islay. A body of water called the Minch separates the mainland from the Outer Hebrides, an archipelago stretching 140 miles (225 km) from the Butt of Lewis to Barra Head. The Firth of Clyde is home to the islands of Arran, Bute and the Cumbraes. The northern islands beyond the Pentland Firth are divided into two main groups, the Orkneys with 90 islands and further north the Shetlands with 100. Many of the Scottish islands are in extremely isolated locations and have unique histories and cultures. Two of the best known are Fair Isle and St Kilda.

© Ken Paterson/The Still Moving Picture Company

Harris

MONUMENTS, CASTLES AND CHURCHES

Ring of Brodgar, Orkney Islands

Some of the world's best examples of historic monuments are to be found in Scotland and they tell us something of the ancient history of the land. Among the most beautiful are intricately carved Celtic crosses, replete with animal imagery and complex geometric patterns. Most of these crosses were not used as burial stones but designed simply to celebrate the glory of God.

Brochs are round, tower-like, dry-stone structures, located mainly in the north and west and dating from the Iron Age. Hillforts are hill-top enclosures fortified by one or more ramparts and ditches. Many contain the outlines of huts and were probably defended villages. The best examples of defensive dwellings in Scotland are Brown/White Catherthun Forts, Angus, Tayside; Carn Liath Broch, Sutherland, Highland; Dun Carloway Broch, Isle of Lewis, Outer Hebrides; Gurness Broch and Settlement; Rennibister Earth-house, Orkney (nearest town, Kirkwall); and Skara Brae Neolithic settlement, Orkney.

Cairns are another common ancient monument in Scotland. They comprise a round or long mound of stones, often covering a chamber or burial. Good examples are Balnuaran of Clava chambered cairns, Inverness, Highland; Corrymony chambered cairn, Inverness, Highland; Camster Two chambered cairns, Caithness, Highland; Cairnpapple

hill cairn with burial grave and henge, West Lothian, Lothian; Isbister (Tomb of the Eagles) chambered tomb, South Ronaldsay, Orkney; Maes Howe passage grave, Orkney; Cuween Hill chambered cairn, Orkney; Nether Largie cairns, Argyll, Strathclyde; Dunchraigaig cairn, Argyll, Strathclyde; and Ri Cruin cairn, Argyll, Strathclyde.

Lone vertical stones known as standing stones are located throughout most of Scotland, but the biggest concentration is in the area where the Picts lived in the north of the country. The best examples are Achavanich standing stones, Caithness, Highland; Hill o' Many Stanes stone rows, Caithness, Highland; Clach an Trushal standing stone, Isle of Lewis, Outer Hebrides; Nether Largie standing stones, Argyll, Strathclyde; Comet Stone standing stones, Orkney; Stones of Stenness standing stones and henge, Orkney; and Watch Stone standing stone, Orkney.

Scotland's world famous stone circles comprise rings of spaced or contiguous standing stones; sometimes roughly (and very rarely completely) dressed. Their purpose is unknown, but it is believed that their function was related to the seasons and religious rites. Some of the most outstanding are Callanish I-IV stone circles and rows, Isle of Lewis, Outer Hebrides; Cullerlie, Easter Aquhorthies, Sunhoney Recumbent and Loanhead of

Daviot stone circles, Gordon, Grampian; Ring of Brodgar stone circle and henge, Orkney; and Temple Wood stone circle, Argyll, Strathclyde.

The earliest Scottish castles are the stone brochs of the first century AD, the best example of which is Mouse in Shetland. Castle-building in the 12th century changed when Scottish kings invited people from England to take over many Scottish estates. They built their homes to resemble those in England, with Norman moat and bailey castles. Examples of this type of castle can be found at Duffus and Invernochty. The 13th century saw the construction of many finely built stone castles with massive curtain walls for defence, as the country then was flourishing. In the late 1300s a new kind of castle was developed which included a tower house surrounded by a low wall (Scotland had grown poorer, so the grand castles of earlier years were unaffordable). Examples of this type of castle can be found at Threave, Drum and Craigmillar. Over time, defence became a less important factor in the building of castles and comfort became more important. Some of the old plain tower houses were enlarged by the addition of a wing, thus forming an L-shaped castle like the one at Ardblair. Sometimes two wings were added to a tower, forming the Z-shape like Kelburn's. The tower house reached its height in the Grampian area with baronial masterpieces like Craigievar, Crathes, Fyvie and Castle Fraser.

After Flodden, orders were given for the castles in the Borders to build towers for protection from the English, but many

Floors Castle

13

© Mika / The Still Moving Picture Company

Dunrobin Castle

were destroyed during the "rough wooing" of Henry VIII. Some Protestant nobles acquired Catholic church buildings, which they modified into homes after the Reformation. The Restoration brought some new royal works designed by Sir William Bruce: Holyroodhouse Palace is a good example. In the 1800s Robert Adam created the elegant Adam style to be seen in the castles of Culzean and Seaton. The 19th century also saw a revival of medieval styles, as seen at Scone, Abbotsford and Brodick. The 20th century was dominated by Charles Rennie Mackintosh's art nouveau style (which can be seen in Hill House at Helensburgh) and Sir Robert Lorimer's restorations (such as Dunrobin Castle). Visitors to Scotland would miss much if they overlooked the many small buildings found in the countryside. The

"black house" home of the Western Isles and the Highlands, for example, is only found in Scotland. These homes were built with double-thick walls, rounded corners and curved heather thatch weighted with stones because of the strong winds. In some areas new examples of black houses have been reconstructed. Rural Scotland is the location of the "wee cottage", which is a small house, most often white, nestled in the hills of the owner's farmland. It is this common little building which is really more symbolic of the country than the grand houses and castles.

Scotland's cities (especially Glasgow and Edinburgh) have some beautiful and unique buildings, but they also have tenements built when there was a need for cheap and abundant housing for

growing populations. Many of these tenements have been renovated, but in some areas the term "slum" still applies.

Many of the first churches in Scotland were built in the Borders area with monastic houses but were destroyed by the English and in religious conflicts in the 16th century. Good examples of ruins from this period are Dryburgh, Melrose and Jedburgh abbeys. Scotland had some great cathedrals but during the Scottish Reformation the Calvinists destroyed many of them. However, there are still some examples of cathedrals remaining, like the 12th-century cathedral at Dornoch. Probably the most beautiful churches in Scotland are the small village kirks, often surrounded by magnificent scenery. Examples can be found in every area of Scotland.

CLANS AND TARTANS

The Gaelic word clann simply means "children". It began to be used about a thousand years ago. Prior to this the more ancient and broader word cenel described the tribal divisions in the country which became Scotland.

The concept of clanship reaches far into the prehistoric Celtic world. Each community was a little kingdom. Pictland was originally divided into seven and, by the 6th century, the British Kingdoms of Strathclyde in the southwest, Lothian in the southeast, and the Gaelic Kingdom of Dalriada (Argyll) had also emerged.

The social structures and customs that governed these principalities were preserved and developed by the later clan system. Indeed, many chiefs were descended from the ancient kings, according to their genealogists, and, because of the blood-bond which exists between chief and clan, the same can be said of anybody bearing his name. Hence the dignity and pride of the Highlander. "My race is royal" is the motto of Clan Gregor; "I am poor but I am proud. Thank God I am a Maclean" runs a well-known saying.

Modern research suggests that the origins of most clans are more prosaic. Their emergence has much to do with the subordination of the ancient kingdoms to the Scottish Crown during the 12th and 13th centuries, and the opportunities thus created for warlords to "put lands under them" with the assurance of their kindred, and to dominate localities remote from central authority.

The Wars of Independence in the late 13th and early 14th centuries provided further opportunities, and those clans which supported the triumphant cause of Robert the Bruce were rewarded with grants of land, and the right to dispense justice in the name of the Crown. Conversely, those who opposed him lost territory and status.

The relationship between the clans and the Scottish Crown during the following four centuries was uneasy. The Highland clans spoke a different language, dressed differently, had different customs, different loyalties and were as remote culturally as they were physically from the emerging modern state of Scotland. Their often vaunted independence of central authority was threatening; their loyalty only to chief and Name was potentially treacherous. Strong kings led expeditions into the Highlands and

Islands, hanged chiefs, took hostages against good behaviour, set one clan against another, and generally sought to curb their unruly subjects.

Yet during the Great Civil War of the 1640s and the Jacobite risings of 1689, 1715, 1719 and 1745 most of the clans were royalist. Indeed, it was their support for Prince Charles Edward Stuart's desperate venture to restore his father to the Throne that led directly to the obliteration of the clan system, following the Jacobite defeat at the Battle of Culloden in 1746.

There are those who maintain that the kilt is "the garb of Old Gaul" and that the clans have worn individual tartans since time immemorial. Debunkers claim that clan tartans were a 19th-century creation, and the kilt was an invention of an Englishman. The truth lies in-between.

Checked or striped cloth was worn in Scotland from a remote period. The earliest example of such cloth, a fragment of two colour "dog-tooth" checked woollen fabric – the so-called "Falkirk tartan" – dates from about AD235. But, prior to the 16th century, there is no clear evidence of tartan as we would recognise it.

Furthermore, the dress of the Highlandman of the 1500s consisted of a long linen shirt (usually dyed yellow) with a plaid or mantle thrown over it.

The legs were bare or covered in long chequered stockings or tight trousers, called triubhas (hence "trews"). Only during the 16th and 17th centuries did the plaid evolve into the feilidh-mor, the great kilt (literally "great wrap"), which was the precursor of the feilidh-beg, the "little kilt" we wear today.

While there is evidence to support the claim that specific patterns of tartan were worn by individual clans, tartan was not originally an expression of identity. Other emblems, particularly sprigs of plants, worn in the bonnet, served this purpose. The truth is that, in smoke-filled "black houses", the cloth would in all likelihood have been kippered to an indistinguishable hue, and it is certain that plaids were taken as booty on clan raids.

However, there are early references both to identifiable regional colours and patterns, even associated with individual clans. In 1587 Hector Maclean of Duart received a charter for lands in Islay, for which his feu duty was sixty ells of black, white and green cloth. The current Maclean hunting tartan is black, white and green. In a letter to one of his lairds in 1618, Sir Robert Gordon instructed him to "remove the red and white lines from [his tenants'] plaides so as to bring their dress into harmony with the other septs" (i.e. branches of the clan). A German woodcut of 1631 shows "Mackay's Highlanders", in the service of the King of Sweden, wearing a uniform pattern of tartan.

© Paul Tomkins/STB/The Still Moving Picture Company

Statue of Robert Burns, Ayr

Golf

No one knows for sure who invented golf, but Scotland's devotion to the game is largely responsible for its development into one of the most popular sports worldwide. Golf's origins go back to the Middle Ages, but it became the game it is today within the last 200 years. James II of Scotland made the first written reference to golf when he declared it should be prohibited, as it distracted his subjects from their archery practice. Mary Queen of Scots was fond of golf and played the Leith Links, Bruntsfield Links, Falkland, and St Andrews. The game was exported to England when James VI of Scotland became James I of England and established a course at Blackheath Common near London.

The world's first golf clubs were Muirfield and the Royal & Ancient at St Andrews. Most golfers who visit Scotland are keen to play the famous championship courses, which are very challenging. The popularity of such courses sometimes makes it difficult to gain access, so a wiser choice may be to play one of Scotland's excellent smaller courses.

Fishing

Scotland with its fast flowing rivers, ready availability of salmon and some of the most beautiful scenery in Europe attracts anglers from all over the world. However, permits for fishing can often be expensive. Some of the best-known rivers for fishing are the Tweed, Tay, Dee and the Spey. The major types of fishing in Scotland are coarse and game. The former means fishing for freshwater fish except salmon and trout. This includes carp, tench, pike, bream, roach and perch. Because most lochs do not freeze over fishing is done year round. For more information contact the local tourist board. Game fishing includes salmon and trout (brown, rainbow or sea) usually caught using wet and dry flies between February and October. This type of fishing is highly controlled. Contact the Salmon and Trout Association (Scottish Branch), 10 Great Stuart Street, Edinburgh EH3 7TN (tel: (0131) 1225 2417). Other types of fishing include sea fishing from a beach, a rocky shore or a pier; inshore fishing, which means dropping a line into ocean waters within 3 miles (5 km) of the coast line; and deep-sea fishing, which means casting off from a boat more than 3 miles (5 km) offshore. Offshore catches might include several species of shark, including porbeagle, thresher, mako and blue shark.

© Doug Corrance/ The Still Moving Picture Company

Crieff

FESTIVALS

JANUARY
• Hogmanay, 1
• Ba' Games, Kirkwall, 1
• Boys' Walk, Dufftown, 1
• Yetlins, East Weems, 1
• Handsell Monday, 2
• Uphallie Day, 6
• Burning the Clavie, Burghead 11
• Old New Year's Day, 12
• Robert Burns Night, 25
• Up Helly-Aa, Lerwick

FEBRUARY
• Candlemas, 1
• Candlemas Ba', Jedburgh, 2
• Fastern's E'en, Thursday before Lent
• Fastern's E'en Ba', Jedburgh, Thursday before Lent
• Beef Brose and Bannock Night, Thursday before Lent
• Rappy Night, Thursday before Lent
• Five Nations Rugby, continues into March

MARCH
• Whuppity Scourie, 1
• Taillie Day, 30
  Edinburgh Folk Festival
• Horse and Plough, Orkney, moveable feast
• Gryo Night, Orkney, moveable feast

APRIL
• Huntigowk, 1
• Links Market, Kirkcaldy
• Kate Kennedy procession, St Andrews
• Shetland Folk Festival

MAY
• Beltane, 1, 3 and 8
• Mayfest, Glasgow

• Robin Hood Games, 1
• Lanimer Week, Lanark, 3
• Victoria Day, 24
• Empire Day, 24

JUNE
• Midsummer's Eve, 21
• St John's Eve, 24
• Petermas, 29

AUGUST
• Lammas, 1
• Burryman Procession, second week in August
• Marymas, 15
• Edinburgh International Festival
• Edinburgh Military Tattoo

SEPTEMBER
• Fishermen's Walks, various dates
• Feast of St Barr, 27
• Michaelmas Eve, 28
• St Michael's Day, 29

OCTOBER
• St Luke's Eve, 18
• Sour Cakes Day, 18
• Hallowe'en, 31

NOVEMBER
• All Saints' Day, 1
• Bonfire Night, 5
• Martinmas, 11
• St Andrew's Day, 30

DECEMBER
• St Nicholas Eve, 6
• St Thomas' Day, 21
• Barring-out Day, 21
• Sweetie Scone Day, 26
• Hogmanay, 31

Cycling

Cycling is an ideal way to see Scotland. If you have a good mountain bike or touring bike the possibilities are endless. Flat Fife or the islands of Arran or Islay are popular destinations. However, Scotland's weather can make cycling hazardous with strong winds and thick mist so always take appropriate clothing. Cycling is forbidden on highways, trunk roads and motorways. Tourists overcrowd the narrow scenic roads in July and August, so May, June and September are the best months for cycling. The best source of information on cycling is the Scottish Cyclists' Union (Executive Office, The Velodrome, Meadownbrook Stadium, London Road, Edinburgh EH7 6AD; tel: (0131) 652 0187).

Rambling

Rambling, for the uninitiated, is simply walking for pleasure. It is popular in Scotland since there is such a varied landscape. Rambling is the cheapest sport available in the country and suitable for those of all ages. Scotland offers an unlimited number of walking and hiking possibilities. However, weather can change suddenly so make sure you are properly equipped at all times with map, compass and waterproof clothing. In addition to numerous short walks based around individual villages or towns, Scotland has several Long Distance Footpaths, which normally take several days to complete. The best known of these are the Southern Upland Way and the West Highland Way.

For further information contact The Ramblers Association Scotland, 23 Crusader House, Haig Business Park, Markinch, Fife KY7 6AQ (tel: (0131 652 2937).

Horse Riding and Pony Trekking

The beautiful countryside lends itself naturally to horseback trips. There are plenty of trails and riding centres situated throughout the country. Pony trekking originated as an alternative use for Highland ponies. Most treks last between two hours and a full day. Since ponies come in all sizes this is a good activity for most age groups.

Bird Watching

The moors and highlands with their low population density attract millions of birds, making Scotland a superb bird-watching area. One of the most popular destinations for ornithologists is the Orkney Islands where thousands of birds live in close proximity with many prehistoric sites. The Shetland Islands, and Fair Isle in particular, also provide excellent bird watching opportunities. During the winter and early spring the entire Solway shoreline, Loch Ryan, Wigtown Bay, and Auchencairn Bay are good places to see wildfowl and waders. Dumfries and Galloway have barn owls, kestrels, tawnies and merlins.

Skiing

Skiing does not have a large following in Scotland but the industry is starting to grow. The natural snowfall has to be complemented with snow cannons. The principle areas are the Cairngorms near Aviemore, Glenshee and Glen Coe.

In terms of numbers and news interest, soccer is the prime Scottish sport. But Scotland has preserved other games as well. Curling, sometimes called "the roaring game", is a winter form of bowls, in which heavy granite "curling stones" are sent sliding along an ice-covered surface. Modern ice-rink technology has freed curling from the vagaries of the weather and it has become an international sport among northern countries. In the central and western Highlands, shinty is played in a competitive local league. This game, very like Irish hurling, is an exuberant all-male version of hockey. At the many "Highland Games" in the summer and autumn, more specialised sports can be seen, including "tossing the caber", which involves pitching a large pole end over end, and throwing the hammer. These are performed by semi-professional athletes, but other sports like mountain racing, up and down the nearest mountain, are open to all.

Edinburgh International Festival

The Edinburgh International Festival was first held in 1947 and is now the biggest arts festival in the world. The build-up to the Edinburgh Festival and the fringe events attract hundreds of thousands of visitors to the city during August and September every year, especially for the Festival parade. Both the Fringe and the Festival programmes offer an amazing variety and choice in the performing arts, including comedy, cabaret, theatre and music to suit all tastes. Contacts for the major events are:

Edinburgh International Festival, 21 Market Street, Edinburgh EH1 1BW (tel: (0131) 473 2001)

Bank of Scotland Fireworks Concert (tel: (0131) 473 2001)

Edinburgh Festival Fringe, 180 High Street, Edinburgh EH1 1QS (tel: (0131) 226 5257)

Edinburgh International Jazz Festival, 29 Saint Stephen St, Edinburgh EH3 5AN (tel: (0131) 225 2202)

Edinburgh International Film Festival, 88 Lothian Road, Edinburgh EH3 9BZ (tel: (0131) 228 4051)

Edinburgh Book Festival, Scottish Book Centre, 137 Dundee Street, Edinburgh EH11 1BG (tel: (0131) 228 5444)

© Doug Corrance/ The Still Moving Picture Company

Edinburgh Festival Fringe office

Edinburgh Tattoo

One of the most popular events during the Edinburgh International Festival is the Edinburgh Tatoo. Its unique blend of music, ceremony, entertainment and theatre, set against the amazing backdrop of Edinburgh castle, make it one of the world's greatest shows. At the heart of the Tattoo's appeal is the stirring sight and sound of the massed pipes and drums of the Scottish regiments. The word "tattoo" derives from the cry of innkeepers in the Low Countries during the 17th and 18th centuries. At closing time, the fifes and drums of the local regiment would march through the streets, their music signalling a return to quarters, and the shout would go up – 'Doe den tap toe' ('turn off the taps'). Postal bookings for the Edinburgh Tattoo should be sent to: The Tattoo Office, 32 Market Street, Edinburgh EH1 1QB (tel: (0131) 225 1188; fax: (0131) 225 8627).

MUSIC

Music is a very important part of Scottish culture and a discussion of Scottish music would not be complete without mentioning the bagpipe. It is believed that the Romans introduced the bagpipe into Britain. An important military instrument because its sound often terrified the enemy, the bagpipe was integral to all Scottish battle plans until the defeat at Culloden, after which it was outlawed. There are now many types of bagpipe music. The pibroch, a highly

If your programme is to achieve artistic success (and artistic success must be the first aim) then every object you produce must have a strong mark of individuality, beauty, and outstanding workmanship.

Charles Rennie Mackintosh
1868-1928
Taken from *A Little Book of Scottish Sayings* published by Appletree Press

© STB/The Still Moving Picture Company

Gaelic sign

developed theme with variations, was unique to the Highlands. The marches, dances and airs fall into the category of "ceol beag" or small music. The Highland bagpipe has two or more pipes with reeds that the player blows through. The air required is produced by arm pressure on a skin bag. To do all of this well is difficult and it can take about seven years to learn to play the instrument.

Fiddle music is another important part of Scottish music. Scottish fiddlers are first known in the 13th century and collections of fiddle music began as far back as the 15th century. Strathspey and Shetland are the centres of Scottish fiddle music, both in solo and concert form, but the instrument is used all over Scotland for all types of music. Fiddle music has also travelled the world; for example, Scottish fiddle music echoes in the Blue Grass music of the United States.

The harp is the most ancient of the Scottish musical instruments and came to the country with the Scots from Ireland. Queen Mary's Harp and the Lamont Harp in the Royal Museum of Scotland are the earliest surviving examples of the instrument. Its popularity has fluctuated through the years but it is once again enjoying a great revival.

Church music played a big part in Scotland before the Reformation. The earliest sacred music document known to us was written in St Andrews in 1250. The height of sacred music composition began with the reign of James IV, but the Calvinist Reformation destroyed many church music schools and organs in the 17th century. The remoteness of the Gaelic areas helped preserve the "long psalms" in which church congregations sang the lines in response to a leader. "Scottish folk song", wrote Edwin Muir, "is pure feeling; but the ballads express a view of life which is essentially philosophical." Such music dates back to the Middle Ages, and love, death and the

supernatural are among its most popular themes. Songs and ballads belonged to an oral tradition, and as the music travelled it was often changed so as to be made more familiar to local audiences. Most songs and ballads were not written down, but some were preserved in 18th-century pamphlets called chapbooks or broadsides: these did not seem important enough at the time to be kept so many have been lost. Books of songs were sold to professional musicians and middle-class amateurs for drawing room performances. The Scottish middle classes became more involved in such music as a way to preserve their identity after 1707, when the Scottish and English parliaments merged.

Songs and ballads are written down in the Skene Manuscript, which is now in the National Library of Scotland. An Edinburgh wigmaker turned bookseller, Allan Ramsay, compiled Tea-Table Miscellany in 1723, the most comprehensive collection of Scots and English songs to be printed up to that time. Its publication led to the first Scottish songbook with words and music, William Thomson's Orpheus Caledonius. After that many authors wrote lyrics of their own to old melodies which were called pseudo-folk songs, but they were popular enough to be widely sung even today.

By far the most famous of Scottish songwriters is Robert Burns. It is believed that over his lifetime Burns wrote, revised or collected over 370 songs. Besides being an inspired songwriter, Burns faithfully noted both the words and music to traditional songs. He played the fiddle and often set words to tunes, which up until his time had only been instrumental. The Scots Musical Museum published most of Burns's original songs in six volumes.

At the end of the 19th century and the beginning of the 20th century more people were visiting the Highlands and islands and the huge resource of Gaelic songs was added to the Scottish musical scene. This divided Scottish folk music into two traditions: lowland music where the Scottish version of English was spoken and the Gaelic music of the Highlands and Hebrides. The Gaelic songs were not collected until the 19th century, so they differ from clan to clan and it is still possible to hear a song which has never been written down or recorded. The death of the ancient Norse language in the Orkney and Shetland Islands took with it most ancient Norse folk songs. The School of Scottish Studies at Edinburgh is leading a fight to preserve folk songs, a movement first begun by local folk clubs started by people who were dissatisfied with commercial music. The merging of Scottish folk music into a category called Celtic music (which includes Irish, Cape Breton, Brittany and Welsh musics, and to some extent the American blues and country and western) and New Age music helped to spread the music to more people. Professional folk groups like the Corries and the Whistlebinkies became popular, while Gaelic rock groups like Runrig, Capercaillie and Iron Horse became famous. Today, Celtic music is a huge industry and popular all over the world.

Several composers have found inspiration in the natural beauty of Scotland. Felix Mendelssohn wrote Hebridean Overture to celebrate the island's beauty. Hoy in the Orkney Islands had been home to composer Sir Peter Maxwell Davies since 1970. Paul McCartney wrote Mull of Kintyre, which celebrates the Mull of Kintyre Lighthouse, and in 1997 the "Standing Stone Symphony" inspired by the Scottish standing stones.

Dancing

Scottish country dancing is a popular pastime, and almost any dance or ball will include a number of national dances. Reels, jigs, fox-trots, polkas – most date from the 18th and 19th centuries. They are dances to join in rather than to watch, and nowadays there is often a caller to help dancers keep in step. Highland dancing, including the famous "Highland fling", and the Gille-Calum or sword-dance, is more of a spectator sport, seen to best advantage at competitions. A form of Highland dress is always worn when performing these.

Perhaps the best way to experience the more traditional aspects of Scottish culture, though often with a modern twist, is at a ceilidh (pronounced kay-lee). Originally a gathering where people

entertained one another, it is now an evening of song, music and dance. Ceilidhs are frequently put on in tourist centres, but usually you will find many locals, and Scots from other parts, also attending.

LANGUAGE

Scotland's earliest known languages are old Welsh and Gaelic, with old Norse dialects in the northern isles. As English became predominant it incorporated and adapted some terms from the ancient languages. When Scotland was allied to France, particularly during the reign of Mary Queen of Scots, French terms were added to the evolving Scottish language. Scottish English never developed linguistic class divisions to the extent that the language did in England. A movement to accept Scots as a separate language became popular, and in 1997 Scottish educators treated Scots as a

language and included it in their curriculum. Gaelic survived in the northwestern Highlands and the Hebrides, and in islands like Skye over 50 per cent of the population speak the language (Gaelic speakers comprise less than 5 per cent of the total population of the country). Efforts to promote Gaelic have been hampered by the difficulty and complexity of the language, plus a shortage of money for the teachers and supplies needed.

FOOD AND EATING OUT

The food of Scotland was once believed to be inferior to that of other countries but that is not true any more. There are now many good independent restaurants and some hotels have gourmet cuisine. The Scottish Tourist Board has initiated a culinary programme called "Taste of Scotland" where a menu of traditional dishes with the freshest ingredients is

© Doug Corrance/The Still Moving Picture Company

Shopping, Melrose

provided. Some dishes to look out for on a menu are Aberdeen Angus beef, considered some of the best in the world; Abroath Smokies, a small, salted, smoked haddock; Atholl Brose, a mixture of honey, oatmeal and cream; Cock-a-Leekie soup, made with fowl, leeks and prunes; Cranachan, a desert that incorporates raspberries, oatmeal, cream and whisky; Crowdie, similar to cottage cheese; Cullen Skink, a flavourful soup made with smoked haddock; Dunlop cheese from Ayrshire, with an unusual flavour; Finnan Haddie, a salted haddock, which is dried on the beach prior to smoking over a peat fire; Haggis, the national dish of a spiced hash-like filling boiled in a bag; Heather honey; Heather-fed lamb; Kippers, split, salted and smoked herring; Partan Bree, a mouth-watering crab soup; Scots or Barley broth, a vegetable and barley soup; Scottish salmon (farmed or wild), the best in the world; Scottish Cheddar, also among the best in the world; trout freshly caught are mild and tasty; venison, a delicacy that is cooked in many different ways; and red grouse, often present on menus. Scotland also grows a lot of soft fruits such as strawberries, currants and rasps (raspberries).

Whisky (never call it "Scotch" in Scotland) is an important part of life and Scotland's biggest export. It is a social honour to be offered the opportunity to share a "wee dram" with a native. The first major producers of whisky in Scotland were orders of monks in the 15th century. The government placed an extremely high tax on whisky in the 1700s in order to increase its revenue, but this led to elicit stills and smuggling. In 1824 the laws were changed: producers were licensed and paid duty on each gallon produced. Large distilleries were founded, which grew into today's major industry.

Two types of whisky are produced. The unblended straight malt product is known as "single malt"; "blends" contain barley malt and other cereals. Single malts manufactured in Scotland are categorised by location: Speyside comes from distilleries in the valley of the Spey River, while Islay malts have a smokey flavour from being malted over peat. The remaining distilleries are categorised as Highland, even though some of them are near Edinburgh. The process by which whisky is produced from barley, local water and peat smoke is fascinating and over 50 distilleries are open to visitors, providing tours and even a wee dram for tasting.

Scottish Beer is not widely known even though it has been around since AD43. Hops do not grow in Scotland, so Scottish Ales are noted for their very malty taste. The first hops used in Scottish Ale came from Belgium (via England), though the Scottish taste was for more local spices and herbs – ginger, bog myrtle, orange peel, dandelion roots, juniper, liquorice, pepper, spruce, serviceberries and gooseberries. Even heather-flavoured beers were quite common. Hops balance the malt's sweetness, but don't contribute to the aroma. Scottish pale malt resembles English pale malt. Modern commercial examples of Scottish Ale include Grant's, Caledonian 80 Export, Belhaven Scottish Ale and McEwan's Export. Traditional Scotch Ale is much more commonly available, with commercial examples such as McEwan's Scotch Ale, Traquair House Ale and Orkney Brewery's Skullsplitter.

GENEALOGY

Down the centuries Scottish people emigrated all over the world as a result of the Clearances and other hardships. Many visitors to Scotland know they have Scottish blood and want to trace their ancestry back to their homeland. The key to finding your ancestors is to begin with your own records and documents. Begin with the birth certificates of your parents and work back in time as far as you can until you find a descendant from Scotland. Then, once in Scotland, visit the National Library, George IV Bridge, Edinburgh EH1 3YT (tel: (0131) 2264531), where you can check to see if any research has been done on your particular family.

If there is no record of such research contact the New Register House, 3 W. Register Street, Edinburgh EH1 3YT (tel: (0131) 3340380) and obtain a list of their fees and the extent of their records on your particular family. They have details of every birth, marriage and death in Scotland since 1855. Old parish records dating back as far as 1553 are available on baptisms, marriages and burials, but these records are incomplete. Other useful sources of information at New Register House are census data to 1851, data records of foreign marriages of Scots, an adopted children register and war registers.

Property records are available at the Scottish Record office, HM General Register House, Edinburgh EH1 3YY (tel: (0131) 5351314). Once you have narrowed down to a particular family and where they lived, the clan associations might be of help; contact details are available at the local tourist board.

SHOPPING

The most popular purchases for visitors to Scotland are tartans, single malt whisky, local glass products, pottery, soap and local woollen goods. Stores selling these items can be found in all areas, but the best selection is available in the big cities, especially Edinburgh and Glasgow.
Most fun can be had by poking around the small shops in local towns, where proprietors can often provide a wealth of information.
The opening hours for stores vary. In some of the larger cities grocery stores and shopping malls are open on Sundays. In just about every other location newsagents will also be open on Sundays. Some small towns still observe half-day closing, which means on Wednesday or Thursday afternoons the shops will be shut. In many areas shops close at lunchtime for an hour.
The Scots are very serious about their holidays. You should expect the stores to be shut on major holidays (including grocery stores).

PUBLIC TRANSPORT

Air Travel

Although Scotland is a small country, it has its own internal air network. British Airway Express will supply details of flights from Glasgow, Edinburgh, Aberdeen and Inverness to the farthest corners of the Scottish mainland and to the islands, plus information on special offers.

The Scotch do not drink ... During the whole of two or three pleasant weeks spent lecturing in Scotland, I never on any occasion saw whisky made use of as a beverage. I have seen people take it, of course, as a medicine, or as a precaution, or as a wise offset against a rather treacherous climate; but as a beverage, never.

Stephen Leacock
Taken from *A Little Book of Scottish Quotations* published by Appletree Press

Facing page: Glencoe
© *Kenny Ferguson/ The Still Moving Picture Company*

EasyJet also flies between Glasgow, Edinburgh, Aberdeen and Inverness.

Booking Your Flight

Price is just one factor to consider when booking a flight; frequency of service and even a carrier's safety record may be just as important. Major airlines offer the greatest number of departures; smaller airlines – including regional and "no-frills" airlines – usually have fewer daily flights. So called low-cost airlines are cheaper, and their fares impose fewer restrictions such as advance-purchase requirements. The safety record of
low-cost airlines is equal to that of the major carriers.

Try to book a non-stop flight and remember that "direct" flights stop at least once. Connecting flights – which require a change of plane – should be avoided if possible. Two airlines may jointly operate a connecting flight, so ask if your airline operates every stage of the journey – you may find that you're preferred carrier flies you only part of the way. International flights on a country's flag carrier are almost always non-stop but it is important to check, since there are very few flights into Scotland without at least one connection.

Carriers

For international flights there is usually a choice between a domestic carrier, the national flag carrier of the country you wish to visit and a foreign carrier from a third country. British Airways is the national flag carrier for Scotland and has the greatest number of non-stop flights. Domestic carriers may have better connections to your nearest airport and serve a greater number of gateway cities. Other carriers may have a price advantage.

Many carriers prohibit smoking on all their international flights, or else place restrictions on smoking. Others allow smoking only on certain routes or certain departures, so contact your carrier beforehand if you wish to know.

Major Airlines

The best connections into Scotland are by the national flag carrier, British Airways (tel: 0141 2222345). Other major airlines that fly to the United Kingdom are listed below. Those marked with an asterisk also have connections directly to Scotland.

Air Canada*
Tel: (0990) 247226
American Airlines*
Tel: (01293) 524418
Continental Airlines*
Tel: (0141) 8427555
Delta Air Lines
Tel: (028) 90 480526
Egyptair
Tel: (020) 77342395
El Al Airlines (Israel)
Tel: (020) 79574100
Estonian Air
Tel: (020) 73330196
Ethiopian Airlines
Tel: (020) 74912125
Finnair
Tel: (020) 74081222
Ghana Airways
Tel: (020) 74990201
Iberia International Airlines (Spain)
Tel: (020) 79213054
Icelandair
Tel: (020) 73885599
Inter Air (South Africa)
Tel: (020) 77074581
Iran Air
Tel: (020) 74913656
Istanbul Airlines
Tel: (020) 76373031

Japan Airlines
Tel: (020) 74081000
KLM/Northwest Airlines
Tel: (01293) 543281
Korean Air
Tel: (0800) 413000
(freephone within Britain)
Kuwait Airways
Tel: (020) 74120006
LAPA (Argentina)
Tel: (020) 77074576
Malaysia Airlines
Tel: (020) 73412000
Malev Hungarian Airlines
Tel: (020) 74390577
Mexicana Airlines
Tel: (020) 72842550
Middle East Airlines
Tel: (020) 74936321
Nigerian Airways
Tel: (020) 74939726
Pakistan International Airlines
Tel: (020) 87418066
Philippine Airlines
Tel: (020) 74999436
Qantas Airways
Tel: (020) 74972571
Qatar Airways
Tel: (020) 78963636
Royal Brunei Airlines
Tel: (020) 75846660
Royal Jordanian Airlines
Tel: (020) 78786333
Royal Nepal Airlines
Tel: (020) 74940974
Sabena
Tel: (020) 87801444
Saudi Arabian Airlines
Tel: (020) 89957777
Scandinavian Airlines*
Tel: (020) 77346777
South African Airways
Tel: (020) 73125000
Swissair
Tel: (020) 74347200
TAM (Brazil)
Tel: (020) 77074586

© David Robertson/ The Still Moving Picture Company

Inversnaid, Loch Lomond

TAP Air (Portugal)
Tel: (020) 78280262
Tarom Romanian Airlines
Tel: (020) 72243693
Thai Airways International
Tel: (020) 74999113
Trans World Airlines
Tel: (0345) 333333
Tunis Air
Tel: (020) 77347644
US Airways
Tel: (020) 7484210
Virgin Atlantic Airways
Tel: (01293) 562345

**Flights from London to Edinburgh
and Glasgow**

British Airways flies from Heathrow
Tel: (0345) 222111
British Midland flies from Heathrow
Tel: (0345) 554544
easyJet flies from Luton (London)
and Belfast
Tel: (0990) 292929
KLM UK flies from Stansted and
London City
Tel: (0990) 074074
Ryanair flies from Stansted
Tel: (01292) 678000

Flights within Scotland

Charter flights usually have the lowest
fares but are the least dependable.
Departures are infrequent and seldom on
time, flights can be delayed for up to 48
hours and can be cancelled for any reason
up to ten days before scheduled
departure. Itineraries and prices can
change after a flight has been booked.

Checking in and Boarding

Airlines routinely over-book, assuming
that not everyone with a ticket will show
up, but sometimes everyone does. When
that happens, airlines ask for volunteers
to give up their seats. In return these
volunteers usually get a certificate for a
free flight and are rebooked on the next
flight out. If there are not enough
volunteers, the first to be selected for a
later flight are passengers who checked in
late and those flying on discounted
tickets; so check in promptly, especially
during peak periods. Many airlines
still ask you to reconfirm each leg of
your international itinerary. Failure to
do so may result in the cancellation of
your reservation.

Always bring your passport. You will be
asked to show it with your ticket.

Cutting Costs

The least expensive airfares to Scotland
are priced for round-trip travel and

Castlebay and Kisimul Castle, Barra

© Doug Corrance/ The Still Moving Picture Company

usually have to be purchased in advance.
Compare prices of flights to and from
different airports if your destination or
nearest home airport has more than one
gateway. Also seek the price of off-peak
flights, which may be significantly less
expensive. Try several airlines with
different routings and if you are quoted a
low airfare take it immediately, as the
same fare may not be available the next
day. Airlines usually allow you to change
your return date for a fee. (Be aware that
most low-fare tickets are not refundable).
If you intend to fly to Scotland from
London check flights from London's four
airports. First try Ryanair between
London Stansted and Glasgow Prestwick,
and easyJet's bargain fares from London
Luton to Glasgow, Edinburgh, Aberdeen,
and Inverness.

The major gateway to Scotland is
Glasgow Airport. Edinburgh Airport has
good connections to Europe and hourly
flights to London Heathrow and Gatwick

Glasgow Airport, Tel: (0141) 8871111
Edinburgh Airport, Tel: (0131) 3331000

BOATS AND FERRIES

From Europe

P&O Scottish Ferries
Bergen-Lerwick (Shetland)-Aberdeen
(1 weekly, 12 hours; June, July, Aug only)
P&O North Seas Ferries
Rotterdam-Hull (1 daily, 14 hours)
Zeebrugge-Hull (1 daily, 14 hours)
Color Line
Bergen-Stavanger-Newcastle (3 weekly
summer, 2 weekly winter, 24-26 hours)
Scandinavian Seaways
Hamburg-Newcastle
(May-end Sept every 4 days, 23 hours)

Gothenburgh-Newcastle (1 weekly, 22
hours, June, July, August only)
Ijmuiden (Amsterdam)-Newcastle
(April-Sept every 3 days, Oct-Mar
every 4 days)

From Northern Ireland

Argyll and Antrim Steam
Packet Company
Ballycastle-Campbeltown
(2 daily, 3 hours).
For further information contact:
Argyll Antrim Steam Packet Company,
Seacat Terminal, Donegall Quay
Belfast BT1 3AL
Tel: (028) 90 313543
Fax: (028) 90 311801

Stena Line
Belfast-Stranraer
(several crossings daily, Hoverspeed
service 1 hour 30 minutes, ferry 3 hours).
For further information contact:
Stena Line
Ballast Quay, Corry Road
Belfast BT3 9SS
Tel: (028) 90 884090
Fax: (028) 90 884091

P&O European Ferries
Larne-Cairnryan
(Jetliner makes several 1-hour
crossings daily).
For further information contact:
P&O European Ferries
Larne Harbour,
Larne
Co Antrim BT40 1AG
Tel: (0990) 98077
Fax: (028) 28 270949
Seacat
Belfast-Stranraer
(Several crossings daily,
1 hour 30 minutes).
For further information contact:
Seacat, Seacat Terminal

Donegall Quay, Belfast BT1 3AL
Tel: (028) 90 313542
Fax: (028) 90 311801

To the Clyde and Western Isles

With so many islands, plus the great Firth of Clyde waterway, ferry services in Scotland are vital. Most ferries transport vehicles as well as pedestrians but check in advance, as some smaller ferries are for pedestrians only.

Scotland's islands can be divided into two main groups: the Inner and Outer Hebrides off the west coast and Orkney and Shetland off the north coast. Caledonian MacBrayne (Calmac) ferries sail to 23 islands off the west coast of Scotland and most are able to transport vehicles. The summer timetable runs from Easter until mid October, with a slightly reduced service during the rest of the year. Vehicle reservations are advisable on some routes, particularly at peak season. Calmac offers an Island Rover runabout ticket – ideal for touring holidays – as well as an island-hopping scheme called Island Hopscotch. For further information call Caledonian MacBrayne at (0990) 650000; fax: (01475) 637607. Western Ferries operate services between McInroy's Point (near Gourock) and Hunters Quay (near Dunoon) in the

Firth of Clyde and between the islands of Islay and Jura.
For further information contact Western Ferries (Clyde) Ltd at (0141) 3329766; fax: (0141) 3320267

ARRAN
Adrossan-Brodick
55 minutes
Tel: (01475) 650100
Cloanaig-Lochranza
30 minutes
Tel: (01475) 650100
Rothesay-Brodick
1 hour 50 minutes
Tel: (01475) 650100
BARRA
Ludag-Eoligarry
35 minutes
Tel: (01878) 810223
Oban-Castlebay
5 hours
Tel: (01475) 650100
BUTE
Colintraive-Rhubodach
5 minutes
Tel: (01475) 650100
Wemyss-Rothesay
30 minutes
Tel: (01475) 650100
COLL
Oban-Coll
3 hours 5 minutes
Tel: (01475) 650100

COLONSAY
Oban-Colonsay
2 hours 10 minutes
Tel: (01475) 650100
Port Askaig-Colonsay
1 hour 10 minutes
Tel: (01475) 650100
COWAL
Gourock-Dunoon
20 minutes
Tel: (01475) 650100
Tarbet-Portavadie
20 minutes
Tel: (01475) 650100
McInroys Point-Hunter's Quay
20 minutes
Tel: (01369) 704452
CUMBRAE
Largs-Cumbrae Slip
10 minutes
Tel: (01475) 650100
ERISKAY
Ludag-Eriskay
20 minutes
Tel: (01878) 720261
Ludag-Eriskay
10 minutes
Tel: (01878) 720238
GIGHA
Tayinloan-Gigha
20 minutes
Tel: (01475) 650100
HARRIS
Uig (Skye)-Tarbert
1 hour 45 minutes
Tel: (01475) 650100
IONA
Fionnphort-Iona
5 minutes
Tel: (01475) 650100
ISLAY
Kennacraig-Port Ellen
2 hours 10 minutes
Tel: (01475) 650100
Kennacraig-Port Askaig
2 hours
Tel: (01475) 650100
JURA
Port Askaig-Feolin
5 minutes
Tel: (0141) 3329766
LEWIS
Ullapool-Stornoway
3 hours 30 minutes
Tel: (01475) 650100
LISMORE
Oban-Lismore
50 minutes
Tel: (01475) 650100
MULL
Lochaline-Fishnish
15 minutes
Tel: (01475) 650100
Oban-Craignure
40 minutes
Tel: (01475) 650100
Kilchoan-Tobermory
35 minutes
Tel: (01475) 650100

© Richard Welsby/ The Still Moving Picture Company

Old Man of Hoy, Orkney Islands

Cliffs, Orkney Islands

NORTH UIST
Uig (Skye)-Lochmaddy
1 hour 50 minutes
Tel: (01475) 650100
Otternish-Berneray
5 minutes
Tel: (01475) 650100
Otternish-Leverburgh
1 hour 5 minutes
Tel: (01475) 650100
RAASAY
Sconser-Raasay
15 minutes
Tel: (01475) 650100
SCALPAY
Kyles Scalpay-Scalpay
10 minutes
Tel: (01475) 650100
SKYE
Glenelg-Kylerhea
5 minutes
Tel: (01599) 511302
Mallaig-Armadale
30 minutes
Tel: (01475) 650100
SMALL ISLES
Mallaig-Eigg
1 hour 30 minutes
Tel: (01475) 650100
MUCK
2 hours 30 minutes
Tel: (01475) 650100
RUM
3 hours 30 minutes
Tel: (01475) 650100
CANNA
4 hours 30 minutes
Tel: (01475) 650100
SOUND OF SLEAT
Mallaig-Kyle of Lochalsh
2 hours

Tel: (01475) 650100
SOUTH UIST
Oban-Lochboisdale
5-7 hours
Tel: (01475) 650100
TIREE
Oban-Tiree
4 hours 15 minutes
Tel: (01475) 650100

To Orkney and Shetland

P&O Scottish Ferries
Serves both Orkney and Shetland:
Aberdeen-Lerwick
14 hours
Scrabster-Stromness
1 hour, 45 minutes
Aberdeen-Stromness
8 hours
Stromness-Lerwick
8 hours.
The main crossing from the mainland to
Orkney is from Scrabster (near Thurso) to
Stromness. There are daily sailings on this
route all year (except Sundays between
November and March). The main
crossing to Shetland is from Aberdeen.
Ferries depart Monday-Friday all year
except between January and March when
sailings are subject to alteration. It is also
possible to sail to Shetland via Orkney
twice weekly in June, July and August
and once a week September to May. It is
advisable to book in advance. For further
information contact:
P&O Scottish Ferries, PO Box 5
Jamieson's Quay
Aberdeen AB11 5NP
Tel: (01224) 572615
Fax: (01224) 57411

John o' Groats Ferries
John o' Groats Ferries operate a service
for pedestrians only from the end of
April to the end of September from
John o' Groats to Burwick on South
Ronaldsay, the most southerly of the
Orkney Islands. Crossing time is
45 minutes. Tours are also available to
Orkney from John o' Groats and
Inverness. For further details contact:
John o' Groats Ferries Ltd
Ferry Office
John o' Groats
Caithness KW1 4YR
Tel: (01955) 611353
Fax: (01955) 611301
Orkney Ferries
Orkney Ferries operate inter-island
services between the various Orkney
Islands. For further information contact:
Orkney Ferries Ltd
Shore Street, Kirkwall
Orkney KW15 1LG
Tel: (01856) 872044
Fax: (01858) 72921
Shetland Islands Council
Shetland Islands Council operates a
ferry service within Shetland.
For information contact:
Shetland Islands Council
Roads and Transport Department
Grantfield, Lerwick, Shetland ZE1 0NT

To Orkney and Shetland, and Between Islands

Aberdeen-Lerwick
14 hours
Tel: (01224) 572615
Fair Isle-Sumburgh
2 hours 30 minutes

© Richard Welsby/ The Still Moving Picture Company

Tel: (01595) 760222
Fair Isle-Lerwick
4 hours
Tel: (01595) 760222
Foula-Walls
2 hours
Tel: (01595) 532232
Foula-Scalloway
3 hours
Tel: (01595) 532232
Gutcher-Belmont
10 minutes
Tel: (01957) 722259
Gutcher-Oddsta
25 minutes
Tel: (01957) 722259
Skerries-Lerwick
2 hours 30 minutes
Tel: (01806) 515226
Skerries-Vidlin
1 hour 30 minutes
Tel: (01806) 515226
Symbister-Laxo
30 minutes
Tel: (01806) 566259
Ulsta-Toft
20 minutes
Tel: (01957) 722259

West Burrafirth-Papa Stour
40 minutes
Tel: (01595) 810460

Orkney Islands
Aberdeen-Stromness
8 hours
Tel: (01224) 572615
John o' Groats-Burwick
45 minutes
Tel: (01955) 611353
Kirkwall-Eday
Contact Operator
Tel: (01865) 872044
Stronsay
Contact Operator
Tel: (01865) 872044
Sanday
Contact Operator
Tel: (01865) 872044
Papa Westray
Contact Operator
Tel: (01865) 872044
Westray
Contact Operator
Tel: (01865) 872044
North Ronaldsay
Contact Operator

Tel: (01865) 872044
Kirkwall-Shapinsay
30 minutes
Tel: (01865) 811397
Longhope-Lyness
20 minutes
Tel: (01865) 811397
Flotta-Houton
30 minutes
Tel: (01865) 811397
Stromness-Graemsay
30 minutes
Tel: (01865) 811397
Scrabster-Stromness
1 hour 45 minutes
Tel: (01224) 572615
Stromness-Lerwick
8 hours
Tel: (01806) 566259
Tingwall-Rousay
Contact Operator
Tel: (01865) 751360
Egilsay
Contact Operator
Tel: (01865) 751360
Wyre
Contact Operator
Tel: (01865) 751360

© Paul Tomkins/STB/ The Still Moving Picture Company

DRIVING IN SCOTLAND

Legal Requirements and Insurance

Anyone with their own valid driving licence can drive in Scotland for one year. For vehicles registered abroad it is necessary to have your registration papers and a nationality plate of approved size. Insurance cover is compulsory and an international insurance certificate (Green Card), although no longer a legal requirement, is the most effective proof of insurance cover, and is recognised by police. Some motoring organisations (AA, RAC) run accident insurance and breakdown service schemes covering holiday periods. There are car rentals in most towns of any size in Scotland. Cars usually have manual transmissions but automatics are available. A valid driving licence is required. Most companies will not rent to someone between 21-25 years of age or over 70.

Some Rules of the Road

The minimum driving age is 17. Traffic drives on the left and overtakes on the right. Traffic on main roads and on roundabouts has priority. In case of breakdown a red warning triangle or hazard warning lights are required. Full or dipped headlights should be switched on in poor visibility and at night: use sidelights only when the vehicle is

Wester Ross

stationary in an area without street lights. It is mandatory that everyone in the front seat wear seat belts. Children under 14 must travel in the back seat and if seat belts are available all back-seat passengers should wear them. Drivers suspected of speeding or drink driving are liable to prosecution. On single-track roads be extremely careful and use the passing places to allow traffic to pass. Maximum speed limits are 30 mph in towns and cities; 60 mph on single carriageways; 70 mph on motorways and dual carriageways.

Bus

A number of companies offer express services in Scotland on a daily basis throughout the year. Overnight travel is available on most major routes. Scottish Citylink runs most of the internal Scottish routes. They link up with National Express so through tickets are available to the rest of the UK. Light refreshments and toilet facilities are available on many routes. Special discount tickets are available throughout the year on both Scottish Citylink and National Express, including reduced fares for students, senior citizens, young people with a coach card and children. Contact Scottish Citylink Coaches at (0990) 505050; Website: www.citylink.co.uk; and National Express at (0990) 505050; Website: www.nationalexpress.co.uk.

Lothian Regional Transport runs buses between Edinburgh Airport terminal and Waverly Bridge in the city centre. The buses run every 15 minutes on weekdays and less frequently (roughly every hour) during off-peak hours and at weekends. The journey takes about 30 minutes. Express buses run from Glasgow Airport to near Glasgow Central railway station and to the Glasgow Buchanan Street bus station. There is a service every 15 minutes throughout the day (every 30 minutes in winter).

In some rural areas where there is no other form of transport the mail delivery vehicle carries fare-paying passengers. Seats are limited and there is no Sunday service. Timetables are available from Royal Mail Communications at (0131) 228 7407; fax: (0131) 229 2050.

Backpackers can use jump on/jump off bus services to hostels and backpacker accommodation. Contact Go Blue Banana at (0131) 556 2000; fax: (0131) 558 1177; Haggis Backpackers at (0131) 557 9393; fax: (0131) 558 1177; or Macbackpackers, tel/fax: (0131) 220 1869.

Rail

The rail service in Scotland is excellent, with good connections between English and Scottish towns and cities.

All suburban services and lines north and west of Inverness operate on one class of ticket only. Some trains carry buffet and dining cars. There are very few Sunday trains in the Highlands. A wide range of reductions and special deals is available. Two particularly beautiful routes within Scotland are Oban to Mallaig on the west coast and Inverness to Thurso and Wick on the northern mainland.

ScotRail operates the Caledonian Sleeper from London to Edinburgh, Glasgow, Aberdeen, Inverness and Fort William every night from Sunday to Friday, with cabins for one or two passengers.

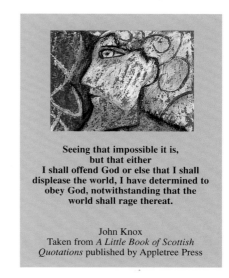

Seeing that impossible it is, but that either I shall offend God or else that I shall displease the world, I have determined to obey God, notwithstanding that the world shall rage thereat.

John Knox
Taken from *A Little Book of Scottish Quotations* published by Appletree Press

© Harvey Wood/ The Still Moving Picture Company

WHERE TO STAY

Accommodation in Scotland varies greatly and is divided into six major classes: hotels; guest houses/bed and breakfast; self-catering (rent normally charged weekly for a furnished house, apartment or cottage with cooking facilities); camping/caravans; wild camping; and youth hostels. The Scottish Tourist Board grading system is a useful guide to quality and standards. It is best to book through local tourist boards.

Scottish Tourist Board Grading System

Deluxe: excellent quality
Highly Commended: very good quality
Commended: good quality
Approved: acceptable quality

The number of Scottish Tourist Board crowns indicates the range of facilities available: the more crowns there are, the better the facilities and services.

Embassies and Consulates

As Scotland is part of the United Kingdom, the chief foreign embassies are in London. However, a number of representatives for other nations have consular offices within Scotland and these can be found in the Yellow Pages. They include: The Australian Consulate, 25 Bernard Street, Leith, Edinburgh EH6 6SH (tel: (0131) 555 4500): The USA Consulate General, 3 Regent Terrace, Edinburgh (tel: (0131) 556 8315).

USEFUL INFORMATION

Area Tourist Boards

• Aberdeen and Grampian Tourist Board, 27 Albany Place, Aberdeen
Tel: (01224) 632727; fax: (01224) 581367
Website: www.holiday.scotland.net

• Angus and City of Dundee Tourist Board, 21 Castle Street, Dundee
Tel: (01382) 434664; fax: (01382) 527550
Website: www.carnoustie.co.uk.

• Argyll, the Isles, Loch Lomond, Stirling and Trossachs Tourist Board, Old Town Jail, St John Street, Stirling
Tel: (01786) 475019; fax: (01786) 471301
Website: www.holiday.scotland.net

• Ayrshire and Arran Tourist Board, Burns House, Burns Statue Square, Ayr
Tel: (01292) 288688; fax: (01292) 288686
Website: www.ayrshire-arran.com

• Dumfries and Galloway Tourist Board, 64 Whitesands, Dumfries
Tel: (01387) 253862; fax: (01387) 245555
Website: www.galloway.co.uk

• Edinburgh and Lothians Tourist Board, 4 Rothesay Terrace, Edinburgh
Tel: 0131 473 3800; fax: (0131) 473 3881
Website: www.edinburgh.org

• Greater Glasgow and Clyde Valley Tourist Board, 11 George Square, Glasgow
Tel: (0141) 204 4400; fax: (0141) 204 4772
Website: www.holiday.scotland.net

• Highlands of Scotland Tourist Board, Peffery House, Strathpeffer
Tel: (01997) 421160; fax: (01997) 421168
Website: www.host.co.uk

• Kingdom of Fife Tourist Board, 70 Market Street, St Andrews, Fife
Tel: (01334) 474609; fax: (01334) 478422
Website: www.sta.co.uk

• Orkney Tourist Board, 6 Broad Street, Kirkwall, Orkney
Tel: (01856) 872856; fax: (01856) 875056
Website: orkneyislands.com

• Perthshire Tourist Board, Lower City Mills, West Mill Street, Perth
Tel: (01738) 627958; fax: (01738) 630416
Website: www.perthshire.co.uk

• Scottish Borders Tourist Board, Shepherds Mills, Whinfield Road, Selkirk
Tel: (0175) 20054; fax: (01750) 21886
Website: www.holiday.scotland.net

• Shetland Islands Tourism, Market Cross, Lerwick, Shetland
Tel: (01595) 693434; fax: (01595) 695807
Website: www.shetland-tourism.co.uk

• Western Isles Tourist Board, 26 Cromwell Street, Stornoway, Isle of Lewis
Tel: (01851) 703088; fax: (01851) 705244
Website: www.witb.co.uk

Travel

Air

• Glasgow Airport tel: (0141) 8871111
• Edinburgh Airport tel: (0131) 3331000
• British Airways Express tel: 345 222111 (in Britain only)
• EasyJet tel: (0990) 292929
• KLM UK tel: (01279) 660400

Car Rental

Glasgow
• Avis (tel: (0141) 887 2261)
• National (tel: (0141) 887 7915)
• Europcar (tel: (0141) 887 0414)
• Hertz (tel: (0141) 848 4245)

© David Robertson/The Still Moving Picture Company

The Town House, Culross, Fife

Edinburgh
• Avis (tel: (0131) 333 1866)
• Hertz (tel: (0131) 333 1019)
• Budget (tel; (0131) 333 1926)

Local Tourist Boards
The most important resource for any
traveller in Scotland is the local tourist
Board. The following is the listing
of all the local offices.

A
Aberdeen
St Nicholas House
Broad Street, AB9 1DE
Tel: (01224) 632727
Fax: (01224) 620415
Jan-Dec

Aberfeldy
The Square, PH15 2DD
Tel: (01887) 820276
Jan-Dec

Aberfoyle
Main Street, FK8 3UQ
Tel: (01877) 382352
April-Oct

Abington
Welcome Break Service Area
Junction 13, M74, ML12 6RG
Tel: (01864) 502436
Fax: (01864) 502765
Jan-Dec

Alford
Railway Museum
Station Yard,
AB33 8AD
Tel: (019755) 62052
Easter-Sep

Alva
Mill Trail Visitor Centre
FK12 5EN
Tel: (01259) 769696
Jan-Dec

Anstruther
Scottish Fisheries Museum
KY10 3AB
Tel: (01333) 311073
Easter-Sept

Arbroath
Market Place,
DD11 1HR
Tel: (01241) 872609
Fax: (01241) 878550
Jan-Dec

Ardgartan
Arrochar,
G83 7AR
Tel: (01301) 702432
Fax: (01301) 702432
April-Oct

Glencoe

© David Robertson/ The Still Moving Picture Company

Auchterarder
90 High Street,
PH3 IBJ
Tel: (01764) 663450
Fax: (01764) 664235
Jan-Dec

Aviemore
Grampian Road
Inverness-shire,
PH22 1PP
Tel: (01479) 810363
Fax: (01479) 811063
Jan-Dec

Ayr
Burns House
Burns Statue Square,
KA7 1UP
Tel: (01292) 288688
Fax: (01292) 288686
Jan-Dec

B

Ballachulish
Argyll, PA39 4JB
Tel: (01855) 811296
Fax: (01855) 811720
April-Oct

Ballater
Station Square,
AB35 5QB
Tel: (013397) 55306
Easter-end Oct

Balloch
The Old Station Building
Balloch Road,
G83 8LQ
Tel: (01389) 753533
April-Oct

Banchory
Bridge Street, AB31 5SX
Tel: (01330) 822000
Easter-Oct

Banff
Collie Lodge, AB45 1AU
Tel: (01261) 812419
Fax: (01261) 815807
Easter-Sept

Bettyhill
Clachan, Sutherland,
KW14 7SZ
Tel: (01641) 521342
Fax: (01641) 521342
April-Sept

© Derek Laird/ The Still Moving Picture Company

Edinburgh Castle from Castle Street

Biggar
155 High Street,
ML12 6DL
Tel: (01899) 221066
Easter-Oct

Blairgowrie
26 Wellmeadow, PH10 6AS
Tel: (01250) 872960
Fax: (01250) 873701
Ski Line (01250) 875800
Jan-Dec

Bo'ness
Seaview Car Park
EH51 0AJ
Tel: (01506) 826626
April-Sept

Bowmore
Isle of Islay, PA43 7JP
Tel: (01496) 810254
Easter-Oct

Braemar
The Mews, Mar Road
AB35 5YL
Tel: (013397) 41600
Fax: (013397) 41643
Jan-Dec

Brechin
St Ninians Place, DD9 7AH
Tel: (01356) 623050
April-Sept

Broadford
Isle of Skye, IV49 9AB
Tel: (01471) 822361
Fax: (01471) 822141
April-Oct

Brodick
The Pier, Isle of Arran
KA27 8AU
Tel: (01770) 302140/302401
Fax: (01770) 302395
Jan-Dec

C

Callander
Rob Roy & Trossachs Visitor Centre
Ancaster Square
FK17 8ED
Tel: (01877) 330342
Fax: (01877) 330784
Mar-Dec
Jan & Feb weekends only

Campbeltown
Mackinnon House
The Pier
Argyll, PA28 6EF
Tel: (01586) 552056
Fax: (01586) 553291
Jan-Dec

Carnoustie
1 B High Street, DD7 6AN
Tel: (01241) 852258
April-Sept

Carrbridge
Main Street, Inverness-shire
PH23 3NA
Tel / Fax: (01479) 841630
May-Sept
Castlebay

Main Street, Isle of Barra
H59 5XD
Tel: (01871) 810336
Easter-Oct

Castle Douglas
Markethill Car Park
DG7 1AE
Tel: (01556) 502611
Easter-Oct

Coldstream
High Street, TD12 4DH
Tel: (01890) 882607
Easter-Oct

Craignure
The Pier, Isle of Mull
PA65 6AY
Tel: (01680) 812377
Fax: (01680) 812497
Jan-Dec

Crail
Museum & Heritage Centre
62 - 64 Marketgate
KY10 3TL
Tel: (01333) 450869
Easter-Sept

Crathie
Car Park, Balmoral Castle
AB35 5TB
Tel: (013397) 42414
Easter-Oct

Crieff
Town Hall, High Street
PA7 3AU
Tel: (01764) 652578
Jan-Dec

D

Daviot Wood
A9 by Inverness

IV2 5XL
Tel: (01463) 772203
Fax: (01463) 772022
April-Oct

Dornoch
The Square
Sutherland,
IV25 3SD
Tel: (01862) 810400
Fax: (01862) 810644
Jan-Dec

Drymen
Drymen Library
The Square,
G63 0BL
Tel: (01360) 660068
May-Sept

Dufftown
Clock Tower,
The Square
AB55 4AD
Tel: (01340) 820501
Easter-Oct

Dumbarton
Milton
A82 Northbound
G82 2TZ
Tel: (01389) 742306
Jan-Dec

Dumfries
Whitesands, DG1 4TH
Tel: (01387) 253862
Fax: (01387) 245555
Jan-Dec

**Cha do bhrist fear riamh a bhogha nach
d'fheum fear eile 'n t-sreang.**

**No man ever broke his bow but another
man found a use for the string.**

Taken from *A Little Book of Gaelic
Proverbs* published by Appletree Press

Dunbar
143 High Street, EH42 1ES
Tel: (01368) 863353
Fax: (01368) 864999
Jan-Dec

Dunblane
Stirling Road, FK15 9EP
Tel: (01786) 824428
May-Sept

Dundee
7-21 Castle Street
DD1 3AA
Tel: (01382) 527527
Fax: (01382) 434665
Jan-Dec

Dunfermline
13/15 Maygate,
KY12 7NE
Tel: (01383) 720999
Fax: (01383) 730187
Easter-Oct

Dunkeld
The Cross, PH8 0HN
Tel: (01350) 727688
Jan-Dec

Dunoon
7 Alexandra Parade
Argyll, PA23 8AB
Tel: (01369) 703785
Fax: (01369) 706085
Jan-Dec

Dunvegan
2 Lochside, Dunvegan
Isle of Skye, IV55 8WB
Tel: (01470) 521581
July-Oct

Durness
Sango, Sutherland,
IV27 4PZ
Tel: (01971) 511259
Fax: (01971) 511368
April-Oct

E

Edinburgh
Edinburgh & Scotland
Information Centre
3 Princes Street,
EH2 2QP
Tel: (0131) 473 3800
Fax: (0131) 473 3881
Jan-Dec

Edinburgh Airport
Tourist Information Desk
EH12 9DN
Tel: (0131) 333 2167
Jan-Dec

Elgin
17 High Street, IV30 1EG

Tel: (01343) 542666
        (01343) 543388
Fax: (01343) 552982
Jan-Dec

Eyemouth
Auld Kirk, Manse Road
TD14 5JE
Tel: (018907) 50678
April-Oct

F

Falkirk
2-4 Glebe Street,
FK1 1HU
Tel: (01324) 620244
Fax: (01324) 638440
Jan-Dec

Forfar
40 East High Street
DD8 1BA
Tel: (01307) 467876
April-Sept

Forres
116 High Street, IV36 0NP
Tel: (01309) 672938
Easter-Oct

Fort Augustus
Car Park, Inverness-shire
PH32 4DD
Tel: (01320) 366367
Fax: (01320) 366779
April-Oct

Fort William
Cameron Square
Inverness-shire, PH33 6AJ
Tel: (01397) 703781
Fax: (01397) 705184
Jan-Dec

Forth Bridges
by North Queensferry
KY11 IHP
Tel: (01383) 417759
Jan-Dec

Fraserburgh
Saltoun Square, AB43 9DA
Tel: (01346) 518315
Easter-Sept

G

Gairloch
Auchtercairn
Ross-shire, IV21 2DN
Tel: (01445) 712130
Fax: (01445) 712071
Jan-Dec

Galashiels
St John Street, TD1 3JX
Tel: (01896) 755551
Easter-Oct

Gatehouse of Fleet
Car Park, Castle Douglas
DG7 2HP
Tel: (01557) 814212
Easter-Oct

Girvan
Bridge Street,
KA26 9HH
Tel: (01465) 714950
Easter-Oct

Glasgow
11 George Square,
G2 1DY
Tel: (0141) 204 4400
Fax: (0141) 221 3524
Jan - Dec

Glasgow Airport
Tourist Information Desk
PA3 2PF
Tel: (0141) 848 4440
Fax: (0141) 849 1444
Jan-Dec

Glenshiel
Kintail, Kyle of
Lochalsh, Ross-shire,
IV40 8HW
Tel: (01599) 511264
April-Oct

Grantown on Spey
High Street,
Morayshire
PH26 3EH

Tel / Fax: (01479) 872773
April-Oct

Greenock
7a Clyde Square
Greenock, Renfrewshire
PA15 1NB
Tel: (01475) 722007
Fax: (01475) 730854
Jan-Dec

Gretna Green
Old Blacksmith's Shop
DG16 5EA
Tel: (01461) 337834
Easter-Oct

H

Hamilton
Road Chef Services
(M74 Northbound)
ML3 6JW
Tel: (01698) 285590
Fax: (01698) 891494
Jan-Dec

Hawick
Drumlanrig's Tower
TD9 9EN
Tel: (01450) 372547
Fax: (01450) 373993
Easter-Oct

Helensburgh
The Clock Tower,
G84 7PA

Tel: (01436) 672642
April-Oct

Helmsdale
Coupar Park, Sutherland
KW8 6HH
Tel: (01431) 821640
Fax: (01431) 821640
April-Sept

Huntly
The Square,
AB54 8BR
Tel: (01466) 792255
Easter-Oct

I

Inveraray
Front Street, Argyll
PA32 8UY
Tel: (01499) 302063
Fax: (01499) 302269
Jan-Dec

Inverness
Castle Wynd,
IV2 3BJ
Tel: (01463) 234353
Fax: (01463) 710609
Jan-Dec

Inverurie
18 High Street
AB51 3XQ
Tel: 01467 625800
Jan-Dec

© David Robertson/ The Still Moving Picture Company

Lagangarbh cottage

Irvine
New Street, KA12 8BB
Tel: (01294) 313886
Fax: (01294) 313339
Jan-Dec

J

Jedburgh
Murray's Green,
TD8 6BE
Tel: (01835) 863435/863688
Fax: (01835) 864099
Jan-Dec

John O'Groats
County Road,
Caithness
KW1 4YR
Tel: (01955) 611373
Fax: (01955) 611448
April-Oct

K

Kelso
Town House,
The Square, TD5 7HF
Tel: (01573) 223464
Easter-Oct

Kilchoan
Argyll, PH36 4LH
Tel: (01972) 510222
Easter-Oct

Killin
Breadalbane Folklore Centre
Falls of Dochart,
Main Street,
FK21 8XE
Tel: (01567) 820254
Fax: (01567) 820764
March-end Oct
Feb weekends only

Kilmarnock
62 Bank Street,
KA1 1ER
Tel: (01563) 539090
Fax: (01563) 572409
Jan-Dec

Kincardine Bridge
Pine 'n' Oak
Kincardine Bridge Road
Airth, by Falkirk,
FK2 8PP
Tel: (01324) 831422
April-Sept

Kingussie
King Street
Inverness-shire,
PH21 1HP
Tel: (01540) 661297
May-Sept

Kinross
Kinross Service Area

Linlithgow Palace

off Junction 6, M90
KY13 7NQ
Tel: (01577) 863680
Fax: (01577) 863370
Jan-Dec

Kirkcaldy
19 Whytescauseway
KY1 1XF
Tel: (01592) 267775
Fax: (01592) 203154
Jan-Dec

Kirkcudbright
Harbour Square,
DG6 4HY
Tel: (01557) 330494
Easter-end Oct

Kirkwall
6 Broad Street
Orkney, KW15 1DH
Tel: (01856) 872856
Fax: (01856) 875056
Jan-Dec

Kirriemuir
Cumberland Close
DD8 4EF
Tel: (01575) 574097
April-Sept

Kyle of Lochalsh
Car Park
Inverness-shire,
IV40 8AG
Tel: (01599) 534276
Fax: (01599) 534808
April-Oct

L

Lairg
Sutherland, IV27 4PZ
Tel: (01549) 402160
Fax: (01549) 402160
April-Oct

Lanark
Horsemarket
Ladyacre Road, ML11 7LQ
Tel: (01555) 661661
Fax: (01555) 666143
Jan-Dec

Langholm
High Street, DG13 0JH
Tel: (01387) 380976
Easter-Sept

Largs
Promenade,
KA30 8BG
Tel: (01475) 673765
Fax: (01475) 676297
Jan-Dec

Lerwick
The Market Cross
Shetland, ZE1 0LU
Tel: (01595) 693434
Jan-Dec

Linlithgow
Burgh Halls, The Cross
EH49 7EJ
Tel: (01506) 844600
Fax: (01506) 671373
Jan-Dec

© Doug Corrance/ The Still Moving Picture Company

Lochboisdale
Pier Road
Isle of South Uist
HS8 5TH
Tel: (01878) 700286
Easter-Oct

Lochcarron
Main Street
Ross-shire,
IV54 8YB
Tel: (01520) 722357
Fax: (01520) 722324
April-Oct

Lochgilphead
Lochnell Street, Argyll
PA31 8JL
Tel: (01546) 602344
April-Oct

Lochinver
Main Street, Sutherland
IV27 4LT
Tel: (01571) 844330
Fax: (01571) 844373
April-Oct

Lochmaddy
Pier Road, Isle of North Uist,
HS6 5AA
Tel: (01876) 500321
Easter-Oct

M

Mallaig
Inverness-shire,
PH41 4QS
Tel: (01687) 462170
Fax: (01687) 462064

April-Oct
Melrose
Abbey House,
TD6 9LG
Tel: (01896) 822555
Easter-Oct

Millport
28 Stuart Street
Isle of Cumbrae,
KA28 0AJ
Tel / Fax: (01475) 530753
Easter-Oct

Milton
See Dumbarton

Moffat
Churchgate, DG10 9EG
Tel: (01683) 220620
Easter-end Oct

Montrose
Bridge Street, DD10 8AB
Tel: (01674) 672000
April-Sept

Musselburgh
See Old Craighall

N

Nairn
62 King Street, Nairnshire
IV21 4DN
Tel / Fax: (01667) 452753
April-Oct

Newtongrange
Scottish Mining Museum
Lady Victoria Colliery
EH22 4QN
Tel: (0131) 663 4262
Easter-Oct

Newton Stewart
Dashwood Square
DG8 6GQ
Tel: (01671) 402431
Easter-Oct

North Berwick
Quality Street,
EH39 4HJ
Tel: (01620) 892197
Fax: (01620) 893667
Jan-Dec

North Kessock
Ross-shire, IV1 1XB
Tel: (01463) 731505
Fax: (01463) 731701
Jan-Dec

O

Oban
Argyll Square, Argyll,
PA34 4AR

© David Robertson/ The Still Moving Picture Company

Neist Lighthouse

Tel: (01631) 563122
Fax: (01631) 564273
Jan-Dec

Old Craighall
Granada Service Area (A1)
Musselburgh,
EH21 8RE
Tel: (0131) 653 6172
Fax: (0131) 653 2805
Jan-Dec

P

Peebles
High Street,
EH45 8AG
Tel: (01721) 720138
Fax: (01721) 724401
Jan-Dec

Penicuik
Edinburgh Crystal
Visitor Centre,
Eastfield
EH26 8HJ
Tel: (01968) 673846
Easter-Sept

Perth
45 High Street,
PH1 5TJ
Tel: (01738) 638353
Fax: (01738) 444863
Jan-Dec

Perth
Caithness Glass

Inveralmond
(A9 Western City Bypass)
PH1 3TZ
Tel: (01738) 638481
Jan-Dec

Pitlochry
22 Atholl Road,
PH16 5DB
Tel: (01796) 472215/472751
Fax: (01796) 474046
Jan-Dec

Portree
Bayfield House
Bayfield Road
Isle of Skye,
IV51 9EL
Tel: (01478) 612137
Fax: (01478) 612141
Jan-Dec

R

Ralia
A9 North by Newtonmore
Inverness-shire,
PH20 1DD
Tel / Fax: (01540) 673253
April-Oct

Rothesay
15 Victoria Street
Isle of Bute,
PA20 0AJ
Tel: (01700) 502151
Fax: (01700) 505156
Jan-Dec

S

St Andrews
70 Market Street,
KY16 9NU
Tel: (01334) 472021
Fax: (01334) 478422
Jan-Dec

Sanquhar
Tolbooth,
High Street, DG4 6DJ
Tel: (01659) 50185
Easter-Sept

Selkirk
Halliwell's House,
TD7 4BL
Tel: (01750) 20054
Easter-Oct

Shiel Bridge
See Glenshiel

Spean Bridge
Woollen Mill Car park
Inverness-shire
PH34 4EP
Tel: (01397) 712576
Fax: (01397) 712675
April-Oct

Stirling
Dumbarton Road
FK8 2LQ
Tel: (01786) 475019
Fax: (01786) 450039
Jan-Dec

Stirling Castle © David Robertson/ the Still Moving picture company

© STB/ The Still Moving Picture Company

Tobermory

Stirling
Pirnhall
Motorway Service Area
Junction 9 (M9), FK7 8ET
Tel: (01786) 814111
April-Oct

Stirling
Royal Burgh
of Stirling
Visitor Centre,
FK8 1EH
Tel: (01786) 479901
Jan-Dec

Stonehaven
66 Allardice Street,
AB39 2AA
Tel: (01569) 762806
Easter-Oct

Stornoway
26 Cromwell Street
Isle of Lewis, H51 2DD
Tel: (01851) 703088
Fax: (01851) 705244
Jan-Dec

Stranraer
Burns House
28 Harbour Street,
DG9 7RD
Tel: (01776) 702595
Fax: (01776) 889156
Easter-Oct

Strathpeffer
The Square, Ross-shire,
N14 9DW
Tel: (01997) 421415
Fax: (01997) 421460
April-Nov

Stromness
Ferry Terminal Building
The Pier Head, Orkney
KW16 3AA
Tel: (01856) 850716
Fax: (01856) 850777
Jan-Dec

Strontian
Argyll, PH36 4HZ
Tel: (01967) 402131
Fax: (01967) 402131
April-Oct

T

Tarbert
Harbour Street, Argyll
PA29 6UD
Tel: (01880) 820429
April-Oct

Tarbert
Pier Road
Isle of Harris,
HS3 3DG

Tel: 01859 502011
Easter-Oct

Tarbet-Loch Lomond
Main Street,
G83 7DE
Tel: (01301) 702260
Fax: (01301) 702224
April-Oct

Thurso
Riverside,
KW14 8BU
Tel: (01847) 892371
Fax: (01847) 893155
April-Oct

Tobermory
Isle of Mull,
PA75 6NU
Tel: (01688) 302182
Fax: (01688) 302145
Apr-Oct

Tomintoul
The Square, AB37 9ET
Tel: (01807) 580285
Fax: (01807) 580285
Easter-Oct

Troon
Municipal Buildings
South Beach, KA10 6EJ
Tel: (01292) 317696
Easter-Oct

Tyndrum
Main Street,
FK20 8RY
Tel: (01838) 400246
April-Oct

U

Uig
Ferry Terminal,
Isle of Skye, IV51 9XX
Tel: (01470) 542404
Fax: (01470) 542404
April-Oct

Ullapool
Argyle Street,
Ross-shire, IV26 2UR
Tel: (01854) 612135
Fax: (01854) 613031
April-Nov

W

Wick
Whitechapel Road
Caithness, KW1 4EA
Tel: (01955) 602596
Fax: (01995) 604940
Jan-Dec

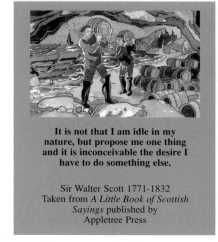

**It is not that I am idle in my
nature, but propose me one thing
and it is inconceivable the desire I
have to do something else.**

Sir Walter Scott 1771-1832
Taken from *A Little Book of Scottish
Sayings* published by
Appletree Press

Facing Page: Yachts at Dawn, Tayvallich
© David Robertson/ The Still Moving Picture Company

TOURING IN SCOTLAND

Scotland's roads lead to some of the country's most spectacular scenery and places of greatest interest to visitors. During the summer months and major local holidays these areas can become very crowded, so you may wish to visit off-season from March to April, October to November or January to February.

Car hire is available at all of Scotland's major airports. It is also possible to hire a car in most of Scotland's towns and cities, while local garages often have cars for rent. Consult the local tourist board for information.
Visitors on a budget can use Scotland's excellent public transportation system to travel to their tour areas and then hire a car when it is needed. Remember that it can be very expensive to take a car on major ferries.

The cost of renting a car in Scotland is relatively high compared to other countries, so try to shop around for the best deal. (Fuel in Scotland is also expensive, especially in remote areas.) Customers are responsible for any damage or loss to their vehicle.
Check to see if you are covered by your personal motor insurance, otherwise purchase temporary insurance from the car rental agency. This insurance will cover you in the event of collisions but probably not for stolen vehicles.

Your own driving licence is acceptable in Scotland, but universally recognised International Drivers' Permits can be obtained from national automobile associations. Such permits can be a wise precaution, as they establish your right to drive your vehicle to the satisfaction of the police.

Southern Scotland has a small network of high-speed motorways, which have two or three lanes to each carriageway and a central reservation.
There are no right turns, traffic lights or roundabouts on motorways. On road signs and maps motorways are designated by the letter "M".

"A" roads with one or two lanes connect all major towns throughout Scotland. Such roads have right turns, traffic lights and roundabouts. On road signs and maps they are designated by the letter "A".
"A" roads also connect with smaller roads which travel to remote areas. These are designated by the letter "B". "B" roads were originally coach and turnpike roads built for horse and carriage and often have majestic views of the countryside. They can be very winding and narrow, but if you drive appropriately they are perfectly safe.

Facing page: Glencoe
© *Kenny Ferguson/ The Still Moving Picture Company*

Boats at Burravoe, Shetland Islands

© David Robertson/ The Still Moving Picture Company

Minor roads are unlettered and unnumbered, and must be driven on slowly and with great care. They are the way into the heart of the countryside and provide the best way to see the real Scotland. (It is on the most challenging of these roads that Postbus tours are so advantageous.) In the islands and in the north and west of Scotland there are single-track roads the width of one vehicle only. These roads have passing places: small areas where vehicles pull in to allow traffic to pass. It is considered discourteous to hold up traffic on these roads, so allow vehicles to pass whenever necessary. It is illegal to park in vehicle passing places.

Another hazard in rural Scotland is sheep on the road. Vast tracts of Scotland are open range, where sheep and other livestock wander freely. Most sheep are well used to cars but they should never be trusted! Exercise caution when sheep are wandering on the road or grazing close by.

Roundabouts are designed to allow an orderly flow of traffic at busy road junctions. Visitors to Scotland can sometimes feel nervous about roundabouts, but provided you know the rules there is nothing to worry about.

Traffic already on the roundabout always has priority and always approaches from your right (never left). Once you have joined a roundabout simply follow the flow of traffic until you reach your exit. There is no need to panic if you miss your exit: just continue round the roundabout and try again.

In Scotland traffic drives on the left and drivers sit in the right-hand side of their vehicles. If you are not used to driving on the left give yourself plenty of time to adjust to the change. For example, it is wise not to drive in a city on your first day.

The speed limit in urban areas is usually 30 miles (50 km) per hour and 40 miles (64 km) per hour on main roads. All speed limits are clearly and regularly indicated on circular red road signs. Outside towns and villages the speed limit is generally 60 miles (96 km) per hour; on motorways it is 70 miles (113 km) per hour. Never assume you know the speed limit: look for a sign first.

Scotland enforces very tough laws for driving under the influence of alcohol, so under no circumstances should you drink and drive.

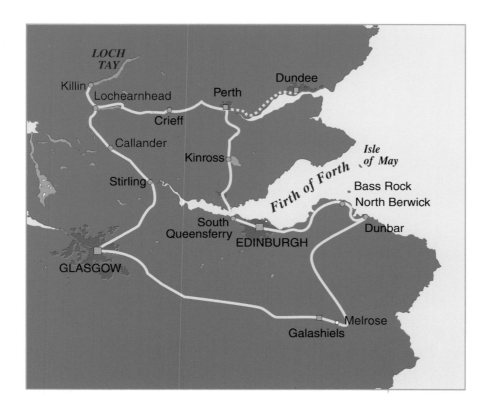

National Gallery of Scotland with its classical design and collection of Old Masters; the Sir Walter Scott Memorial; Charlotte Square; the Royal Botanical Garden with its world-famous rhododendron exhibit; Edinburgh Zoo; and George Street for shopping. Edinburgh has so much to offer it could easily take a week to see everything.

Day 3: Edinburgh-Perth 40 miles (64 km) Leave Edinburgh by proceeding north (M90). Stop to visit Dunfermline, which was the seat of Scotland's kings from Malcolm III in the 11th century until the Union of the Crowns in 1603. Dunfermline Abbey (founded in 1072) is where Robert the Bruce is buried. Andrew Carnegie was born in Dunfermline and his birthplace has become a fascinating museum. Loch Leven Castle at Kinross is your next stop before arriving in Perth for the night. Places of interest in Perth are St John's Kirk, Balhousie Castle, Perth Museum, and the Caithness glass factory. A 20-mile drive on the road to Dundee, the two-acre Branklyn Garden is known as the finest garden of its size in Britain and is well worth the short journey.

Day 4: Perth-Stirling 38 miles (61 km) Travel westward (A85) to Crieff, which has a 19th-century spa, Drummond Castle and sunken Italian Garden, and Glenturret, the Scottish mainland's oldest distillery. East of Crieff (A85) is beautiful Loch Tay. A short journey north (A827) takes you to Killin on Loch Tay with its Folklore Museum. Turn south (A84) for an overnight stay in Stirling.

Day 5: Stirling
Stirling has much to investigate. Its magnificent castle houses the Museum of the Argyll and Sutherland Highlanders,

NINE TOURING IDEAS

These car tours encompass some of Scotland's most spectacular scenery and will help you see the best of both urban and rural Scotland. All tours are circular and you can begin at any point on the route. The major road to use to reach each location is indicated in brackets.

The Southern Uplands and Cities
A seven-day tour over 208 miles (333 km). If you decide to stay in Glasgow or Edinburgh the tour can be longer. Suggested starting point: Melrose.

Day 1: Melrose-Edinburgh 33 miles (53 km)The red-stone Melrose Abbey is situated among the beautiful Eildon Hills. Built in 1136, it is known today as the finest ruined abbey in Scotland.

Stop two miles west of Melrose at Abbottsford House - Sir Walter Scott's home – before proceeding north to explore the Lothians. Go east towards the coast and stop at ancient Dunbar, whose castle looks out over the harbour and cobbled streets of the town. Then travel north (A1) to North Berwick, a popular seaside resort. This royal burgh has a hill formed by volcanic activity called North Berwick Law, at the summit of which is the ruin of a watchtower built during the Napoleonic War and an arch constructed from the jaw-bone of a whale. Just visible three miles out to sea is Bass Rock with

its famous lighthouse. Bass Rock once served as a prison for Covenanters. The ruin of the 14th-century former Douglas Clan headquarters, Tantallon Castle, sits on a wild headland three miles east of town. End the day here or proceed 23 miles (37 km) into Edinburgh for an early start on the big city.

Day 2: Edinburgh
Some recommended sites are Edinburgh Castle; Greyfriars Church (with the graves of 1400 Covenanters); the 15th-century St Giles Cathedral; John Knox's house; the Palace of Holyroodhouse (neglected, but still the official residence of the royal family of Scotland); the

© S J Taylor/ The Still Moving Picture Company

National Gallery of Scotland

while the Wallace Monument provides an audio-visual presentation and fine views from the tower. Other places of interest are Callander, a touring centre for the Trossachs; Queen Elizabeth Forest Park; Inchamahome Priory; and the Bannockburn Battlefield, where Robert the Bruce defeated Edward II in 1314.

Day 6: Stirling-Glasgow 27 miles (43 km)
Travel southwest (M80) to Glasgow, Scotland's largest city and the third most populous in Britain. Glasgow was once an industrial city but is now known for its many cultural attractions. Some of the most popular are the Gallery of Modern Art; the Burrell Collection of textiles, furniture and ceramics; the Art Gallery and Museum in Kelvingrove Park; the Museum of Transport; and the Hunterian Museum and Art Gallery. A concert by the Royal Scottish National Orchestra, the Scottish Opera, or the Scottish National Orchestra at the Royal Concert Hall is worth an overnight stay before returning to the Borders and Melrose through superb countryside.

Malt Whisky

This five-night tour of malt-whisky distilleries encompasses 404 miles (646 km). Unless otherwise stated, all the distilleries on the tour have visitor centres which provide historical information. You can also purchase the whisky, and in some places enjoy a free taste.

Day 1: Edinburgh-Pitlochry
68 miles (109 km)
Edinburgh's Scotch Whisky Heritage Centre provides detailed information on the production and history of whisky (useful background for the rest of the tour). Head north (M90) to Perth and turn west through the Tay valley, via the grand Aberfeldy Bridge (A9 and A827) to Aberfeldy and the Aberfeldy Distillery, which was established in 1896. Further north (A9) there is an even older and extremely interesting distillery: Blair Atholl Distillery in Pitlochry. If you visit Pitlochry in the summer months be sure to check the schedule for their famous Festival in the Hills.

Day 2: Pitlochry-Inverness
119 miles (190 km)
Leave Pitlochry early in the morning and continue north (A9) to the Dalwinnie Distillery, which was established in 1897-98 and is the highest distillery in Scotland. Scotland's largest distillery is north (A9) at Tomatin. The Tomatin Distillery dates from 1897 and offers whisky tasting. Travel north (A9) to Tain to visit the Glenmorangie Distillery. This distillery does not have a visitor centre, but visitors are welcome if they phone in

advance (tel: (01862) 892043). Stay overnight at Tain to visit the beautiful Collegiate Church of St Duthac, Loch Eye, the Pilgrimage Visitor Centre and the ruins of Lochslin Castle, or else head 35 miles (56 km) to Inverness for the night.

Day 3: Inverness-Dufftown
62 miles (99 km) Proceed west (A96) from Inverness to Forres, where the Dallas Dhu Distillery is no longer licensed but operates as a living museum. This is the first of the six distilleries and a cooperage that together comprise the Malt Whisky Trail: watch for road signs identifying the Whisky Trail and its various distilleries. South (A941) from Elgin to Craigellachie, stop at the

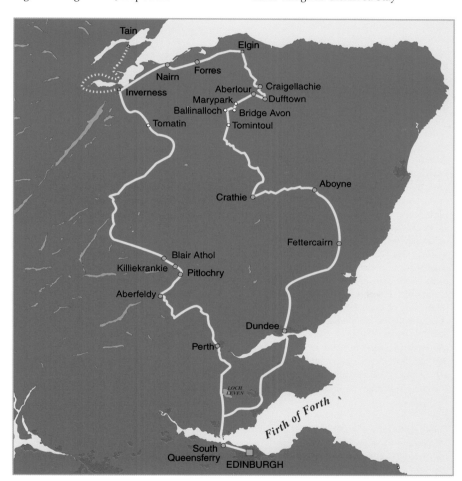

Speyside Cooperage, a working cask- and barrel-making plant. Its "Acorn to Cask" exhibit tells the story of the cooperage industry. There are 16 distilleries between Elgin and Dufftown, two of which are open to visitors. Glen Grant – established in 1840 – has a restored historic woodland garden. The final distillery before an overnight stay in Dufftown is Glenfiddich, which was founded in 1886 and welcomes over 100,000 visitors a year. Its extensive facilities include a bottling plant.

Day 4: Dufftown-Tomintoul
28 miles (45 km)

From Dufftown turn south (A941/A95) toward Aberlour, home to two distilleries only one of which – Cardhu, built in 1824 – is open to the public. Continue west (A95) to Marypark and the Glenfarclas Distillery. Approximately 4 miles from the Bridge of Avon junction is the Tormore Distillery. This distillery does not have a visitor centre but features a breathtaking woodland garden with magnificent topiary. Backtrack east (A95) until you come to the River Avon, and then turn south (B9008) to Ballindalloch and the Glenlivet Distillery. The Tamnavulin Distillery with its charming old mill and sheltered picnic area has a visitor centre in the same village as Glenlivet. Stay overnight in Tomintoul where you will find another distillery, Tomintoul Glenlivet, but it does not have a visitor centre.

Day 5: Tomintoul-Royal Deeside
124 miles (198 km)
Leave the official Whisky Trail and continue south (A939) to Royal Deeside. In the small town of Crathie you will find the Royal Lochnagar Distillery – established in 1826 – with its renowned visitor centre. The distillery is called "Royal" because of its royal patronage. Be sure to visit neighbouring Balmoral

Castle, the summer home of Britain's royal family. Follow the Dee River (A93) and then turn south (B976) at Aboyne and take the beautiful Cairn o' Mount road through the mountains. Your final stop is Fettercairn Distillery, after which you can head south (A94) back to Edinburgh.

Land of the Campbells, Donalds and Hamiltons:

Argyll, Island of Islay and Arran

This five- or six-day tour of 257 miles (331 km) traverses the homeland of three of the largest Scottish clans: the Campbells, the MacDonalds and the Hamiltons. These clans ruled for centuries over beautiful mountains, giant lochs, some of the most famous Hebridean Islands, and many historic sites of great interest.

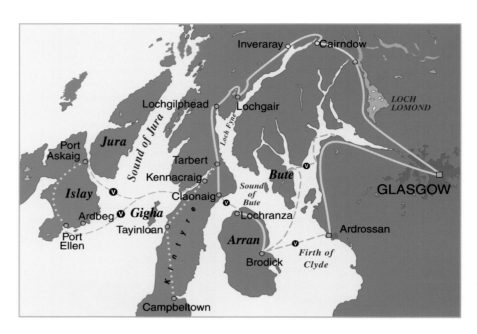

Day 1: Glasgow-Inveraray

58 miles (93 km)

Leave Glasgow and head north (A82) around spectacular Loch Lomond with its tree-covered shoreline and waters reflecting the grandeur of Ben Lomond and the mountains to the east. Stop for refreshments at Tarbet and wander through the pleasant shoreline park to enjoy the stunning splendour of the loch. Proceed east (A83) through high mountains to Cairndow, where you will cross the bridge over the northern tip of Loch Fyne, which stretches 40 miles inland from the sea – one of the longest sea lochs in Scotland. This is the boundary of the ancient territory of the Campbells. Continue east (A83) along the north side of Loch Fyne to the home of the Campbell Clan chiefs, Inveraray Castle. The castle has a well-kept formal garden and a large display of Scottish armour. Stay overnight in Inveraray, whose attractions include Inveraray Jail, the Argyll Wildlife Park and the imposing Bell Tower.

Day 2: Inveraray-Tarbet 38 miles (61 km)

Proceed south from Inveraray by following Loch Fyne (A83) through glorious mountains. The road passes two spectacular gardens: a lovely woodland garden at Crarae on the side of Beinn Ghlas and a more formal garden at Kilmory Castle. The next stop is Kilmartin House, a centre for archaeology and landscape interpretation at Lochgilphead. South of Lochgilphead is Tarbert, a fishing port with the Tairbeart Heritage Centre. Tarbert is the entrance to the Kintyre Peninsula, the ancient homeland of the Scots. At Tarbert two optional tours are available, each of which necessitates an overnight stay:

Option 1
Days 2 and 3: Kintyre Peninsula and

Gigha 37 miles (59 km)

South (A83) at Tayinloan a 15-minute ferry ride across Gigha sound will take you to lush and tranquil Gigha Island and the world-famous Achamore Gardens. Gigha also produces some of the best cheese in Scotland. After visiting the island head for Campbeltown for the night. Campbeltown has a heritage centre. You can explore the rugged mountainous area of the Mull of Kintyre. There are three major lighthouses (Davaar, Sanda, Mull of Kintyre), spectacular views of the Isle of Arran, Machrihanish, and a famous golf course. There is also a ferry to Ballycastle in Northern Ireland.

Option 2
Days 2 and 3: Island of Islay

50 miles (80 km)Take the two-hour ferry ride from Kennacraig (5 miles south of Tarbert) to Port Ellen on the Island of Islay, homeland of the MacDonalds. Islay has no less than six world-renowned distilleries which produce the peat– and smoke-flavoured whiskies known as "Island Malts". A visit to one of the distilleries is part of the Islay experience and three of them are near Port Ellen: Laphroaig, Lagavulin and Ardbeg. The southernmost of the Hebridean Islands, Islay was the seat of the Lords of the Isles and the first home of Clan Donald. The mostly flat green island has many ruins and remnants of the past, such as standing stones, cairns and Dunivaig Castle. The west side of the island has great surfing, bird watching and white sandy beaches. Drive down the Rinns peninsula (A847) to see the beautiful village of Portnahaven and the Rinns of Islay lighthouse. Return north (A847 junction with A846) to Port Askaig. The road passes the side road to Loch Finlaggan and Dunivaig Castle, which

was home to the Lord of the Isles and is a definite place to visit. Proceed north to Port Askaig; if time permits take the short ferry ride to the Island of Jura with its famous Paps Mountains and Corrievreckan tidal whirlpool located at the northern tip of the island. The return ferry to the mainland and Kennacraig takes 1 3/4 hours.

Day 4: Isle of Arran 53 miles (85 km)

Six miles east from Kennacraig (B8001) is Claonaig, from where – in the summer only – you can take a 30-minute ferry ride to the Isle of Arran. Arran is known as "Scotland in Miniature" because the geological fault that separates Scotland's highlands and lowlands neatly divides the island into its own highland and lowland areas. Follow the "String Road" (A841) for 48 miles (77 km) around the island. This journey reveals the island's great diversity, from Goat Fell (the highest mountain in southern Scotland) to the Duke of Hamilton's Brodick Castle, which contains exquisite works of art and racing memorabilia. Brodick Castle has extensive formal gardens, wild garden walks and famous rhododendron gardens. Scattered along the coast are quaint fishing villages with their artists' colonies. You can stay overnight at Brodick.

Day 5: **Glasgow** 29 miles (46 km)

Take the ferry to Ardrossan for a short trip back to Glasgow.

Lighthouse Tours

These three circular tours of the beautiful lighthouses of Scotland also take in some of the country's most spectacular scenery.

West and East Coast Lights

A six-day tour of the lighthouses on the

I will arise now, and go
to Inverness,
And a small villa rent there,
of lath and plaster built;
Nine bedrooms will I have there,
and I'll don my native dress,
And walk around in a damned
loud kilt.

Harry Graham
Taken from *A Little Book of
Scottish Quotations* published by
Appletree Press

east and west coasts of central Scotland covering 749 miles (1205 km) of beautiful Scottish shoreline.

Day 1: North Berwick-Aberdeen
163 miles (261 km)
At North Berwick take a boat to Bass Rock Lighthouse, a remote and desolate rock light station. Bypass Edinburgh centre and head north (A1 and A199) toward Leith where Fidra, a major light, was built just offshore in 1885. Some minor lights are located on the south coast of the Firth of Forth heading west (A198). As you cross the Firth of Forth on the Forth Road Bridge (A90) you can see Oxcars Light (with a distinctive red stripe) standing in the water near the southern end of the Forth Railway Bridge. Turn west after crossing the Forth (A921) for a short stop at Kinghorn to view the castle-like Inchkeith Lighthouse, built in 1804. Continue north (A915) to join the A917 to turn south toward Anstruther, where a boat is available to visit the location of Scotland's first lighthouse on the Isle of May. Further north (A917) is Fife Ness Lighthouse with its white and red beacons. Go north through Dundee, turning east (A92) to follow the coast to Scurdie Ness Lighthouse with its 39-metre tower at Montrose, the Todd Head Lighthouse built in 1897 at Roadside, and Girdle Ness less than a mile east of Aberdeen. Stay overnight in Aberdeen.

Day 2: Aberdeen-Inverness
150 miles (240 km)
Proceed north (A92 to the A952) to the Stevenson-engineered Buchan Ness Lighthouse at Peterhead. Rattray Head Lighthouse – with its brick and granite tower built in 1895 – can be found on a side road to the east just before Crimond. Continue on to Fraserburgh to see Kinnaird Head, where the first lighthouse was built by the Northern Lighthouse Board in 1787. The facility now contains Scotland's lighthouse museum with many artefacts from the history of the Scottish lights and guided tours of the lantern room. Follow the coastline west to Elgin where a short trip north will take you to the all-white Covesea Skerries Lighthouse built in 1846 at Lossiemouth. Head for Inverness for an overnight stay and to see some minor lights in Moray Firth.

Day 3: Inverness-Sleat
178 miles (285 km)
Leave Inverness for a stunning drive through the mountains (A82, A887, A87) to Kyle of Lochalsh and the Kyleakin Lighthouse, which stands at the foot of the Skye toll bridge. Go over the bridge and continue north (A87, A863) to Dunvegan with its beautiful castle. Turn west (B884) toward Millovaig until the road ends. Leave the car to walk 45 minutes around a large headland to visit Neist Point Lighthouse with its spectacular views. Backtrack from Neist Point to Broadford to turn south along the magnificent Sound of Sleat (A851) for a view of the Isleornsay Lighthouse, which stands on an island just offshore surrounded by some of Scotland's most beautiful panoramic views. At low tide you can walk to the light. You can stay overnight in Sleat.

Day 4: Sleat-Ardnamurchan
140 miles (224 km)
Leave Skye and proceed south (A87) through Fort William to Corran Ferry where two minor lights, Corran and Corran Narrows, can be seen. Proceed

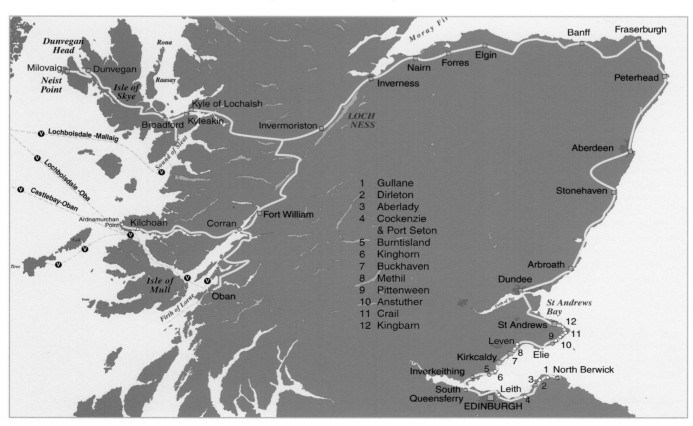

1 Gullane
2 Dirleton
3 Aberlady
4 Cockenzie
   & Port Seton
5 Burntisland
6 Kinghorn
7 Buckhaven
8 Methil
9 Pittenween
10 Anstuther
11 Crail
12 Kingbarn

Càit am biodh na puirt nach faigheadh na clàrsairean?

Where would be the melodies the harpers could not find?

Taken from *A Little Book of Gaelic Proverbs* published by Appletree Press

due west (A861) to a narrow road with passing places (B9007), which follows Loch Sunart and ends near Ardnamurchan Lighthouse. This is the most westerly point of the Scottish mainland and has spectacular views of the islands of Rum, Eigg and Muck. Stay overnight in the area.

Day 5: Ardnamurchan-Oban

110 miles (176 km)
Retrace your journey to the A828 and turn south to Oban, where you will find the Northern Lighthouse Board's depot. Oban is also the home port for the Pharos, which tends all the lights from the sea (during the winter months the ship may be seen at anchor). Oban has many minor lights such as Dubh Sgeir, Dunollie and North Spit of Kerrera. Stay overnight in Oban.

Day 6: Oban and return south

115 miles (184 km)
An option before returning south is to take a ferry to some of the Inner Hebridean islands to see their lights. These include Lismore, built in 1833 on the Isle of Lismore; Rubha nan Gall on the north end of Mull; Scarinish on the island of Tiree; and Skerryvore, which stands on a solitary reef 25 miles west of Mull on the southern tip of Tiree. Otherwise head back to Inverness.

Northern Scotland Lights

This tour has many options for viewing the lights of northern Scotland, including a voyage to the Orkney Islands, the Shetland Islands or the Western Isles of Lewis and Harris. The basic tour lasts four days.

Day 1: Inverness-Wick

104 miles (166 km)
Leave Inverness heading north (A9) and turn east (A832) to reach the Chanory Lighthouse, built in 1894. Continue north (A832) to Cromarty Point Light where a ferry crosses the Cromarty Firth.

After leaving the ferry, continue north (B9175) and then turn east (B1965) to the beautiful red and white banded tower of Tarbert Ness Lighthouse, built in 1830. Return west to the A9 north and travel through beautiful mountains which reach right to the sea. A good stopping place is Clythness Lighthouse, built in 1916 near Lybster. Next stop is Wick (A9), just north of which is the 1849 Stevenson-engineered Noss Head Lighthouse, which has excellent views northwards of the lights yet to come. Near John o' Groats is Duncansby Head Lighthouse, built in 1824 (its famous stacks are nearby). On a clear night seven lighthouses guarding the Pentland Firth can be seen from Duncansby, which makes John o' Groats a good place for an overnight stop.

Day 2: John o' Groats-Durness

94 miles (150 km)
Turning eastward (A836) from John o' Groats, Stroma Island can be seen offshore, with Stroma Lighthouse at its north end. A short distance ahead is Dunnet, where a secondary road north (B855) leads to Dunnet Head Lighthouse, which is the most northerly point on the Scottish mainland and affords spectacular views of the Orkney Islands. The next stop west is Holburn Head Lighthouse on the west coast of busy Scrabster Harbour, just outside of Thurso. (At Scrabster you can catch a

ferry to visit the lighthouses on the Orkney Islands and the Shetland Islands.) Another 12 miles (19 km) further west (A836) a road sign directs you 2 1/2 miles north to Strathy Point Lighthouse, the last staffed lighthouse built by the Northern Lighthouse Board. Continuing west the road wanders through the mountains and lochs of Sutherland's isolated and breathtaking beauty before you arrive at Durness for an overnight stay.

Day 3: Durness-Ullapool

115 miles (184 km)
Begin the day with a ferry trip across the Kyle of Durness to catch the minibus to Cape Wrath Lighthouse, built in 1828 on a cliff 300 feet (91 m) above the sea. Travel 37 miles (60 km) south (A89) and turn east (A837) at Skiag Bridge and head west to Stoer Head Lighthouse, built in 1870. Retrace your steps 28 miles (45 km) south (A837) to stay overnight in the beautiful fishing village of Ullapool (the ferry port for the Western Isles, from where you can take a ferry to see the Isle of Harris and Isle of Lewis lighthouses).

Day 4: Ullapool return to Inverness

83 miles (133 km)
Leaving Ullapool continue south (A835) for 12 miles (19 km) to the junction with the A832 west. Proceed west (A832) for 42 miles (68 km) to Gairloch, from where

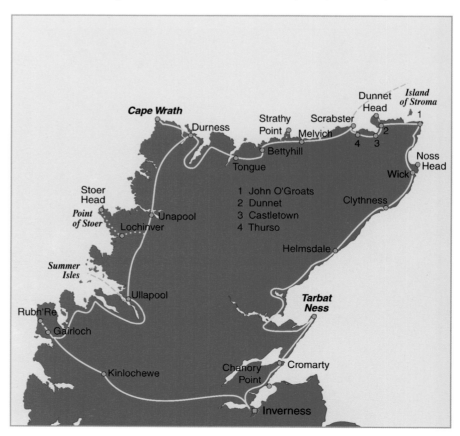

a single-track road (B8021) will take you to beautiful Rubh' Re Lighthouse, built in 1912. It is approximately 25 miles (40 km) to the lighthouse and back and well worth it for the views. Continue south (A832), with the spectacular Sutherland mountain scenery for company.

The Clyde Lights
A tour of the lights which guard the Firth of Clyde.

Day 1: Glasgow-Stranraer
121 miles (194 km)

Leave Glasgow heading west (M8, A8) to Greenock and take the A770 out to the coast to see the Cloch Lighthouse, built in 1797. Follow the A770 along the shore until you turn south (A78). A little farther south you should be able to see Little Cumbrae Island and its lighthouse, built in 1757 and rebuilt in 1905. Continue south (A78) until you can turn west (A719) to follow the coastline. At Turnberry there is a secondary road just north of the clubhouse which enters the golf course. Follow this road to a car park where a short walk across the golf course ends at Turnberry Lighthouse, built in 1873. After Turnberry head straight south (A77): you will see the island of Ailsa Craig offshore with the Ailsa Craig Lighthouse rock station visible on a clear day. Just before you reach Stranraer you will see a beautiful minor light at Cairn Point. Stay overnight in Stranraer.

Day 2: Stranraer-Ardrossan
135 miles (216 km)

Leave Stranraer and proceed south (A716) to the Mull of Galloway Lighthouse with its thrilling views of the coastline and the tidal pools in the sea below. Retrace the way (A716) until the junction with the A77 towards Portpartrich. Turn north (B738) until you reach the road marked Killantringan Lighthouse. This lighthouse – built in

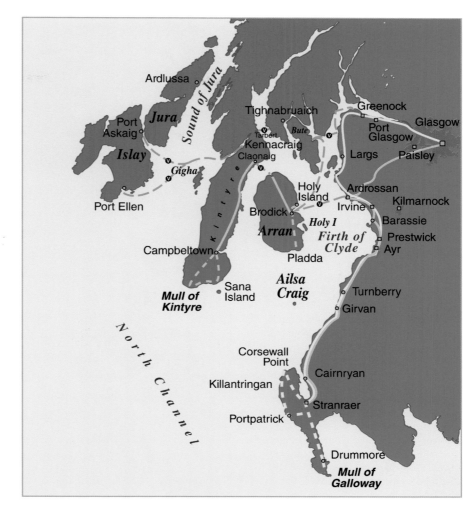

1900 – has beautiful views and a wreck visible in the bay beneath it. After Killantringan continue north (B738) to the roundabout marked Corsewall Point Lighthouse, which is now a hotel. After Corsewall proceed to Stranraer and then north (A77) to Ayr.

Follow the A719 south out of Ayr, to pass minor lights at Barassie and Ardrossan before reaching Anrdrossan, where a ferry leaves for the Isle of Arran. On Arran there are two lights: Holy Isle built

in 1905 and the much older Pladda Lighthouse built in 1790 just off the south coast. Stay overnight at Brodick.

Day 3: Brodick-Campbeltown
50 miles (80 km)

In winter take the ferry and head back to Glasgow. In summer it is possible to visit the lighthouses on the Kintyre Peninsula from Arran: take the ferry to Claonaig and turn south (B842) to Campbeltown, on an island in the harbour. Ten miles

© *Doug Corrance/ The Still Moving Picture Company*

(16 km) south (B842) is Sanda Island with the beautiful Sanda Lighthouse. An adventurous drive from South Carrine on a mountainous single-track road leads to the Mull of Kintyre Lighthouse, made famous by Paul McCartney's Mull of Kintyre. The Mull has magnificent scenery. Stay overnight in Campbeltown.

Day 4: Campbeltown-Glasgow
134 miles (214 km)
Take the A83 and head back to Glasgow.

Wildlife Tour

This tour travels 719 miles (1150 km) to see examples of the diverse wildlife of Scotland.

Day 1: North Berwick-Perth
73 miles (117 km)
East of Edinburgh, a boat trip from North Berwick takes you to Bass Rock in the Firth of Forth. Bass Rock has a famous gannet colony of over 50,000 birds. Travel north towards Perth (M90) and visit Vane Farm on Loch Leven, a nature reserve near Kinross run by the Royal Society for the Protection of Birds (RSPB) for wintering wildfowl. Kinross has many other attractions including a castle and gardens. Stay overnight in the Perth area.

Day 2: Perth-Braemar 99 miles (158 km)
Begin by journeying north (A9) to Dunkeld for the nearby Loch of the Lowes, noted for its summer-visiting ospreys (there are now over 100 pairs of ospreys in Scotland, breeding mostly in the highlands). There is excellent hill walking in this area. Continue (A923) to Blairgowrie and then north towards Braemar (A93) to the Cairnwell pass. At 2182 feet (665 m) above sea level this is Britain's highest road pass: there are two ski resorts and breathtaking panoramic views. Continue into Royal Deeside, which is golden eagle and ptarmigan country. Mountain hares – white in winter – also live on these heathered hills. Stay overnight in Braemar, where you can also visit beautiful Braemar Castle.

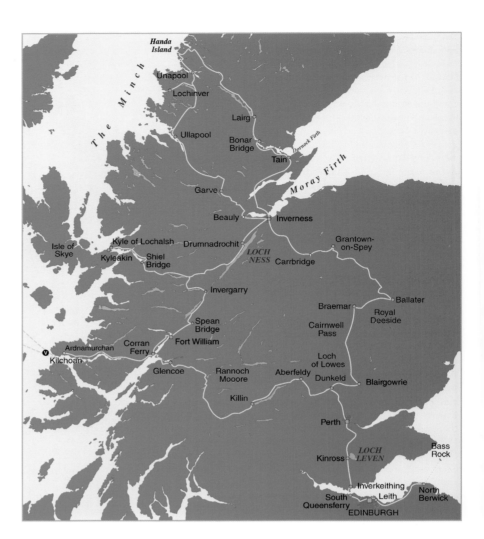

© Niall Benvie/ The Still Moving Picture Company

Day 3: Braemar-Carrbridge
64 miles (102 km)
Beyond Braemar drive through what remains of the once-widespread Caledonian pinewoods, home to Britain's only native bird, the Scottish crossbill. Near the ancient spa town of Ballater lies the Muir of Dinnet Reserve, with its visitor centre and the fascinating Burn o' Vat – a huge glacial pothole. Follow the A939 as it winds over heather moors towards the Lecht and look for red grouse. Grantown-on-Spey begins the Speyside area known for the elusive Capercaillie, the "cock of the north". Continue (A9) to Carrbridge, where the Landmark Visitor Centre tells the story of the pinewoods. Stay overnight at Carrbridge. South of Carrbridge you will find wildlife areas at Aviemore and great hill walking at Abernethy Forest on Loch Garten.

Day 4: Carrbridge-Lochinver
210 miles (338 km)
North of Inverness (A9) the Moray Firth and the Beauly Firth have a large population of bottlenose dolphins. Find out more about the dolphins at the North Kessock Centre, just across the Kessock Bridge. Continue north

(A9) and west (A838) through the beautiful wild countryside of Sutherland to Handa Island, another seabird city. Stay overnight around Lochinver on the spectacular west coast of Sutherland.

Day 5: Lochinver-Kyleakin
124 miles (198 km)Return to Inverness (A82) following Loch Ness (home of legendary "Nessie"), en route to Kyleakin for an overnight stay. An alternative route would be to follow the road (A832) which winds south down the west coast of Scotland, where the views are dramatic but the journey can be slow.

Day 6: Kyleakin-Ardnamurchan
135 miles (216 km)
The Castle Moil seal cruises can be taken at Kyleakin and otters can be seen around the lighthouses at Kyleakin and the Isle of Ornsay. The Skye Environmental Centre at Broadford arranges guided walks. On the mainland continue south beyond Fort William. Divert from the A82 via the Corran ferry for a beautiful drive to Glenmore to visit the wildlife centre (run by a local naturalist) with its wildcat den and river salmon. Continue on to

Red deer stag

Ardnamurchan, the most westerly mainland point in Britain. Stay overnight.

Day 7: Ardnamurchan-Glencoe 74 miles (118 km) Travel east (A830) to the Corran ferry and then on to Fort William (A82). At Fort William you can climb Glen Nevis for wonderful views and close-up encounters with wildlife. Leave Fort William (A82) to reach one of the most dramatically beautiful of Scotland's mountain areas at Glencoe. Wildlife abounds in this area, particularly red deer. To the east is Rannoch Moor, which straddles the A82 to Stirling. If you are lucky enough to visit in the autumn during the red deer rut (breeding) the hills resound with the bellowing of stags.

Castles and Kings

Explore Scottish castles on a nine-day tour covering 729 miles (1166 km). Castles in Scotland range from ruined fortresses to elegant homes closely associated with Scotland's monarchy. These imposing buildings provide an insight into the history of Scotland. You can join and leave the tour at any point, depending on the time available.

Day 1: English Border-Melrose
14 miles (23 km) Head toward Jedburgh (A68) to Ferniehirst Castle, Scotland's frontier fortress and the ancestral home of the Clan Kerr. On to Kelso (A68) for Floors Castle, the 18th-century building which is the home of the Duke and Duchess of Roxburgh and the largest inhabited house in Scotland. It contains fine furniture, tapestries and paintings. King James II was killed near here in 1460 by an exploding cannon. Take a leisurely drive through beautiful Borders countryside (A6404) and watch for signs for Smailholm Tower on the minor roads, which lead to a simple ancient rectangular tower. There are great panoramic views from the rocky outcrop upon which the tower stands.
Stay overnight at Melrose or elsewhere in the area.

Day 2: Melrose-Perth via Edinburgh
75miles (120km) Begin early in the morning by going 14 miles north (A68) to Thirlestane Castle in Lauder, which contains the Border Country Life Museum. Continue north (A68): just to the west near Pathhead (B6367) is Crichton Castle, associated with Mary Queen of Scots and one of whose former owners was chancellor to James II. A little further north on the A68 is Oxenford Castle, home of the Dalrymple family and now a school for girls. Continue into Edinburgh (you may wish to take an extra day to see all of Edinburgh's castles). Begin with Edinburgh Castle,

which houses the crown jewels, the Stone of Destiny and the Scottish National War Memorial. Two miles south of the city centre on the Edinburgh-Dalkeith Road is Craigmillar Castle, where Mary Queen of Scots hid after her secretary Rizzio was murdered. North (A90) is Lauriston Castle, a beautiful Edwardian home with a fine collection of furniture and decorative art, set in tranquil grounds. West and north of Edinburgh (A90) travel west (A904) to see Dundas Castle near South Queensferry before proceeding to Linlithgow Palace, the birthplace of Mary Queen of Scots. Return to the M90, turning west (A91) and south (A912) for the Falkland Palace – a former hunting lodge of the Stuart monarchs – before heading north for Perth for the night.

Day 3: Perth-Stonehaven 75 miles (120 km) Northeast of Perth (A93) visit historic Scone Palace, associated with the crowning of early Scottish monarchs. Twelve miles northwest of Dundee (A90/A928) Glamis Castle is the seat of the Earls of Strathmore. North (A90) is the turn-off for the early 16th-century Edzell Castle with its famous pleasance (walled formal garden). Continue north (A90) to the spectacular cliff fortress of Dunottar, once a refuge for the crown

jewels and used as the location for Mel Gibson's movie of Hamlet. Stay overnight at Stonehaven.

Day 4: Stonehaven-Banff 69 miles (110 km)Travel west from Stonehaven (A957) for 14 miles (23 km) to the Burnett family castle, Crathes Castle, with its magnificent gardens. Continue north (B977) by minor roads to reach Castle Fraser near Dunecht. From here there are signs to many fine castles on the local castle trail such as Fyvie (on the A947), which is a great example of Scots baronial architecture. Continue north (A947) to visit Duff House, an outpost of the National Galleries of Scotland, on the coast near Banff. Proceed to Banff for your overnight stay.

Day 5: Banff-Tain 108 miles (173 km)Travelling west (A96) from Banff you will find Brodie Castle near Forres, which incorporates the old fortalice of the original castle built in 1609. Cawdor Castle (built in 1362) lies southwest of Nairn on the Moray Firth coastline: Shakespeare refers to Cawdor Castle in Macbeth. Continue to Inverness, where King David built the first castle in the 12th century. The present castle in the middle of the town was built in 1834.

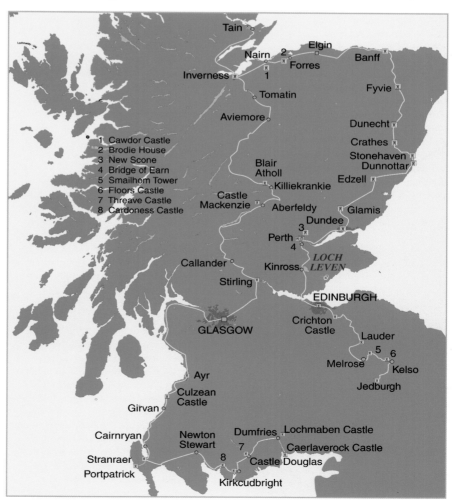

Map keys:

1. Muirfield
2. Gullane
3. Luffness
4. Longniddry
5. Prestonpans
6. Musselburgh
7. Pencaitland
8. Dalkeith
9. Aberdour
10. Burntisland

1. West Kilbride
2. Seamill
3. Ardrossan
4. Saltcoats
5. Irvine
6. Gailies
7. Barassie
8. Troon
9. Preswick
10. Ayr

Two other Inverness castles are Castle Stuart six miles east on the A96 and Aldourie Castle on the northernmost tip of Loch Ness. Continue on to Tain to stay overnight.

Day 6: Tain-Aberfeldy
134 miles (181 km)
Tain was a place of pilgrimage for Scottish kings (its story is told in Tain through Time at the visitor centre). Return through Inverness to begin the southward part (A9) of the tour with Blair Castle near Blair Atholl. The castle dates back to 1269 and was visited by both Mary Queen of Scots and Bonnie Prince Charlie. Nearby is Killiecrankie, where the Jacobites defeated a government army in 1689. Stay overnight at Aberfeldy.

© David Robertson/ The Still Moving Picture Company

Day 7: Aberfeldy-Stirling
48 miles (77 km)
Near Aberfeldy is Castle Menzies, erected in the latter part of the 16th century and now owned by the Clan Menzies Society, who opened it to the public. Enjoy the scenery along Loch Tay before turning south (A84) to Stirling. Stirling Castle was one of the principal courts of the Stuart monarchs of Scotland. The town of Stirling has many places of historic interest, including the Wallace Memorial and the site of the Battle of Stirling Bridge. Stirling is your overnight stay.

Day 8: Stirling-Ayr
66 miles (106 km)
From Stirling, travel via Glasgow (M80) down to the Ayrshire coast. First stop (A719) is the neoclassical opulence of Culzean Castle, the "jewel in the crown" of the National Trust. Morton Castle at Douglas – known also as Douglas Larder – is worth a visit. Stay overnight in Ayr.

Day 9: Ayr-Dumfries
140 miles (224 km)
Continuing southward (A77), Dumfries and Galloway have many castles: they include Cardoness Castle at Gatehouse of Fleet, St John Castle at Stranraer, Dunskey Castle at Portpatrick, Lochmaben Castle (seat of Robert the Bruce) and MacLellan Castle at Kirkcubrigh. Two castles of particular note are the stern tower of the 14th-century Threave Castle near Castle Douglas and the unique triangular design of the 13th-century stronghold of the Maxwells, Caerlaverock Castle at Dumfries. Stay overnight in Dumfries.

Golf Tours
The following four tours of golf courses are not divided into days of travel but simply by locality, so you can play as many rounds as you like a teach course!

Tour 1: Edinburgh and the Lothians
65 miles (104 km)
Begin in Edinburgh with two historic courses: the Bruntsfield Links (18 holes, 6407 yards;tel: (01313) 361479) in Davidsons Mains and the Royal Burgess (18 holes, 6494 yards; tel: (01313) 392075) in Linlithgow. These two courses have over 500 years of golf history between them. Take the A198 at Prestonpans near Musselburgh on the way to Longniddry Golf Course, which is part links, part parkland. You will pass Seton, where Mary Queen of Scots practised her golf 400 years ago. Longniddry Golf Course (18 holes, 6210 yards; tel: (01875) 852141) has beautiful views of the seaand is 13 miles east of Edinburgh.
One short detour to the sea (A198) leads you to Kilspindie(18 holes, 5410 yards; tel: (01875) 870358), Luffness New (18 holes, 5750 yards; tel: (01620) 843114) and three courses at Gullane before you reach historic Muirfield (18 holes, 6941 yards; tel: (01620) 842123), with its unique layout of outer and inner loops. Continue on to the West Links in North Berwick (18 holes, 6033 yards; tel: (01620) 892135). The West Links design has been copied all over the world. Turn south on the A198 to find the Dunbar Golf Course(18 holes, 6426 yards; tel: (01368) 862317), a narrow links which follows the coastline. Turn west (A1) until Haddington and then turn south (B6368) to pass a few

Wallace Monument from Stirling Castle

courses near Gifford. Newbattle Golf Course (18 holes, 6025 yards; tel: (01316) 631819) can be reached by turning north at the junction with the A68. Go around Edinburgh (A720) and west (M8) to reach Deer Park (18 holes, 6636 yards and continue onto Bathgate Golf Course (18 holes, 6362 yards; tel: (01506) 630533), a moorland course.

Tour 2: Southern Scotland
311 miles (498 km)
Courses in Galloway, Dumfries and the Borders are not world renowned but there are some enjoyable challenges nevertheless. Begin in the Borders with the unique Kelso Golf Course (18 holes, 6066 yards; tel: (01573) 23009) which lies inside the racetrack near Kelso. Head west (A699) toward Selkirk for the nine-hole Selkirk Course (5620 yards; tel: (01750) 20621). Turn south (A7) to Hawick for the Hawick Golf Course (18 holes, 5929 yards; tel: (01450) 372293) and the Minto Golf Course (18 holes, 5460 yards; tel: (01450) 870220). Continue on the A7 until Langholm, with its nine-hole course (5744 yards; tel: (01387) 381247), and then turn west (B7068) towards Lockerbie where you can find Lochmaben Golf Course (18 holes, 5537 yards; tel: (01387) 810552). A short trip to the south (B7238) will bring you to Powfoot Golf Course (18 holes, 6266 yards; tel: (01461) 700276), a difficult semi-links course with lots of heather and gorse. Proceed west and north (B725) amid spectacular views of the Solway Firth to Dumfries, with its 18-hole Dumfries and County Golf Course (5803 yards; tel: (01387) 253585). Continue south (A710) to one of Scotland's most famous links: Southerness Golf Course is the only championship links course built since 1945 (18 holes, 6566 yards; tel: (01387) 880677). Proceed to Castle Douglas via the A745 where you turn west (A75) until you reach Newton Stewart. Fourteen miles south (A714) is Wigtown, where you will find an excellent nine-hole course, Wigtown and Bladnoch Golf Course (2732 yards; tel: (01988) 403354) and a good 18-hole course, Newton Stewart (5970 yards; tel: (01671) 402172). Head for Stranraer (A75) with its Stranraer Golf Course (18 holes, 6300 yards; tel: (01776) 703539), a fine parkland course overlooking Loch Ryan. A short journey southwest (A77) of about 10 miles brings you to beautiful Portpatrick with its clifftop course (18 holes, 5644 yards; tel: (01776) 810273). Return to Stranraer and proceed east (A75) to Dumfries for a 15-mile trip (A76) to Thornhill for 18 holes (6011 yards; tel: (01848) 331779). From Dumfries proceed north (A701) to Moffat in the Annandale Valley and play its

Golf, Crail

© Robert Lees/ The Still Moving Picture Company

moorland course (18 holes, 5218 yards; tel: (01683) 220020). Leaving Moffat continue north (A701) to play the course at Peebles (18 holes, 6160 yards; tel: (01721) 720197), a public course set in a beautiful area. Further east (A72) the Innerleithen course can be found. For a round at the Galashiels 18-hole course (5785 yards; tel: (01896) 753724) continue east (A72). Proceed north (A7) and then east (B6362) for nine holes at Lauder (6002 yards; tel: (01578) 772256).

Tour 3: Western Scotland
138 miles (220 km)
In one of the most popular golf areas of Scotland, begin at Turnberry with its two championship courses (18 holes, 6976 yards and 6014 yards respectively; tel: (01655) 331000) on the west coast just south of Ayr. Turnberry is considered by many to be the most beautiful golf course in Scotland, with views of Ailsa Craig, the Isle of Arran, the Mull of Kintyre and its symbol, Turnberry Lighthouse. Leaving Turnberry go north (A719) towards Ayr, where you will find Belleisle (18 holes, 5900 yards; tel: (01292) 441258), a beautiful Parkland course. North of Ayr you will find popular and prominent links courses such as Western Gailes (18 holes, 6639 yards; tel: (01294) 311649), Prestwick, the birthplace of the Open Championship (18 holes, 6544 yards; tel: (01292) 477404), Barassie Glasgow Gailes (18 holes, 6510 yards; tel: (01294) 311347) and Irvine (18 holes, 6408 yards; tel: (01294) 275979). For a change of pace ride the ferry from Ardrossan to the Isle of Arran to play two lovely and exceptional courses: Brodick (18 holes, 4409 yards; tel: (01770) 302349) and Lamlash (18 holes, 6542 yards; tel: (01770) 600296). Back on the mainland the star of this area is the world-famous Royal Troon which has staged six Open Championships. The Royal Troon has two 18-hole courses, the Old Troon (7097 yards) and the Portland (6386 yards; tel: (01292) 312464). Farther north (A78) you will find the West Kilbride links (18 holes, 6542 yards; tel: (01294) 823911) and the wooded Largs (18 holes, 6220 yards; tel: (01475) 673594) courses. The Isle of Bute has the Rothesay

18-hole course (5370 yards; tel: (01700) 502244). Glasgow has many famous courses but access is difficult. There are two municipal courses with fairly easy admission and reasonable prices: Lethamhill (18 holes, 5836 yards; tel: (01417) 706220) and Little Hill (18 holes, 6240 yards; tel: (01417) 721916). Head north from Glasgow (A82) to the Loch Lomond Golf Club (18 holes, 7053 yards; tel: (01436) 860223), beautifully set on the world-famous "bonnie banks of Loch Lomond".

Two courses are accessible by air from Glasgow. On the Isle of Islay at Port Ellen is the 18-hole links course of Machrie (6226 yards; tel: (01496) 302310). Machrihanish (18 holes, 6228 yards; tel: (01586) 810213) is on the Mull of Kintyre near Campbeltown. It is the most geographically remote of all the great courses on the British Isles.

Tour 4: Fife
75 miles (120 km)
Begin at Dunfermline with two parkland courses, Dunfermline (18 holes, 6244 yards; tel: (01383) 723534) and Pitreavie (18 holes, 6032 yards; tel: (01383) 722591). Admission is simple if prior arrangements are made. Go southeast to the Firth of Forth shore for some difficult challenges and some lovely views over the Firth of Forth at Burntisland Golf Course (18 holes, 5908 yards; tel: (01592) 873247). An interesting 18 holes is available at Aberdour (A921) (5460 yards; tel: (01383) 860080). Proceed east (A921) to Kirkcaldy where you will find two courses: Dunnikier, a public course (18 holes, 6601 yards; tel: (01592) 261599) and Kirkcaldy (18 holes, 6004 yards; tel: (01592) 260370). Beyond Kirkcaldy (A921) on the spectacular east coast of Scotland are the "famous five". Leven Links (18 holes, 6433 yards; tel: (01333) 421390) and Lundin Links (18 holes, 6377 yards; tel: (01333) 320202) are the least known of these courses. Elie (18 holes, 6267 yards; tel: (01333) 330301), a popular, charming and very natural links with beautiful views over the Firth, lies south on the A917. East of Elie (A917) is the seventh-

oldest golf club in the world, the Crail
Golfing Society with the Balcomie links
(18 holes, 5922 yards; tel: (01333) 450686).
In St Andrews, the mecca of golf, take
time to visit the British Golf Museum
next to the first tee on the Old Course.
The Old Course is open to visitors, but
play must be arranged in advance.
There are five other 18-hole links at St
Andrews (tel: (01334) 475757): the New
Course (6604 yards), the Jubilee (6805
yards), the Eden (6112 yards), the new
Strathyrum Course (5087 yards) and the
inland Duke's Course (7271 yards).
Go west (A91) to one of Fife's beautiful
inland courses, Cupar (5350 yards; tel:
(01334) 653549). Cupar is one of the
oldest nine-hole golf courses in Scotland
and well worth visiting. Turning south
(A92) it is only a short distance to
Ladybank (18 holes, 6641 yards; tel:
(01337) 830814) – a few miles north of
Leven – with its delightful mixture of
pine and heather. A few miles farther
south is Glenrothes (18 holes, 6444
yards; tel: (01592) 758686), one of the
newer courses.

Viking Country

The Orkney Islands and the Shetland
Islands have a long and interesting
history, much of which has been closely
connected with the Norse peoples of
Scandinavia. The following circular tour
covers the Orkneys and the
Shetlands, but individual island tours
can be taken separately. The whole nine-
day tour covers 207 miles (333 km) by
road and sea.

Orkney Islands

Day 1: Aberdeen-Stromness
Catch the PO Scottish ferry from
Aberdeen to Stromness Harbour in the
Orkney Islands. The trip lasts eight hours.
If you also wish to visit Hoy there is a
ferry connection from Stromness.

Day 2: Stromness-Lerwick
38 miles (61 km)
The harbour in Stromness was first
constructed in the 1700s: it has been a
port for whaling ships and the Hudson
Bay Company. Points of interest are the
Stromness Museum, Old Orkney
Distillery and the Pier Arts Centre.
Leave Stromness and head north (A967)
toward Birsay through the Sandwick
area, which includes Raven Ale, the
Orkneys' only brewery; the Bay of Skaill;
the 17th-century Skaill house; the
beautiful cliffs at Rora Head; and
Borwick's historic broch. The B9056 leads
to Birsay Bay with its historic and
beautiful grassy island the Brough of
Birsay, with good bird watching and a
lighthouse. Continue east (A966) toward
Evie and enjoy the north coast of the
Orkney mainland with views of Rousay.
Burgar Hill with its aerogenerators and
the Broch of Gurness, one of Orkney's
best-preserved brochs, are in this area.
Turn south toward Kirkwall (A965) and

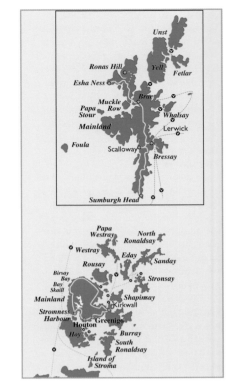

pass through the Firth area. At Finstown
– with its unusual Binscarth trees – turn
east for several historic sites such as the
Chambered Cairn at Cuween Hill and the
Rennibister Earth House. Stay overnight
at Kirkwall

Day 3: Kirkwall
Kirkwall is the capital of the Orkney
Islands and has many places to see, such
as St Magnus Cathedral, Bishop's Palace,
Earl's Palace, Tankerness House Museum
and Gardens, Highland Park Distillery,
Kirkwall Golf Course and the Orkney
Wireless Museum. Ferries
sail to the northern Orkney Islands of
Shapinsay, Eday, Westray, Papa
Westray, North Ronaldsay and Stronsay
from Kirkwall.

Day 4: Kirkwall-Stromness
21 miles (34 km)
Proceed west (A964) toward Houton
where you will find Scapa Distillery, an
excellent view of Scapa Flow from
Greenigoe, and an RSPB bird reserve. At
Houton you can catch the ferries to Hoy
and Flotta. Continuing on the A964 you
will reach Stenness, the heart of Neolithic
Orkney with the Ring of Brodgar,
Standing Stones of Stenness, the
Maeshowe chambered Cairn, Unstan
tomb, Bookan Cairn and Ring, and the
Barnhouse complex. Proceed to
Stromness for the night, after which you
can catch the ferry to mainland Scotland
or on to the Shetlands.

Day 5: Stromness-Lerwick
The ferry ride from Stromness to Lerwick
in the Shetland Islands takes eight hours.

© David Robertson/ The Still Moving Picture Company

St Ninian's Isle, Shetland Islands

© Robert Lees/ The Still Moving Picture Company

Applecross

Day 6: Lerwick

With a population of 8,000 Lerwick is the largest settlement in the Shetlands. The Shetland Museum, which explains folk life, shipping, art and archaeology, is a good place to begin your visit. Some of Lerwick's attractions include Clickhimin Broch, a broch built within an Iron Age fort; Fort Charlotte, built in 1665; and Gremista, an 18th-century fishing booth. The finest example of a broch is Mousa Broch on the Island of Mousa, a short ferry ride from Lerwick (only in the summer). Another short ferry ride is to Bressay's Noss National Nature Reserve, where there are thousands of puffins and gannets. Ferries are also available from Lerwick to the Out Skerries and Norway.

Day 7: Lerwick-Esha Ness

69 miles (139 km)

While in the Shetlands keep an eye out for the famous but rare Shetland miniature ponies. Go north (A970) until the junction with the B9078, which leads to the cliffs and awesome rock features of Esha Ness on the northwest coast (the cliffs at Esha Ness are considered to be the most dramatic in all of Britain). The Holes of Scraada, the Heads of Grocken and the Grind of the Navir are especially grand. South (B9078) of Esha Ness you will find the Drongs – large sea stacks – in the bay. Backtrack to the A970 and continue north to Ronas Hill; its low-altitude arctic environment encourages many arctic and alpine plants. Stay overnight in Brae on the Mavis Grind, where the Shetland mainland is almost split in two except for the narrow rock on which the road is built.

Day 8: Brae-Scalloway

23 miles (37 km)

As you return south (A970) the next stop is Scalloway, the second-largest settlement in the Shetlands and older than Lerwick. The town is dominated by the ruins of Scalloway Castle, built in the 1600s. The museum which tells the story of the "Shetland Bus" – the operation which rescued Norwegian refugees from occupied Norway during the Second World War – is an interesting stop. Stay overnight in Scalloway.

Day 8: Scalloway-south of Shetland mainland 56 miles (90 km)

Go south (A970) toward Sumburgh, where there is a lighthouse and an easily accessible colony of puffins at Sumburgh Head. The main attraction in this area is Jarlshof, an ancient site of Norse buildings. Sumburgh is also the location for Shetland's airport. Return to Lerwick for the ferry back to the Scottish mainland or fly home from here.

Postbus Tour

Postal and passenger services to remote rural areas in Scotland began in 1968.

There are now more than 140 Postbuses, which offer visitors a unique way of seeing the country. The two tours by Postbus described here are for those who really want to see the countryside but do not want to drive themselves. Travelling by Postbus means that you can reach some of the most isolated areas of Scotland and not have to worry about difficult roads. There are Postbus tours of most of the remote areas of Scotland. Postbuses run from Monday to Saturday. You can stop at any of the small towns, since most of them have hunting/fishing lodges or bed and breakfast accommodation. Except on Sundays, you can pick up the Postbus for your return journey whenever you want. Brochures are available from Royal Mail Scotland & Northern Ireland, 102 W. Port, Edinburgh EH3 9HS; tel: (0345) 740740.

Tour 1: Lairg-Durness

175 miles (280 km) Begin at Lairg to travel north (A836) through the mountains to arrive at Altnaharra on beautiful Loch Naver. Turning west, go deep into the mountains following the Meadle Burn through Corburnuisach to arrive at Cashel Dhu at the south end of Loch Hope. From the Postbus there are spectacular mountain views around Loch Hope and north to the village of Hope, and then west (A838) to Polla at the south end of Loch Eriboll. Continuing on to the west side of Loch Eriboll the Postbus arrives in Durness, where there is overnight accommodation. In the Durness area you can take a sea cruise and visit the historic Smoo Cave or cross the Kyle of Durness by ferry to visit Cape Wrath Lighthouse.

Tour 2: Shieldaig-Applecross Peninsula

27 miles (43 km)

The Postbus travels from Shieldaig along the shores of Loch Shieldaig and Loch Torridon around the north side of the remote and glorious Applecross Peninsula, which was inaccessible by car until a few years ago. Along the west shore of the peninsula there are views of the Isles of Rona, Raasay and Skye across the Inner Sound. At Toscaig Jetty in Applecross there are more beautiful views of the islands and the mountains.

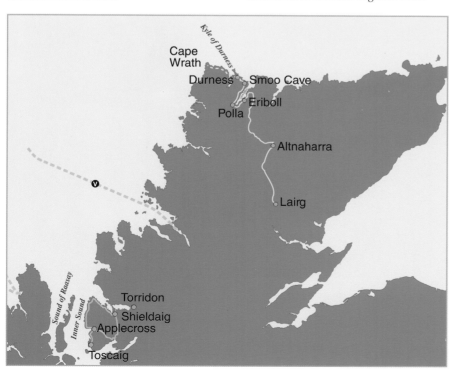

EDINBURGH

The capital of Scotland, Edinburgh is a beautiful city set on a series of hills. The city has a rich historic past and is divided into two towns, the Old and the New.

Calton Hill

From this area of neo-classical buildings there is a magnificent panoramic view of the city (Robert Louis Stevenson's favourite view). **The James Craig Observatory** is the only surviving building by New Town planner James Craig. The New Observatory provides an audiovisual presentation of Edinburgh's history (open: April-Oct, Mon-Fri 10.30am-5.30pm, Sat-Sun 10.30am-5pm; tel: (01315) 564365). Other interesting buildings are **Waterloo Place; St Andrews House; the Dugald Stewart Memorial** (loosely based on the temple of Lysicrates in ancient Athens); the 12-column portico of the unfinished **National Monument** (commemorating those Scots who died in the Napoleonic Wars); and the **Nelson Monument**, a 106 feet (32 m) tiered circular tower with magnificent views of Edinburgh (open: April-Sept, Mon-Sat 10am-6pm; Oct-Mar, Mon-Sat 10am-3pm; tel: (01305) 562716). The Royal High School has an imposing porticoed front.

Canongate is the section of Royal Mile from High Street to the entrance of Holyroodhouse. Canongate was once a town with trading rights granted by the monarch. The graveyard of Canongate Kirk, built in 1688, is the final resting place of many famous Scots. A statue near the wall of the graveyard is of Agnes McLehose, the "Clarinda" to whom Robert Burns wrote passionate letters during his recovery from an injured leg. **Acheson House**, built in 1633, across from the graveyard, is a fine example of a town mansion (open June-Sept, Mon-Sat 10.30am-4.30pm; tel: (01315) 563515). **Canongate Tolbooth,** built in 1591, is a good example of the customs houses where tolls were gathered and which later became town halls and prisons. It now contains the People's Story Museum, which describes how the area was once a thriving commercial centre (open: Mon-Sat 10am-5pm; tel: (01315) 294057).

Charlotte Square In 1791 Robert Adam was commissioned to design what is now New Town's most impressive square, at the centre of which is a statue of Prince Albert on horseback. The headquarters of the **National Trust for Scotland** are located at no. 5 (open: Mon-Fri 9am-5.30pm; tel: (01312) 265922). **Bute House** (no. 6) is the official residence of the Secretary of State for Scotland. The **Georgian House** at no. 7 is refurbished

in the style of a typical Georgian home of the late 1700s (open: April-Oct 10am-5pm; tel: (01312) 263318). On the west side, **St George's Church** is the focal point for George Street and has been converted into the West Register House with a good historical exhibition (open: Mon-Fri 9am-4.45pm; tel: (01315) 568921). George Street meets Charlotte Square and ends at St Andrew Square. Once solely residential, it has become a bustling commercial area. Toward the east end are the Assembly rooms, built in 1784 and patronised by luminaries such as Sir Walter Scott and Robert Burns. The Church of St Andrew and St George – with its towering spire – was built in 1785 and was the birthplace of the Free Church of Scotland. St Andrew Square has a 150-feet (46 m) statue of Henry Dundas, Viscount Melville, better known as "King Harry IX" for his successful administration of Scotland from 1782 to 1805. There are many more splendid buildings in the area, among them Buchan House, Dundas House and the domed Royal Bank of Scotland.

City Art Centre Market Street.

This six-floor art gallery displays its own impressive collection of Scottish paintings and periodically exhibits other important collections.

Craigmillar Castle 3 miles (5 km) southeast of St Leonard's Street. Believed to be where the plot to kill Mary Queen of Scots' husband was first conceived, Craigmillar Castle is an imposing 14th-century fortress. Its inner curtain wall – built in 1427 – is quartered with round towers with gun holes and topped with machicolations (open: April-Sept 9.30am-6.30pm; otherwise 9.30am-4.30pm; tel: (01316) 614445).

Edinburgh Castle Open April-Sept 9.30am-5.15pm; Oct-Mar 9.30am-4.15pm; tel: (01312) 259846. Probably Scotland's most famous landmark, Edinburgh Castle dominates the skyline of the city. Archeological investigations have established that the rock on which the castle is built has been occupied since the Bronze Age. The Picts fortified the rock in the 3rd and 4th centuries AD, but the oldest building today is the tiny 11th-century St Margaret's Chapel, named after King Malcolm III's wife, Queen Margaret. The chapel was the only building spared when the Scots won back the castle from the English in 1313. The terrace in front of the chapel affords fine views of northern Edinburgh, including Princes Street.

The Crown Chamber contains the Honours of Scotland: the crown, sceptre and sword worn by the Scottish monarchy. The Stone of Scone on which the Scottish monarchs once sat at their coronation is also in the Crown Chamber.

Facing page: Edinburgh Castle
© *David Robertson/ The Still Moving Picture Company*

In Queen Mary's apartments, Mary Queen of Scots gave birth to the future James VI of Scotland, who also ruled England. The castle was almost destroyed by English artillery in 1573 when it defended Mary as the rightful Catholic Queen of Scotland. King James IV's great hall built in the 16th century displays arms and armour under an impressive hammerbeam roof. The Scottish National War Memorial on the north side resembles the exterior of Stirling Castle and has beautiful stained-glass windows depicting war scenes. On the west side is the Scottish United Services Museum which has displays of uniforms, medals, badges, colours and weapons of the Scottish regiments in the British army. The Mons Meg cannon built in Belgium in the 15th century has been silent since 1682 and is located in an ancient hall behind the Half-Moon Battery, a curving rampart that gives the castle its distinctive profile. The battery's gun is fired every day at 1pm. The huge

of 30 King and 100 Gentoo penguins is its main attraction. The zoo has a good collection of native Scottish wildlife, including wild cat, pine marten and golden eagles. The zoo also has great views of Edinburgh, the Pentlands and the mountains around Loch Lomond.

Lauriston Castle Cramond Road South. Open April-Oct, Sun-Thurs 11am-1pm, 2pm-5pm; otherwise weekends 2pm-4pm; tel: (01313) 362060. Built in 1593 on the site of a tower destroyed in 1544, Lauriston Castle was owned by the mathematician John Napier, who invented logarithms. It has beautiful Edwardian interiors.

The Royal Yacht Britannia, one of the greatest examples of Scottish shipbuilding, has been in her new home in the Edinburgh port of Leith since May 1998. After travelling more than one million miles across the globe during her 44-year active life – the equivalent of one

people in Scottish history, from the Stuart monarchs to Sean Connery.

National Gallery of Scotland and RSA The Mound. Open Mon-Sat 10am-5pm, Sun 2pm-5pm; tel: (01315) 568921. Built in 1857 by William Playfairs, the Gallery is in a light neo-classical design. It contains some of the best Old Masters in the United Kingdom, plus a fine collection of Impressionists and a huge collection of Scottish paintings. Playfairs Royal Scottish Academy (same hours as National Gallery) is to the rear of the National Gallery. The RSA Annual exhibition runs from April to July.

Palace of Holyroodhouse Open April-Oct 9.30am-5.15pm; Nov-Mar 9.30am-3.45pm; tel: (01315) 561096. Holyroodhouse is an official residence of the royal family in Scotland. The original palace started by King James IV was a guesthouse to the adjacent Holyrood

Royal Mile

© S J Taylor/The Still Moving Picture Company

forecourt of the castle, the Esplanade, was built in the 18th century as a parade ground. It is now a car park for most of the year, but is alive with colour during the famous Edinburgh Military Tattoo, a magnificent display which takes place in August as part of the Edinburgh International Festival.

Edinburgh Zoo Corstorphine Road. Open April-Sept 9am-6pm; Oct-Mar 9am-4pm; tel: (01313) 349171. Edinburgh Zoo is a huge complex of barless _ and sometimes glassless – enclosures for all sorts of animals on the south side of Corstorphine Hill. The famous collection

voyage round the world each year – she has come home to Scotland. The ship is the first visitor attraction in Scotland to introduce a system of entry by pre-booked tickets. The public is asked to obtain tickets by phoning the Britannia booking line (tel: (0131) 556 5566).

National Portrait Gallery Queen Street. Open Mon-Fri 10am-5pm; tel: (01315) 568921. Funded by John Ritchie Findlay, who owned the Scotsman newspaper, the Scottish National Portrait Gallery was designed as a Gothic palace by architect Rowand Anderson. The collection contains portraits of prominent

Abbey. It was damaged during the "rough wooing" of King Henry VIII and only the northwest tower remained. It was burned again and finally remodelled in the 1670s. A plaque marks the spot on which Riccio, secretary to Mary Queen of Scots, was murdered. Other monarchs who resided at Holyroodhouse include Bonnie Prince Charlie, King George IV and Victoria and Albert. The building fell into disrepair after 1850 and was not restored until the 20th century. Inside, portraits of monarchs are surrounded by tapestries and fine furniture from the royal collections.

John Knox's House

© S J Taylor/The Still Moving Picture Company

Princes Street Originally planned as a residential area, Princes Street grew inexorably into the commercial centre it is today. It is flanked by the castle to the south and in the east by the 200-feet (61 m) Gothic spire of the Scott Monument. Princes Street Gardens, with its lawns, benches and monuments, is popular with tourists and residents. At the east end of the street is Robert Adam's splendid General Register House, home of the Scottish Record Office, with a projecting portico and end pavilions crowned by cupolas.

Royal Botanic Garden Inverleith Row. Open May-June 10am-8pm; Mar, April, Oct 10am-6pm; Nov-Feb 10am-4pm; tel: (01312) 251331. Situated in the heart of the city, the Royal Botanic Garden has one of the world's largest rhododendron collections, a magnificent rock garden and many glasshouse displays.

Royal Mile From Castle to Palace. The principal thoroughfare of Old Town runs from the castle on the hill to the abbey and the palace. It comprises four streets: Castle Hill, Lawnmarket, High Street and Canongate. **The Scotch Whisky Heritage Centre** shows how Scotland's many whiskies are made (open: 10am-5.30pm; tel: (01312) 200441). **The Outlook Tower**

and Camera Obscura provide a fascinating view of the city and have their own photographic exhibits *(open: April-Oct 9.30am-6pm; otherwise 10am-5pm)*. **Gladstone's Land**, a narrow six-storey tenement, is typical of 17th-century Edinburgh. The first floor is refurbished as an excellent example of a 17th-century townhouse (open: April-Oct 10am-5pm; tel: (01312) 265856). **Lady Stair's House** is now home to the Writer's Museum, which displays some of the manuscripts of Scotland's great writers, including Burns, Scott and Stevenson (open: Mon-Sat 10am-6pm; tel: (01312) 252424). **St Giles Cathedral** is the high kirk of Edinburgh. This 15th-century structure has been rebuilt many times (open: Mon-Sat 9am-7pm, Sun 1pm-6pm; tel: (01312) 559442). The Scottish Parliament met at **Parliament House** from 1639-1707; the building is now the Supreme Court of Scotland. Its hall has a beautiful hammerbeam roof and paintings by Scottish artists (open: Mon-Sat 10am-4pm; tel: (01312) 252595).

Just outside Parliament House is the Mercat Cross where merchants gathered to transact business; it is still the site of royal proclamations. The Edinburgh City Chambers, formerly the Royal Exchange, was built in 1753. Its unique design

incorporates an 11-storey facade on its north side. A screen at pavement level shelters the Edinburgh Stone of Remembrance. Tron Kirk, named after a weigh-beam used in the weigh-house, was built before Parliament House and is now the traditional gathering place for Hogmanay celebrations. **The Museum of Childhood** exhibits toys, costumes, books, dolls and games from past to present (open: Mon-Sat 10am-4pm; tel: (01315) 294142). **The Brass Rubbing Centre** at Trinity Apse, Chalmers Close has Pictish stones and markers, plus rare Scottish and medieval church brasses (open: Mon-Sat 10am-5pm; tel: (01315) 564364). **John Knox House** was built in 1490 and provides a rare insight into what a house of that period was like. It has a large display on the history of the man who started Scotland's Reformation (open: Mon-Sat 10am-4.30pm; tel: (01315) 562647).

Royal Museum of Scotland
Chambers Street. Open 10am-5pm; tel: (01312) 257534. The Royal Museum comprises the national collection of scientific, natural, historic, geological, archeological and cultural artefacts in a grand Victorian building with soaring columns. Special lectures and talks are given all year round. A new section was added in 1998 for the

© Doug Corrance/ The Still Moving Picture Company

Milne's Court, off Royal Mile

Museum of Scotland, which focuses on Scotland's heritage.

South of the Royal Mile

Royal Mile to George Heriot's School. Grassmarket was for centuries the agricultural market for the city. The cobbled St Andrews cross enclosed behind rails marks the site of the town gallows, where many 17th-century Covenanters met their deaths. Greyfriars Church was originally built in 1612 on the site of a 15th-century friary and has undergone a great deal of alteration. **The historic National Covenant** was signed here in 1638 (open: April-Oct, Mon-Fri 10.30am-4.30pm, Sat 10.30am-2.30pm; Nov-Mar, Thurs 1.30pm-3.30pm; tel: (01312) 251900). George Heriot's School was founded in 1659 for the education of "fatherless bairns of Edinburgh freemen". The building is a good example of Renaissance architecture, with a fine clock tower. A remnant of the 16th-century Flodden wall can be seen west of the school.

Scottish Agriculture Museum

Ingliston. Open 10am-5pm; tel: (01313)

332674. Adjoining Scotland's premier agricultural show ground, the Scottish Agriculture Museum describes the history of rural Scotland, its trades and its social life.

Scottish National Galley of Modern Art

Belford Road. Open Mon-Sat 10am-5pm, Sun 2pm-5pm; tel: (01315) 568921. Close to New Town, this former school building features paintings and sculpture, including the work of Picasso, Braque, Matisse and Derain. One of the most popular parts of the museum is its whole food restaurant.

University Area

George Square to Chambers Street.. George Square was the first residential development outside of Old Town. It dates from the 1760s and is mostly neo-classical in style. The Meadows was once a fashionable place to promenade. The Old University was founded in 1581 and occupied premises within Kirk o' Field Collegiate Church, itself founded in 1450. It houses the **Talbot Rice Gallery** and the **Torrie Collection**, which alternates with touring exhibitions (open: Tue-Sat 10am-

5pm; tel: (01316) 501212). The Chambers Street area was once a mid-Victorian slum before it was redeveloped. On the north side it is now home to the Old College, while on the south side there is the Royal Museum of Scotland and Heriot Watt University, founded in 1821.

The impression Edinburgh has made on me is very great; it is quite beautiful, totally unlike anything else I have ever seen; and what is even more, Albert, who has seen so much, says it is unlike anything he ever saw.

Queen Victoria
An extract from *A Little Book of Scottish Quotations* published by Appletree Press

Facing page: Greyfriars Bobby
© S J Taylor/ The Still Moving Picture Company

GLASGOW

Glasgow and the Clyde Valley

Scotland's largest city is also one of the greatest cities in Europe. Once best known for its shipbuilding and its massive iron and steel industries, Glasgow is now more famous for its cultural and artistic renaissance. Older than Edinburgh, the city developed near a ford 20 miles from the mouth of the River Clyde as a medieval ecclesiastical centre, but by the 17th century the city's life-blood was its commerce.

The Strathclyde district – in which Glasgow is located – has existed since the Middle Ages. Some 1,500 years ago Irish chroniclers spoke of the kingdom of "Stratha Cluatha", while later in Roman times it was called the land of the Damnonni, the capital of which was Dumbarton. In 1707 the Treaty of Union between Scotland and England enabled Scotland to trade with England's colonies in America. The Clyde estuary became the gateway to the New World and was the port of entry for tobacco, rum and cotton. Many people were made wealthy by the trade, so much so that prosperous merchants became known as "tobacco lords".

During the Industrial Revolution the city grew very quickly and became one of the industrial powerhouses of the British empire.

Barras East of Glasgow Cross. Open Sat-Sun 9am-5pm; tel: (0141) 552 7258. Scotland's largest indoor/outdoor market was named after the barrows (pushcarts) formerly used by the stallholders. The 80-year-old market-place really comprises nine separate markets, at which virtually everything can be bought. Always great fun and a spectacle, with lots of street entertainment.

Botanical Garden Great Western Road. Gardens open 7am-dusk; Kibble Palace open 10am-4.45pm; tel: (0141) 334 2422. The Royal Botanical Institute of Glasgow built this garden in 1842. All types of flora are on display, including herbs, tropical plants and a magnificent collection of orchids. Kibble Palace (built in 1873) contains tree ferns and plants from temperate areas, and with its domed, interlinked greenhouses is a unique example of a Victorian iron conservatory.

Bridgegate Gorbals Street. Once the main thoroughfare to the city's first stone bridge built in 1345, all that is left of original construction is the 1659 Merchant's Hall steeple, rising in tiers to a height of 164 feet (50 m). The steeple served as a lookout post for cargo ships coming up the Clyde.

Burrell Collection Pollok Park. Open Wed-Mon 10am-5pm; tel: (0141) 649 7151. A museum in the grounds of Pollok House contains a collection amassed by one man, Sir William Burrell, a wealthy ship owner. In 1944 he gave the city 8,000 artefacts and half a million pounds to pay for a suitable home for them, on the condition that the building should be in a rural location and free from pollution. The condition led to enormous delay, but the exhibition finally opened in 1983 in Pollok Park. The collection includes the work of ancient civilisations, oriental art, medieval and post-medieval European art, paintings, drawings and bronzes. Only part of the collection can be shown at one time, so displays change periodically.

Cathedral Square Cathedral Street. The Bishop's Castle and Canon's Manse once overlooked this area but were torn down to make way for the 1792 Royal Infirmary (the present building was built in the 20th century). It was at the infirmary that Sir Joseph Lister pioneered the use of carbolic acid as an antiseptic.

Central Station Central Station's bridge over Argyle street is known as Heilanman's Umbrella because it was a meeting place and shelter for so many Highlanders who came to Glasgow in search of a better life in the 19th century.

City Chambers George Square. Open Mon-Fri 10.30am-3.30pm, council business permitting; tel: (0141) 287 4017. Opened by Queen Victoria in 1888, City Chambers was built to restore confidence after the financial collapse of the City of Glasgow Bank. Dominating the East Side of George Square, its exterior has a turreted and colonnaded facade in Venetian style, topped by a tower decorated with carvings. Inside there is a vaulted-ceiling entrance hall, marble and alabaster staircases, banqueting hall and many other rooms each fitted out in a different wood.

Clyde Estuary Anderston Quay. Open June-Aug; tel: (0141) 221 8152. The paddle steamer Waverley visits resorts along the Firth of Clyde, including Helensburgh, Dunoon, Rothesay, Largs, Millport and Ayr. The Waverley is the last of the famous Clyde paddle steamers which used to take Glaswegians "doon the watter" for the day.

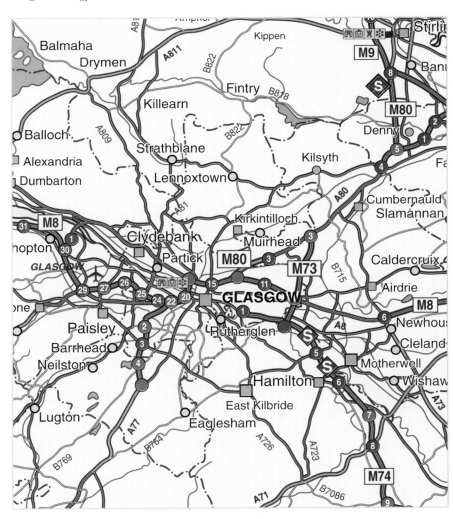

Facing page: St Mungo, Kelvingrove Museum & Art Gallery,
© David Robertson/ The Still Moving Picture Company

Botanic Gardens

Egyptian Halls Union Street. Victorian architect Alexander "Greek" Thompson invariably incorporated Egyptian and Greek elements into his designs. This building dates from 1871.

George Square Between George and St Vincent Streets. The centre of Glasgow's business district, George Square is lined with statues of the famous, including Queen Victoria, Robert Burns, James Watt, William Gladstone and – the biggest statue of the lot – Sir Walter Scott. On the east side of the square is the magnificent City Chambers, on the west the handsome Merchant's House.

Glasgow Cathedral Cathedral Street. Open for all services and April-Sept, Mon-Sat 9.30am-6pm, Sun 2pm-5pm; Oct-Mar, Mon-Sat 9.30am-4pm, Sun 2pm-4pm; tel: (0141) 552 8198. This is the fourth church to be built on the site beside the Molendinar Burn, where St Mungo built his wooden church in the 7th century. The cathedral was begun in the 12th century and completed about 300 years later. Glasgow's trade guilds regarded it as their church and protected it during the Reformation, which destroyed so many other cathedrals in Scotland. St Mungo is buried in a beautiful crypt in the lower church. The cathedral's most unusual features are the double doors at the East End, one on top of the other, as there are actually two churches in a stack.

Glasgow Cross Junction of Saltmarket, Trongate, Gallowgate and London Road. The Mercat Cross, topped by a unicorn, marked the very centre of the medieval city (the present replica

cross dates from 1929). It was a meeting place for Glasgow's merchants and place of execution for criminals. The tron or weigh-beam was installed here in 1491. Anyone entering the old city paid a toll at the elegant tolbooth, all that remains of which is the seven-storey steeple built in 1629.

Glasgow Gallery of Modern Art Queen Street. Open Mon, Wed-Sat, 10am-5pm, Sun 11am-5pm; tel: (0141) 229 1996. In 1780 William Cumminghame, one of the wealthiest of the tobacco lords, built his mansion on Queen Street. The building was later to become the Royal Exchange, where merchants and traders met. For a time it was the Stirling Library before it became the Gallery of Modern Art, with collections of modern art, crafts and design. The gallery is extensive, with displays on each floor designed to reflect the four elements of earth, air, fire and water. As a result, the gallery has a unique atmosphere and allows for interaction between the various exhibits.

Glasgow Green North side of the Clyde. Glasgow's oldest park and one of the city's most historic sites, Glasgow Green has hosted common grazing livestock, public hangings, military reviews, the Glasgow Fair and public meetings. It is now part of the Glasgow Eastern Area Renewal Scheme. The park has monuments to Queen Victoria, Lord Nelson and James Watt.

Glasgow School of Art Renfrew Street. Tours Mon-Fri 11am, 2pm; Sat 10.30am; tel: (0141) 353 4526. Designed by Charles Rennie Mackintosh when he was 28, this famous art nouveau building is studied by architects and designers from

around the world. It has one of the world's largest collections of Mackintosh furniture, designs and paintings. Its most famous room is the three-storey Library, which has a wonderful suspended ceiling. Other rooms have their original stained glass, metalwork designs and light fittings. It is a working school of art, so numbers of visitors sometimes have to be limited.

Glasgow University University Avenue. Open Mon-Sat 2pm-5pm; May-Sept, also Sun 2pm-5pm; guided tours May-Sept, Wed, Fri, Sat 11am-2pm; Oct-April, Wed only, 11am; tel: (0141) 330 5511. Founded by Bishop William Turnbull in 1451, the university first met at the cathedral. Prior to 1642 the university's chancellors were the bishops and archbishops of Glasgow. The university moved to High Street, where the Old College was built (later destroyed when the university moved to an estate on Gilmorehill in the West End). Today the

"Heaven seems vera little improvement on Glesga", a Glasgow man is said to have murmured, after death, to a friend who had predeceased him. "Man, this is no Heaven", the other replied.

Anonymous
Taken from *A Little Book of Scottish Quotations* published by Appletree Press

© Gerry Coutts/The Still Moving Picture Company

university has over 13,000 students and has eight faculties (Arts, Divinity, Engineering, Law, Medicine, Science, Social Science and Veterinary Medicine). The massive Gothic Gilmorehill Building overlooks Kelvingrove Park. In Professors' Square at the west end of the building is the Lion and Unicorn Staircase, originally in the Old College. The visitor centre has informative displays, interactive computers and a camera showing the panorama from the university tower.

Glasgow Zoopark 6 miles (10 km) from city centre, London Road. Open daily 9.30am-5pm; tel: (0141) 777 1185. Famous for its breeding of reptiles, this moderately sized zoo is popular with children.

High Street A plaque marks the site of Glasgow University's Old College, located here from 1632 to 1870. The former British Linen Bank sports a figure of Pallas Athene, goddess of wisdom and weaving, while the stained-glass window above its door portrays a flax boat.

House for Art Lovers Bellahouston Park, Dumbreck Road. Open Sat-Sun 10am-5pm; tel: (0141) 353 4770. Built to a design originally submitted by Charles Rennie Mackintosh to a German competition in 1901, this villa was actually built in 1996. It hosts exhibitions relating to the architect's work and decorative pieces created by Mackintosh and his wife. The building also functions as Glasgow School of Art's postgraduate study centre.

Hunterian Art Gallery Glasgow University, Hillhead Street. Open Mon-Sat 9.30am-5pm; tel: (0141) 330 5431. A famous London physician, William Hunter, trained at Glasgow University and later gave it his substantial art collection. Among its 17th- and 18th-century paintings are works by Rembrandt and Rubens, and 19th- and 20th-century artists like McTaggart and Gillies are also represented. Sixty of James McNeill Whistler's paintings are on display (the gallery owns his artistic estate). The work of Charles Rennie Mackintosh is displayed at his townhouse, which is furnished with his own art nouveau chairs, tables, beds and cupboards. The print gallery hosts travelling exhibitions and displays the techniques of print-making. The courtyard has a good display of contemporary sculpture.

Hunterian Museum Glasgow University. Open Mon-Sat 9.30am-5pm; tel: (0141) 330 4221. The city's oldest museum was established in 1807 as the part of Glasgow University in the Gilmorehill Building, two miles (3 km) west of the city. The museum has everything from dinosaur fossils to coins, manuscripts and scientific instruments. One display is devoted to Captain Cook's voyages to the South Seas. As well as other temporary exhibits, there is a coffeehouse and bookstore.

Hutcheson's Hall Ingram Street. Open Mon-Sat 10am-5pm; tel: (0141) 552 8391. Originally a hospice founded by two brothers, George and Thomas Hutcheson, this elegant neo-classical building is a visitor centre and gift shop for the National Trust for Scotland.

Kelvingrove Museum and Art Gallery/Glasgow Art Gallery and Museum Kelvingrove Park. Open Mon-Sat 10am-5pm, Sun 11am-5pm; tel: (0141) 287 2699. Opened in 1902, this museum was partially financed from the profits of the 1888 International Exhibition held in the same area. The 20th-century red sandstone building

A House for An Art Lovers

looks like a combination of castle and cathedral. Glasgow's main museum and art gallery, it comprises one of Britain's finest civic collections. The collection started by the McLellan Bequest in 1854 includes 17th-century Dutch art, the French Barbizon school, French Impressionists and Scottish art from the 17th century to the present.

Kelvingrove Park Northwest of city centre, bounded by Sauchiehall Street, Woodlands Road and Kelvin Way. Purchased in 1852, the park takes its name from the River Kelvin that flows through it. A peaceful retreat from the hustle and bustle of the city, the park contains statues, a small open theatre, a duck pond, play area and many exotic trees.

Merchant City Hutcheson Street. Handsome Georgian and Victorian buildings are now home to fashionable shops. Look out for the City and County Buildings built in 1842, with their bays and Corinthian columns.

Merchant House West side of George Square. Open Mon-Fri 10am-12am, 2pm-5pm; tel: (0141) 221 8272. Topped by a golden sailing ship as a reminder of the importance of trade to Glasgow's prosperity, this Victorian building was constructed in 1874 and is now home to Glasgow Chamber of Commerce. Inside there are many portraits and stained-glass windows.

Mitchell Library North Street. Open Mon-Thurs 9am-8pm, Fri-Sat 9am-5pm; tel: (0141) 287 2931. Founded by Stephen Mitchell in 1874, the Mitchell Library is reputed to be the largest public reference library in Europe, with over a million volumes. The library also claims to have the world's largest collection of the works of Robert Burns. Minerva, goddess of wisdom, sits proudly on the library's dome.

Museum of Transport Kelvin Hall, Bunhouse Road. Open Mon, Wed-Sat 10am-5pm, Sun 11am-5pm; tel: (0141) 287 2720. The Museum of Transport is a

© Marcus Brooke / The still moving Picture Company

fascinating collection of historic transport-related exhibits, much of it devoted to Glasgow's impressive train locomotives. Its models of ships built in Glasgow are world famous; there are also Scottish motor cars and a recreation of a street scene from the 1950s.

Necropolis A formal burial garden of 1833, located behind the cathedral on the Moendinar Burn. Watched over by a statue of John Knox, the garden affords good views of the cathedral and the city.

People's Palace Entrance, Morris Place. Open Wed-Mon 10am-5pm; tel: (0141) 554 0223. Opened in 1898 as a cultural centre and winter garden for the East End, the People's Palace is now a museum of local and social history which tells the story of Glasgow from its beginnings to the present day. The tobacco lords, weavers and the campaign for women's suffrage are all highlighted. The winter garden has some exotic plants.

Piping Centre The Piping Centre is located at 32 McPhater Street in the Cowcaddens Church built in 1873 and restored in 1996. The centre has a concert hall, instruction on playing the pipes, a small museum of piping memorabilia and a shop, which sells a good selection of piping CDs. A small hotel and restaurant are also located on site (tel: (0141) 353 0220).

Pollok House Pollok Avenue. Open Mon, Wed-Sat 10am-5pm, Sun 11am-5pm; tel: (0141) 649 7151. This classical Georgian building in Pollok Country Park was built in the mid-1700s and contains the art collection of Sir William Stirling Maxwell, who was an authority on Spanish painting. The collection includes work by El Greco, Murillo, Goya, Signorelli, Morales, Piombo, Jordaens and many more. Work by William Blake is displayed in the main hall and there is also a good collection of 18th- and 19th-century furniture, silver, glass and porcelain. A beautiful garden overlooks the White Cart River and Pollok Park.

Provand's Lordship High Street. Open Wed-Mon 10am-5pm; tel: (0141) 552 8819. Glasgow's oldest house, a former prebendal manse built in 1471, is the only survivor of the medieval town besides the cathedral. Mary Queen of Scots is said to have stayed here. The exhibits show the house as it would have been when she visited.

Queen's Cross Church Garscube Road. Open Mon-Fri 10.30am-5pm, Sun 2.30pm-5pm; tel: (0141) 946 6600. This church was designed by Charles Rennie Mackintosh and now has exhibitions on other Mackintosh buildings in Glasgow, among them the Scotland Street School,

© David Robertson/The Still Moving Picture Company

Glasgow Cathedral

© Doug Corrance/The Still Moving Picture Company

Glasgow by night

Glasgow School of Art, the Martyrs Public School and the interiors of the Hunterian Art Gallery. It is the headquarters of the Charles Rennie Mackintosh Society.

Regimental Museum of the Royal Highland
Fusiliers Sauchiehall Street. Open Mon-Thurs 9am-4.30pm, Fri 9am-4pm; tel: (0141) 332 0961. Exhibits tell the story of this famous regiment and include displays of medals, badges and uniforms.

Royal Concert Hall
Sauchiehall Street. Tel: (0141) 287 4000. This 2,500-seat hall is the home of the Royal Scottish Orchestra and hosts concerts throughout the year.

St Mungo Museum of Religious Life and Art
Castle Street. Open Wed-Mon 10am-5pm; tel: (0141) 553 2557. This museum was built in 1993 to house a collection of religious artefacts grouped in three different galleries. Religious Art has Dali's St John of the Cross, a bronze Shiva and Islamic prayer rug. Religious Life tells the story of religion in everyday life. Religion in Scotland focuses on the variety of religions in the country in the last 5,000 years. A fourth gallery has temporary exhibits.

St Vincent Street Church
Pitt and St Vincent Streets. Built in 1859 and Greek Revival in style, this church has an abundance of Ionic columns, sphinx heads, Greek ornamentation and a rich interior.

Scotland Street School
Scotland Street. Open Mon-Sat 10am-5pm, Sun 2pm-5pm; tel: (0141) 429 1202. Built to another Mackintosh design, the Scotland Street School has twin glass stair towers, fine stonework on the south side, drill halls and – of course – classrooms.
The building houses the Museum of Education, which has reconstructions of various period classrooms and tells the history of education.

Scottish Stock Exchange
Nelson Mandela Place. Designed in 1877 by John Burnet in the French Gothic style, the building is a copy of the London Law Courts in the Strand. Today it is the hub of Scottish commerce.

Templeton Business Centre
Built in 1889 as a carpet factory, this highly unusual and colourful building is richly decorated like the Doge's Palace in Venice. It certainly provides a touch of exoticism.

Tenement House
Buccleuch Street. Open Mar-Oct 2pm-5pm; tel: (0141) 333 0138. From 1911 to 1965 Agnes Toward occupied a flat consisting of a hall and four rooms. When she died her relatives realised it was a "time capsule" of life in a Glasgow tenement, for she seemedto have thrown nothing away. The flat has a large black cooking range with coalbunker, box beds and gas lamps. The red sandstone tenement building dates from 1892.

Virginia Court
Virginia Street. Wagon-wheel ruts are still visible in the roadway from the time the tobacco merchants traded with the Americans. Nearby are the Virginia Galleries of Antique & Craft, with a famous indoor cafe.

© Derek Laird/The Still Moving Picture Company

People's Palace

© Gerry Coutts/The Still Moving Picture Company

Greenock 24 miles (39 km) west of Glasgow. The birthplace of James Watt, who developed the steam engine, Greenock has always been an important shipbuilding centre. Lyle Hill behind the town is an excellent place from which to obtain sweeping views of the Clyde estuary from Helensburgh to Dunoon. Members of the Free French Naval Forces who lost their lives between 1940 and 1945 are commemorated with a Lorraine Cross and anchor nearby.

Helensburgh 27 miles (43 km) west of Glasgow. Open April-Oct 1.30pm-5.30pm, access sometimes restricted at peak times; tel: (0143) 667 3900. Sir James Colquhoun, 8th Baronet of Colquhoun and Luss, built a new town named after his wife Helen. Ever since, Helensburgh has been a place of elegant homes and become known as the "museum of villas". Finest of all the houses is the National Trust for Scotland's Hill House, which stands on hills overlooking the Clyde. Built for Glasgow publisher Walter W. Blackie to a design by Charles Rennie Mackintosh, Hill House is considered the best example of the architect's work.

Irvine 12 miles (19 km) north of Ayr. Robert Burns came to Irvine to learn to dress flax, the raw material from which linen is made. The heckling shed where he worked and the house where he lived have become the **Glasgow Vennel Museum and Art Galley** (open: June-Sept, Mon, Tues, Thurs-Sat 10am-1pm, 2pm-5pm, Sun 2pm-5pm; Oct-May, Tues, Thurs-Sat 10am-1pm, 2pm-5pm). The Irvine Burns Club is one of the oldest in the world. Floating in the harbour, the **Scottish Maritime Museum** has a variety of boats on display, including a lifeboat, tug and a puffer. Inside the museum is a typical shipyard worker's cottage and a Victorian boat shed, one of the largest ever built (open: April-Oct; tel: (01294) 278283).

Isle of Bute 5-minute ferry from Wemyss Bay. Tel: (0147) 565 0100. Isle of Bute's biggest attraction is **Mount Stuart**, a palace built on a beautiful stretch of sandy shoreline against the backdrop of the Argyll hills. Built for the 3rd Marquess of Bute, an eccentric scholar with a great interest in architecture, the massive Victorian Gothic palace is about 5 miles south of Rothesay. The exterior is in red sandstone, but it is the interiors which are truly amazing. The marble hall has a star-studded vaulted ceiling, columns in rare polychrome marble with capitals decorated with flowers of white

Glasgow Lampost

marble, magnificent stained-glass windows and a gilt bronze balustrade. For many, the simple chapel in white marble is the most beautiful spot on the estate. (Open: house, May-mid-Oct, Mon, Wed, Fri-Sun 11.30am-4.30pm; gardens, May-mid-Oct, Mon, Wed, Fri-Sun 10am-5pm; tel: (01700) 503877.)

Largs Barrfield, Greenock Road. In 1263 a major battle near Largs broke the power of the Vikings in Scotland. To celebrate that victory a Viking festival is held each September. The **Vikingarl** or **Viking Heritage Centre** tells the story of the Viking influence in Scotland in film and displays (open: April-Sept 9am-6pm; Oct-Mar 10am-4pm; tel: (0147) 568 977). **Clark Memorial Church** on the seafront has magnificent stained-glass windows dating from 1890.

The Earl of Glasgow's historic estate is now the Kelburn Castle and Country Park, with fine woodland walks and a Secret Forest maze. Children will enjoy the adventure centre and commando-assault course (open: Easter-Oct 10am-6pm, Nov-Easter 11am-5pm).

Prestwick 32 miles (51 km) southwest of Glasgow. Prestwick's recorded history goes back as far as 984 and it is one of the oldest baronial burghs in Scotland. A Mercat Cross stands outside the registry in the heart of the old town. Bruce's Well is behind St Ninian's Episcopal Church, the water from which is believed to have helped cure Robert the Bruce of leprosy. Today, Prestwick is known mostly for its airport, which once was a major international destination before it was superseded by Glasgow.

Rothesay Isle of Bute. Popular as an anchorage for pleasure craft, Rothesay is the Isle of Bute's only town. Rothesay Castle is surrounded by a water-filled moat and a wall with the remains of four round towers, one of which now acts as a dovecote (open: April-Sept 9.30am-6.30pm; Oct-Mar 9.30am-4.30pm; tel: (01700) 502691).

Troon 31 miles (50 km) southwest of Glasgow. The early history of Troon is now lost, but its name derives from the strangely shaped promontory that extends out into the Clyde estuary. This piece of land was called Trwyn, which means "nose". The town is world famous for its golf links, particularly the Old Troon course.

Wemyss Bay The magnificent Italian-cum-Tudor railway station built by the Caledonian Railway in 1903 is considered the finest in Scotland and still serves as the main railhead for the Isle of Bute. The covered walkway between the train and the ferry is trimmed in wrought iron.

Glasgow

City! I am true son of thine;
Ne'er dwelt I where great mornings shine
Around the bleating pens;
Ne'er by the rivulets I strayed,
And ne'er upon my childhood weighed
The silence of the glens.
Instead of shores where ocean beats,
I hear the ebb and flow of streets.

Draw thy fierce streams of blinding ore,
Smite on a thousand anvils, roar
Down to the harbour-bars;
Smoulder in smoky sunsets, flare
On rainy night, with street and square
Lie empty to the stars.
From terrace proud to alley base
I know thee as my mother's face.

When sunset bathes thee in his gold,
In wreaths of bronze thy sides are rolled,
Thy smoke is dusky fire;
And from the glory round thee poured,
A sunbeam like an angel's sword
Shivers upon a spire.
Thus have I watched thee, Terror! Dream!
While the blue Night crept up the stream.

Alexander Thomson (1830-1867)
Taken from *A Little Book of Scottish Verse*
published by Appletree Press

Port Bannatyne, Isle of Bute

SOUTHERN SCOTLAND

Southern Scotland is a region of blue rolling hills, stately homes and fortified castles; of characterful towns and lovely villages. Its tales and legends, buildings and relics tell of countless battles with the English to the south, and of famous Scots such as Robert Burns, Walter Scott and Robert the Bruce. The wonderful coastline is warmed by the North Atlantic Drift (Scotland's very own bit of the Gulf Stream) and even has the occasional palm tree. Coastal farms give way to high moors and some rocky inland hills. North of Galloway there are lush river valleys, woods and hedgerows, while the terrain of Arran and Kintyre resembles that of the Highlands. Scotland's densely populated central corridor also begins here.

Ayr A commercial port and Ayrshire's principal town, Ayr is also the leading resort on the Firth of Clyde and Scotland's premier racecourse, hosting the Scottish Grand National and the Ayr Gold Cup. Two of Scotland's most famous golf courses are nearby at Troon and Turnberry.

The neo-classical columns of the Burns monument testify to Ayr's connections with Scotland's national poet. The Auld Kirk is where Robert Burns was baptised and wrote a humorous poem about the Twa Brugs (two bridges) that cross the nearby river. Alloway, three miles (5 km) from the town centre in Ayr's southern suburbs, is the location of **Burns Cottage**, where the poet was born in 1759 (open: April-Oct 9am-6pm; Nov-Mar, Mon-Sat 10am-4pm; tel: (01292) 441215). Down the road from the cottage the **Tam o' Shanter Experience** includes a ten-minute video presentation on Burns, the most exciting segment of which presents his most famous poem on three screens (open: April-Sept 9am-6pm; Oct-Mar 9am-5pm; tel: (01292) 443700). Alloway is also the location of the Auld Brig o' Doon and Alloway Kirk, both immortalised in Tam o' Shanter.

Ten miles (16 km) northeast of Ayr in Mauchline is the **Burns House Museum** (open: daily, summer only; tel: (01292) 288688), where Burns – after his triumphant return from Edinburgh in 1788 – rented an upstairs room in this Castle Street house. Four of his daughters are buried in Mauchline churchyard, and Poosie Nansie's pub – where he used to drink – still serves drinks today. Just up the road is the Burns Memorial Tower, with panoramic views of the countryside. Tarbolton (a few miles from Mauchline) was the muslin- and silk-weaver's village where Burns and his friends formed a debating society in 1780, in a building known today as the **Bachelors Club.**

Burns learned to dance and became a Freemason here (open: Easter, May-Sept, daily 1.30pm-6.30pm; Oct, Sat-Sun 1.30pm-6.30pm; tel: (01292) 541940).

A rare volume of Burns's poetry is on display in Kilmarnock, home of Johnny Walker whisky, at **Dean Castle**. The castle also has displays of early musical instruments and a collection of European armour (open: daily 12pm-6pm; tel: (01563) 522702).

Twelve miles (19 km) southwest of Ayr is the dramatic cliff-top **castle of Culzean** (pronounced "ku-lain") and its country park, the National Trust for Scotland's most popular property. This neo-classical mansion was designed by Robert Adam (1728-92) and has a grand walled garden. The seaward facade, with its great drum tower, is the house's most imposing architecture. The people of Scotland gave a National Guest Flat in the castle to General Eisenhower in appreciation for his services during the Second World War. He stayed there a few times and his relatives still do (open: castle, April-Oct 10.30am-5.30pm; country park, 9.30am-sunset; tel: (01655) 760269).

Biggar 19 miles (30 km) southwest of Edinburgh. Biggar is a pleasant stone-built market town at the headwaters of the Clyde, on the moors of southern Scotland. The town was associated with Flemish immigrants who arrived under the patronage of the Scottish kings. **Gladstone Court Museum** offers a delightful portrayal of life in the town, with reconstructed Victorian shops, bank, telephone exchange and school (open: April-Oct, Mon-Sat 10am-12.30pm, 2pm-5pm; Sun 2pm-5pm; tel: (01899) 221050). **The Moat Heritage Centre** occupies a

former church and is largely dedicated to geology and prehistory, but also has an interesting embroidery collection (open: Easter-mid-Oct, Mon-Sat 10am-5pm, Sun 2pm-5pm; tel: (01899) 22150). **Gasworks**, built originally in 1839, is a fascinating exhibition about what it took to produce gas for lighting and heating in Scotland (open: June-Sept 2pm-5pm; tel: (01899) 221050). A 17th-century farm, relocated stone by stone, is at **Greenhill Covenanter's House**, itself a good place to start to get a better understanding of the Covenanting movement (open: Easter-mid Oct, Mon-Sat 10am-5pm, Sun 2pm-5pm; tel: (01899) 22150). **The Biggar Puppet Theatre** regularly presents performances by Purves Puppets and also offers tours led by the puppeteers in which visitors can try things for themselves (performances: Mon-Sat 10am-5pm; Easter-Sept, also Sun 2pm, 5pm; tel: (01899) 220631).

Caerlaverock Castle and National Nature Reserve
7 miles (11 km) west of Ruthwell. The 13th-century Caerlaverock Castle is unique in all of Britain because of its distinctive triangular moated design. Made of red sandstone, it has a double tower gatehouse. (Open: April-Sept, daily 9.30am-6pm; Oct-Mar, Mon-Sat 9.30am-4pm; tel: (01387) 770244.) Combine a visit to the castle with terrific bird watching at the National Nature Reserve, which has a visitor centre and carefully constructed hides. Winter is best, when there are some 13,000 visiting barnacle geese from Spitzbergen (open: all year; tel: (01387) 770244).

Castle Douglas
18 miles (29 km) southwest of Dumfries. A cheerful inland market town now bypassed by the A75, Castle Douglas is located on Carlingwark Loch, which was once the source of marl, a clay used as a fertiliser that made the town famous. **Threave Garden** (1 mile / 1.6 km west of Castle Douglas) is an estate of four farms, woodland, and a mansion presented to the National Trust for Scotland in 1948. Opened in 1960 as the Threave School of Gardening, it trains all Trust gardeners. Its main gardens are devoted to roses, peat, rock and heather; herbaceous borders, walled gardens, glasshouses, patio, arboretum and woodland walks. There is a good visitor centre (open: daily 9.30am-sunset; tel: (01556) 502575). **Threave Castle** (not the garden's mansion house) is a few minutes away from the garden (access is via a muddy path to the riverside, where visitors ring for a boatman to take them to an island on the River Dee). The castle was once the home of Black Douglas, the Earl of Mithsdale, and the lords of Galloway. It was built in the 14th century

Facing page: Ayr by night
© *Angus Johnston/The Still Moving Picture Company*

and besieged in 1455 by the king's forces (open: April-Sept 9.30am-6pm; tel: (01316) 688800).

Castle Kennedy Gardens 3 miles (5 km) east of Stranraer. Built by the Earl of Stair, who employed his troops to shape the landscape, Castle Kennedy Gardens surround the shell of the original Castle Kennedy, built in 1716 but later burned. The gardens have superb views, a monkey puzzle avenue, woodland walks and lakes. The best time to visit is in the spring when the rhododendrons bloom spectacularly (open: April-Sept 10am-5pm; tel: (01776) 702024).

Chatelherault South of Hamilton. Chatelherault, the imposing "Dog Kennel," is all that is left of Hamilton Palace, which was demolished in 1927. Today, there is beautiful parkland on the edge of the River Avon gorge and a restored house. The visitor centre has an audiovisual presentation on the area and is part shooting lodge, part glorified dog kennel. The house – used for hunting parties – has been refurbished. Of special note are the magnificent ceilings, modelled on the originals: those in the banqueting hall and duke's room are extremely elaborate (open: April-Sept, Mon-Sat 10am-5pm, Sun 12pm-5.30pm; Oct-Mar, Mon-Sat 10am-5pm, Sun 12pm-5pm; tel: (01698) 426213).

Coldstream 9 miles (14 km) east of Kelso. Situated just inside the Scottish border, Coldstream was once a destination for runaway couples from the south, who were able to marry in Scotland because of its more lenient marriage laws. This romantic history is recounted on a plaque by the lovely tolbooth. The town is also known for the Coldstream Guards, an elite corp in the British army. The small local museum was once the Coldstream Guards' headquarters (open: April-Sept, Mon-Sat 10am-4pm, Sun 2pm-4pm; Oct, Mon-Sat 1pm-5pm; tel: (01890) 882630). This

stretch of the Tweed is lined with beautiful homes and gardens. **The Hirsel** (immediately west of Coldstream) was once the home of Sir Alec Douglas-Home, who was Prime Minister of Britain from 1963 to 1964. The house has beautiful walks around the estate, birds to watch and a craft complex in its farm buildings (the house itself is not open to the public). (Open: grounds, sunrise-sunset; museum and craft centre, Mon-Fri 10am-5pm, Sat-Sun 12pm-5pm; tel: (01890) 882834.)
Paxton House – 15 miles (24 km) northeast of Coldstream – is a Palladian-style mansion with interiors designed by Adam. Furniture includes Chippendale and Trotter, and there is a famous Regency picture gallery run by the National Gallery of Scotland. The house has a beautiful garden, with a restored boathouse, a museum on salmon fishing, a squirrel hide, craft shop and tearoom (open: Easter-Oct 11am-5pm).

Crichton Castle 7 miles (11 km) southeast of Dalkeith. Crichton was a Bothwell family castle built between the late 14th and 16th centuries. Mary Queen of Scots attended the wedding at Crichton of Bothwell's sister to Mary's brother, Lord John Stewart. The oldest part of the castle is a 14th-century keep (open: April-Sept 9.30am-6pm; tel: (01316) 688800).

Dalbeattie 12 miles (19 km) northwest of Southerness. Dalbeattie is unusual for a Galloway town because most of its buildings are made from local silver granite. This granite was shipped as far a Malta at one time. The town is a good base from which to explore the coastline, especially around Rockcliffe and Kippford.

Dawyck Botanic Gardens 10 miles (16 km) Southwest of Peebles. This is a specialist garden of the Royal Botanic Garden of Edinburgh and features great conifers and shrubs with woodland walks (open: summer only).

Dirleton Castle 22 miles (35 km) northeast of Edinburgh. In the centre of its village is the 12th-century Dirleton Castle, surrounded by a high outer wall. Inside there is a 17th-century bowling green surrounded by a fine garden. King Edward I of England occupied the castle in 1298. (Open: April-Sept, daily 9.30am-6pm; Oct-Mar, Mon-Sat 9.30am-4pm, Sun 2pm-4pm; tel: (01316) 688800.)

Dumfries 76 miles (122 km) southwest of Glasgow. Robert Burns spent the last years of his life in Dumfries, a town on the banks of the River Nith. He is buried in a grand mausoleum in St Nicholas churchyard. **The Robert Burns Centre** occupies a sturdy former mill overlooking the river and has an audiovisual presentation and exhibition on the life of the poet (open: April-Sept, Mon-Sat 10am-8pm, Sun 2pm-5pm; tel: (01387) 264808). Dumfries was also where Robert the Bruce stabbed Red Comyn.

Dunbar 13 miles (21 km) east of Edinburgh. This east coast resort town has a beautiful beach and the remains of a medieval fortress, which once controlled an important coastal route. The Scots were defeated here by the English in 1296, as was the Covenanting army by forces led by Oliver Cromwell in 1650. John Muir, the great naturalist responsible for the founding of the United States' National Parks, was born here; his birthplace is now a museum. Adjacent to Dunbar is the John Muir Country Park, an excellent coastal habitat around the estuary of the Rive Tyne. Its splendid walks change with the tides.

Ecclefechan 8 miles (13 km) north of the English Border. It is the birthplace of Thomas Carlyle, essayist, historian, social reformer and literary figure of his age. The Carlyle Birthplace Museum located on the Main Street is an 18th-century house with two of the refurbished rooms containing family belongings (open: May-September, Fri-Mon 1.30pm-5.30pm; tel: (01576) 300666)

Eyemouth 8 miles (13 km) north of Berwick-upon-Tweed. Eyemouth is a busy fishing port with brightly painted boats tied up at its quayside. The Eyemouth Museum focuses on rural skills and crafts: one of its most important displays is about the lives of fisherfolk, the highlight of which is a tapestry commemorating the Great Fishing Disaster of 1881 (open: Easter-Oct, Mon-Sat 10am-12pm, 1.30pm-4.30pm; tel: (01890) 750678).

Galashiels 5 miles (8 km) northwest of Melrose. Galashiels is known for its textile mills and knitwear. The Lochcarron

© Doug Corrance /The Still Moving Picture Company

Dunbar

of Scotland Cashmere and Wool Centre has a museum of the town's history and industry and a tour of the mill (open: Oct-May, Mon-Sat 12pm-5pm; June-Sept, Mon-Sun 12pm-5pm; tours Mon-Fri; tel: (01896) 752091).

Galloway Forest Park 8 miles (13 km) northwest of Creetown. Between the Rivers Cree and Ken, this 384-square mile (618-sq km) forest park provides unlimited access to forest paths, plus fishing and camping. The Southern Upland Way footpath goes through the park. Bruce's Stone commemorates the first victory in the Independence wars. There are also some beautiful views of Glen Trool.

Gatehouse of Fleet 9 miles (14 km) west of Kirkcudbright. This quiet little town has a castle guarding its southwest entrance. **Cardoness Castle** is a typical Scottish tower house. Built in the 15th century, it was once the home of the McCullochs of Galloway and later the Gordons (open: April-Sept, daily 9.30am-6pm; Oct-Mar, Sat 9.30am-4pm, Sun 2pm-4pm; tel: (01316) 688800). The Mill on the **Fleet Heritage Centre** tells the history of the town's cotton industry, partly by means of hard hats with pre-recorded audio commentary issued to visitors (open: Easter-Oct 10am-5.30pm; tel: (01557) 814099).

Gretna Green 10 miles (16 km) north of Carlisle. Following an 18th-century act of Parliament to end clandestine marriages in England, the number of those running away to Scotland to get married increased, since Scottish law only required a declaration before witnesses. Even an 1857 Act requiring a 21-day residence before marriage in Scotland did not reduce the number of weddings. The practice was finally stopped by an act of Parliament in 1940. Gretna Green, being the first place the runaways reached in Scotland, got a lot of business. At one time anyone could conduct the ceremony and on many occasions it was the village blacksmith. The Old Blacksmith's Shop contains some interesting relics (open daily: Apr & Oct 10am-4.30pm; May, June & Sept 10am-5pm; July & Aug 10am-6pm; tel: (01461) 338341).

Haddington 15 miles (24 km) east of Edinburgh. This Lothian town has a splendidly well-preserved medieval street plan. The Town House was built by William Adam in 1748. A plaque on the wall of Sidegate shows the flood levels of the River Tyne. Nungate footbridge is also worth seeing, as is the 15th-century St Mary's church a little upstream. Just south of Haddington is the 15th-century

© Andy Sherman/ The Still Moving Picture Company

Galloway Forest Park

Lennoxlove House, a turreted country home with portraits, furniture, porcelain and items associated with Mary Queen of Scots (open: Easter-Oct, Wed, Mon-Fri 2pm-4.30pm; tel: (01620) 823720).

Hawick 7 miles (11 km) south of Galashiels. The largest Border burgh, Hawick is an industrial knitwear centre, has one of Scotland's oldest agricultural markets and is a busy shopping centre. In the centre of town the 16th-century **Drumlanrig's Tower** hosts the Tourist Information Centre and displays the water-colours of Tom Scott (open: 10am-7pm; tel: (01450) 373457). A few minutes' walk away is an attractive Victorian walled garden with its own museum and art gallery, Wilton Lodge Park (open: April-Sept, Mon-Sat 10am-12pm, 1pm-5pm, Sun 2pm-6pm; tel: (01450) 373457).

Hermitage Castle 10 miles (16 km) south of Hawick. In the bleak and lonely Border country stands this desolate 14th-century castle. Restored in the 19th century, it was the stronghold of the Wardens of the March, strategically placed to guard Hermitage Water and old reivers' routes from England into Scotland. It is best known for Mary Queen of Scots' lightning visit to her wounded lover, the Earl of Bothwell in 1566.

Innerleithen 15 miles (24 km) northwest of Selkirk. A mill town located

on the confluence of Leithen Water and the River Tweed, Innerleithen is famous for Robert Smails Printing Works, a fully operational and restored print shop with reconstructed waterwheel (open: Easter, May-Sept, Mon-Sat 10am-1pm, Sun 2pm-5pm; Oct, Sat 10am-1pm, Sun 2pm-5pm; tel: (01896) 830206). Innerleithen also has Scotland's oldest house in continual occupation. **Traquair House** has a bed in which Mary Queen of Scots slept in 1566, more than 3,000 books and a maze. Its 18th-century brewhouse produces wonderful ale. (Open: April-May, Sept, daily 12.30pm-5.30pm; June-Aug, daily 10.30am-5.30pm; Oct, Fri-Sun 12.30pm-5.30pm.)

Jedburgh 50 miles (80 km) south of Edinburgh. The first major town after the English border, Jedburgh was continually invaded by English armies. Jedburgh Abbey, one of the famous Border Abbeys, was built in 1138 as a priory and became an abbey in 1152. The building was destroyed by the Earl of Hertford's forces in 1544-5 as part of King Henry VIII's "Rough Wooing" campaign. Only the outlines of the foundations are left of this once magnificent building. The complete story is told in the **Jedburgh Abbey Visitor Centre** (open: April-Sept, daily 9.30am-6pm; Oct-Nov, Mon-Sat 10am-5pm, Sun 12pm-4.30pm; tel: (01316) 688800). Also of note is the **Mary Queen of Scots House**, where Mary stayed before she visited her wounded lover, the Earl of Bothwell (open: June-Sept, daily 10am-4.30pm; Oct-Nov, Mon-Sat 10am-5pm, Sun 12pm-4.30pm; tel: (01835) 863254). A former Howard Reform Prison on the site of a destroyed castle is worth visiting for its costumed characters and cells (open: mid-Mar-mid-Nov, daily 10am-4pm; tel: (01835) 83036).

Kelso 12 miles (19 km) northeast of Jedburgh. Kelso is one of the most charming border burghs. Its town square is dominated by the ruin of **Kelso Abbey**, which was burned three times in the 1540s. In 1545 100 soldiers and 12 monks where slaughtered there (open: April-Sept, daily 9.30am-6pm; Oct-Mar, Mon-Sat 9.30am-4pm, Sun 2pm-4pm; tel: (01316) 688800). Two miles (3 km) northwest on the River Tweed stands magnificent **Floors Castle**, ancestral home of the Duke of Roxburgh. The castle is the largest inhabited house in Scotland and contains fine French furniture, porcelain, tapestries and paintings, and has beautiful parkland. A holly tree in the deer park marks the place where James II was killed by an exploding cannon (open: Easter-Sept, daily, 10am-4pm; tel: (01573) 223333). **Mellerstain House** is an attractive Adam mansion built in 1720. The house is known for its ornate plasterwork and decoration (open: Easter, May-Sept, Sun-Fri 12.30pm-5pm; tel: (01573) 410225). In the hills south of Mellerstain is **Smailholm Tower**, with memorable views from its top of a barren and rocky ridge. The tower was one of Sir Walter Scott's favourite spots (open: April-Sept 9.30am-6pm; tel: (01573) 460365).

Kirkcudbright 11 miles (18 km) southwest of Castle Douglas. An 18th-century town of blue slate roofs, Kirkcudbright has a dignified air and contains many crafts and antique stores. In the town centre is **MacLellan's Castle**,

Song of the River-Sprite Nigheag

I am washing the shrouds of the fair men
Who are going out but never shall
come in;
The death-dirge of the ready-handed men
Who shall go out, seek peril and fall.

I am lustring the linen of the fair men
Who shall go out in the morning early,
Upon the well-shod grey steeds
And shall not return in season due.

Taken from *A Little Book of Celtic Verse*
published by Appletree Press

a ruined turreted mansion (open: April-Sept 9.30am-6pm; tel: (01557) 331856). **Broughton House** – with its own Japanese garden – was once the home of the artist Edward Hornel (one of the Glasgow Boys of the 20th century). Many of his paintings are on display (open: April–Oct 1pm-5.30pm; tel: (01557) 330437). Stewartry Museum is a delightful old-style museum packed with treasures from the past in quaint old display cases (open: Oct-April, Mon-Sat 11am-4pm; May, Mon-Sat 1pm-5pm; June, Sept, Mon-Sat 11am-5pm, Sun 2pm-5pm; July-Aug, Mon-Sat 10am-6pm, Sun 2pm-5pm; tel: (01557) 331643).

Linlithgow South shore of Linlithgow Loch. Linlithgow Palace was the birthplace of Mary Queen of Scots. The palace is now an impressive shell standing at the end of the loch, as it was accidentally burned by Hanoverian troops in 1746 at the end of the Jacobite rebellion. Most rooms are ruined, but the gatehouse and central courtyard fountain still stand (open: April-Sept, daily 9.30am-6pm; Oct-Mar, Mon-Sat 9.30am-4pm, Sun 2pm-4pm; tel: (01506) 842896). A short walk from the palace is **St Michael's Kirk**, the largest surviving pre-Reformation church in Scotland. The church took over a century to build (open: May-Sept, Mon-Sat 10am-4.30pm, Sun 12.30pm-4.30pm; Oct-April, Mon-Fri 10am-3pm; tel: (01506) 842188).

Logan Botanic Garden 14 miles (22 km) southwest of Stranraer. A range of plant species usually found only in the southern hemisphere is able to grow at Logan due to the North Atlantic Drift, hence its Australian trees, tree ferns and cabbage palms. Logan is a specialist garden of the Royal Botanic Garden in Edinburgh. (Open: Mar-Oct 9.30am-6pm; tel: (01776) 860231.)

The Machars South of Newton Stewart. Lush green is the colour of the Machars, a triangular promontory south of Newton Stewart. It is an area of gently rolling hills, yellow gorse hedgerows, dairy cattle and a number of prehistoric sites. **The Whithorn Dig and Visitor Centre** (open: April-Oct 10.30am-5pm; tel: (01988) 500508) displays relics dating from around AD 400. It is believed that Whithorn was the cradle of Christianity in Britain: it was certainly a place of pilgrimage for Scottish kings. St Ninian's Chapel stands on the Isle of Whithorn.

Melrose 15 miles (24 km) west of Coldstream. **Melrose Abbey**, a red sandstone shell with windows in the Perpendicular style, delicate tracery and carved capitals, dominates the town. A famous carving on the roof is of a

Floors Castle

bagpipe-playing pig. (Open: April-Sept, daily 9.30am-6pm; Oct-Mar, Mon-Sat 9.30am-4pm, Sun 2pm-4pm; tel: (01896) 822562.) Next to the abbey is the National Trust for Scotland's **Priorwood Gardens**, specialising in dried flowers (open: April-Sept, Mon-Sat 10am-5.30pm, Sun 1.30pm-5.30pm; Oct-Dec, Mon-Sat 10am-4pm, Sun 1.30pm-4pm; tel: (01896) 822493). The **Trimontium Exhibition** is a wonderful account of one of Rome's main forts in Scotland just a few fields away at Newstead (open: April-Oct 10.30am-4.30pm; tel: (01896) 822651). **Abbotsford House**, Sir Walter Scott's beloved home, is only two miles (3 km) west of Melrose. Scott collected bits and pieces of history from all over Scotland, such as the door from the Old Tolbooth in Edinburgh, a desk made from the remains of a Spanish armada ship, Rob Roy's gun, James IV's hunting bottle, Bonnie Prince Charlie's quaich (cup) and the keys of Lochleven Castle. His library holds 9,000 volumes. (Open: Mon-Sat 10am-5pm, Sun 2pm-5pm; June-Sept, also Sun 10am-5pm; tel: (01896) 752043.) Scott was buried at **Dryburgh Abbey**, located on a gentle park in the loop of the Tweed. The abbey is a mixture of Romanesque and early English architecture. The chapel, detached from the main building where Scott is buried, is lofty and pillared. (Open: mid-Mar-Oct, Mon-Sat 10am-5pm, Sun 2pm-5pm; June, also Sun 10am-5pm; tel: (01896) 822555.) Teddy bears are the unusual theme of **Teddy Melrose**, a museum about British teddy bears from the 1900s (open: 10am-5pm; tel: (01896) 752043).

Moffat 32 miles (51 km) southeast of Glasgow. This small town at the head of the Annadale is set in beautiful countryside. Moffat is a market town for the sheep from the surrounding hill farms, as signified by the statue of a ram

© Paul Tomkins/STB/ The Still Moving Picture Company

on Colvin Fountain in the town square. There are great bargains to be had from Moffat's weavers. **The Neuk** is a museum which tells the story of the town through the centuries (open: Easter, Whitsunday-Sept, Mon, Tues, Thurs, Sat 10.30am-1pm, 2.30pm-5pm, Wed 10.30am-1pm, Sun 2.30pm-5pm; tel: (01683) 220868).

New Abbey 7 miles (11 km) south of Dumfries. The heart of this town is **Sweetheart Abbey**, founded in 1273 by Devorgila Balliol in memory of her husband, John (open: April-Sept, daily 9.30am-6pm; Oct-Mar, Mon-Wed, Sat 9.30am-4pm, Thurs 9.30am-12am, Sun 2pm-4pm; tel: (01316) 688800). King Edward of England installed the couple's son as a puppet king. The Scots resented this interference and called him Toom Tabard, meaning "Empty Shirt". The 18th-century **New Abbey Corn Mill** is near the abbey. Its great grinding stones are driven by water and produce oatmeal. **The Shambellie House Museum of Costume** is part of the Royal Museum of Scotland and shows material from the National Costume Collection (open: summer, daily; tel: (01387) 850375).

New Lanark 12 miles (19 km) south of Glasgow. Nominated as a World Heritage site, New Lanark was an experiment in industrial development by David Dale.

Dale took good care of his employees and by the end of the century 1,100 workers tended the machines, 800 of whom were young orphans. Later, his son-in-law took the social experiment to America and the approach became known as "Owenism." After many changes of fortune the mills eventually closed in 1968. A major restoration programme has been completed and one of the mills has become an interpretative centre, which tells the story of the experiment (open: 11am-5pm; tel: (01555) 665876). The waters of the Clyde were harnessed to drive textile machinery before the end of the 18th century. Upstream the Clyde flows through some of the finest scenery in lowland Scotland, with woods and spectacular waterfalls.

Newton Stewart 8 miles (13 km) northwest of Creetown. Newton Stewart is a great place to begin a tour of the outstanding natural beauty of the Galloway area. Galloway Forest Park contains some of the most beautiful scenery in southern Scotland, with abundant trees and wildlife. The delightful 19-mile (30-km) drive on the Queen's Way between New Galloway and Newton Stewart includes access to a stone marking a victory over the English by Robert the Bruce, Clatteringshaw Loch, the Galloway Deer Museum, a red deer park and a wild goat park. North of

Newton Stewart is Wood of Cree Nature Reserve, a huge RSPB nature reserve with the largest oak wood left in the southwest. The woods are home to hundreds of bird species.

North Berwick 26 miles (42 km) northeast of Edinburgh. North Berwick is a popular holiday resort with visitors from Edinburgh, many of whom dock their pleasure craft here. A mile (1.6 km) south of the town centre is a volcanic hill called the North Berwick Law with magnificent views of the town, St Abbs Head, Lammermuir, Traprain and Garlton Hills backed by the Moorfoots and Pentlands. In August every year a hill race is held on the Law. East of town is the 14th-century **Tantallon Castle,** a red stone ruin standing guard on a headland with sea on three sides. The curtain wall of this Douglas stronghold still survives (open: April-Sept, daily 9.30am-6pm; Oct-Mar, Mon-Wed, Sat 9.30am-4pm, Thurs 9.30am-12am, Sun 2pm-4pm; tel: (01620) 892727).

Nearby in East Fortune is the **Museum of Flight**, part of the National Museum of Scotland. The museum's vast hangar contains aircraft, trainer cockpits, engines, flight decks and scale models (open: April-Oct 10.30am-5pm; tel: (01620) 880308). North Berwick also has the Myreton Motor Museum, with all types

© Angus G Johnston/ The Still Moving Picture Company

Logan Botanic Gardens

© Harvey Wood/The Still Moving Picture Company

of road vehicles (open: 10am-6pm; tel: (0185) 870288).

Peebles 6 miles (10 km) west of Innerleithen. Within easy distance from Edinburgh, Peebles is a shopping town. A few minutes west of town on the River Tweed is **Neidpath Castle**, an L-shaped tower house adapted to 17th-century requirements (open: May-Sept, daily).

Rosslyn Chapel 7 miles (11 km) south of Edinburgh. Rosslyn Chapel, set on the edge of the Esk valley, is the finest example of medieval stone carving in Scotland. William Sinclair, 3rd Earl of Orkney, founded the chapel in 1446. (Open: Mon-Sat 10am-5pm, Sun 12pm-4.45pm; tel: (01651) 851286.)

St Abbs The coast north of Eyemouth. The large St Abbs National Nature Reserve comprises coastal grassland, rocky shoreline and cliffs. The cliffs rise to 300 feet (91 m) and provide nesting places for many seabirds. Thousands of birds visit every year, including 10,000 guillemots, razorbills, puffins, fulmars and gulls. The cliffs are truly spectacular and echo with the noise of the visiting birds.

Scottish Mining Museum

South of Newtongrange. The Lady Victoria Colliery was at one time the largest pit in Scotland and is gradually being preserved as a museum. The visitor centre includes six talking tableaux recreating life in 1890s Newtongrange. A guided tour takes visitors to the pithead, the 1894 steam winding machine and coal

hutches up and down the shaft. (Open: Mar-Oct 10am-4pm; tel: (01316) 637519.)

Scottish Railway Preservation Society

4 miles (6 km) north of Linlithgow. A station and 3.5 miles (5.6 km) of track have been rebuilt here by the Scottish Railway Preservation Society. The site includes a booking office, footbridge, signal box, locomotives, rolling stock and railway equipment. Excursions run from the shore inland to Birkhill. (Open: late-Mar-late Oct, Sat-Sun; early July-mid-Aug, Tues-Sun; advanced booking necessary; tel: (01506) 822298.)

Selkirk 7 miles (11 km) south of Galashiels. Selkirk is a hilly town with antique shops and bakeries that sell the Selkirk Bannock (sweet bread with fruit). Sir Walter Scott presided as Sheriff here and his courtroom is open to visitors (open: April-Sept, Mon-Sat 10am-4pm; June-Aug also Sun 2pm-4pm; Oct, Mon-Sat 1pm-4pm; tel: (01750) 20096). Once an ironmonger's shop on the main square, **Haliwell's House Museum** has exhibits about the town and the Common Ridings (open: April-June, Sept-Oct, Mon-Sat 10am-5pm, Sun 2pm-4pm; July-Aug, daily 10am-6pm; tel: (01750) 20096).

South Queensferry 9 miles (14 km) west of Edinburgh. Views from this town of the Forth Bridges are magnificent. The 2,765-yard (2,528-m) long Forth Rail Bridge was opened in 1890. Its newer neighbour, the Forth Road Bridge, is 1,993 yards (1,822 m) long and has been open since 1964. Six miles

(10 km) west of South Queensferry is **Hopetoun House**, an elegant mansion built by William and John Adam, which is filled with many beautiful antiques, including a famous collection of paintings (open: April-Sept 10am-5.30pm; tel: (01313) 312451).

Wanlockhead 15 miles (24 km) northwest of Dumfries. Wanlockhead, amid the bald and bleak Lowther Hills, is the highest village in Scotland. Situated in an important mining area, residents made a fortune in lead until their mine closed in the 1930s. **The Museum of the Scottish Lead Mining Industry** - located in an old mine forge - presents the story of mining with various displays and relics. There is also a unique wooden beam engine and an opportunity to pan for gold. (Open: April-Oct.)

Breac à linne, slat à coille is fiadh à fìreach – mèirle às nach do ghabh gàidheal riamh nàire.

A fish from the river, a staff from the wood and a deer from the mountains – thefts no Gael was ever ashamed of.

Taken from *A Little Book of Gaelic Proverbs* published by Appletree Press

Facing page: St Abb's Head
© W S Paton/The Still Moving Picture Company

CENTRAL SCOTLAND

The physical barrier of the Highland Boundary Fault also separates two distinct cultural areas of the country and two languages, Gaelic and Scots English. The Trossachs and Loch Lomond were the first wild areas of Scotland accessible to the lowlanders, which led to the development of tourist centres such as Pitlochry, Callander, Crieff and Dunkeld. Dramatic hills, waterfalls and wildlife can be seen from the roads or by peaceful hill walking. Trossachs Northeast Fife – with its sandy beaches – is a stark contrast to the Highlands, where there are fishing villages and a more nautical environment. The area is a centre for golf: St Andrews is the world's oldest golf course. Rural Angus has rich green pastures nestled against the rising hills of the Highlands. The industrial revolution led to the development of many specialised industries, including whisky, jam and damask, each of which is a central topic of visitor centres in the area. Central Scotland is rich in historic places and events, of which Stirling Castle, Bannockburn and Scone are the most famous.

Aberfeldy

Aberfeldy 15 miles (24 km) southwest of Pitlochry. Aberfeldy, with its distillery, watermill and famous bridge, is the largest settlement in the Breadalbane area. The Aberfeldy Bridge on the River Tay is a five-arch humpbacked structure with obelisks, designed by William Adam in 1733 for General Wade's military road. Across the bridge and 1.5 miles (2.4 km) further on is **Castle Menzies**, a 16th-century Z-plan tower fortress and the home of Clan Menzies. The clan has a museum in the castle (open: April-mid Oct, Mon-Sat 10.30am-5pm, Sun 2pm-5pm; tel: (01887) 820982). Robert Burns wrote a song entitled the "Birks of

Facing page: Stirling Castle
© David Robertson/ The Still Moving Picture Company

Aberfeldy" about the birch woods located on Moness Burn near the town and which is a great place for a walk.

Aberfoyle

Aberfoyle West of Stirling. Aberfoyle was made famous by the meeting of Rob Roy and Nicol Jarvie. **The Scottish Wool Centre** tells the story of Scottish wool from the "sheep's back to your back" with live examples of the various Scottish breeds, a textile display area where you can try spinning and weaving and a Kid's Farm with lambs and kids (open: April-Sept 9.30am-6pm; Oct-Mar 10am-5pm; tel: (01877) 382850). Above the town is the **Queen Elizabeth Forest Park Visitor Centre**, which provides information on the 170 square mile (273 sq km) park with 62 miles (100 km) of forest road for walking. Even though it is so close to the popular tourist areas it is possible to escape people in the beautiful dense forest around Loch Lomond and the Trossachs.

Anstruther

Anstruther 14 miles (23 km) southwest of St Andrews. Anstruther is a picturesque waterfront village with a beautiful harbour. Facing the harbour is the **Scottish Fisheries Museum**, housed in colourful buildings, one of which was built in the 16th century. The museum's exhibits - documents, artefacts, model ships, paintings and historic vessels tied at the quayside – illustrate the working lives of Scottish fishermen (open: April-Oct, Mon-Sat 10am-5.30pm, Sun 11am-5pm; Nov-Mar, Mon-Sat 10am-4.30pm, Sun 2pm-4.30pm; tel: (01333) 310628).

Arbroath

Arbroath 15 miles (24 km) north of Dundee. A fishing village made famous by Arbroath Smokies, a whole haddock gutted and lightly smoked. In the centre of the town is **Arbroath Abbey,** a red stone ruin, built in 1178. Here, in 1320, Robert the Bruce and the Scottish church sent a plea to Pope John XXII to recognise Scottish independence (the plea is now regarded as one of the most important documents in Scottish history). The pope asked King Edward of England to work for peace, but to no avail (open: April-Sept 9.30am-6pm; Oct-Mar, Mon-Sat 9.30am-4pm, Sun 2pm-4pm; tel: (01316) 688800). Arbroath was the shore base for Robert Stevenson's construction of Bell Rock lighthouse on a barely exposed offshore rock in the early 19th century. A signal tower was built to facilitate communications while the lighthouse was under construction. This tower has been turned into a museum, which tells the story of the construction and the town's various industries, including the manufacture of lawnmowers (open: Sept-June, Mon-Sat 10am-5pm; July-Aug also Sun 2pm-5pm; tel: (01241) 875598). Next to the museum **Kerr's Miniature Railway**

is a popular trip for adults and children and parallels the main ScotRail line (open: summer only).

Balquhidder

Balquhidder 20 miles (32 km) from Callander. The area around Balquhidder is Rob Roy MacGregor country. The Braes of Balquhidder and the Balquhidder Glen with Loch Voil have magnificent scenery. It was once settled by desperate people and the stronghold of the MacLarens and the Macgregors. There is still no road into the area. The grave of Rob Roy is in the Balquhidder churchyard next to that of his wife Helen and their two sons. His house is a private farm and is beyond the car park at the end of the glen road. Access from the car park enables visitors to climb some of the Munros or hike to the Lachine nan Eirennaich.

Blair Atholl

Blair Atholl 8 miles (13 km) north of Pitlochry. Blair Atholl is the location of the white Blair Castle, with its turrets, cross-stepped gables, chimneys and crenellations. The castle is surrounded by forest and in a strategic position to protect the central Highlands. The ancestral home of the dukes of Atholl, the castle was built in 1269 and was prominent in the Jacobite rebellion of 1745 (open: April-Oct 10am-6pm; tel: (01796) 481207). The Duke of Atholl, Chief of Clan Murray, retains the only private army in the British Isles, known as the Atholl Highlanders. The 80-member army is made up of estate workers and is one of the last remnants of the clan system. An annual parade by the Highlanders takes place on the last Sunday in May. In the village's old school is a museum, which provides insights into the history of the area (open: July-Sept, Mon-Fri 10am-5pm, Sat-Sun 1.30pm-5pm; tel: (01796) 481232). Three miles (5 km) from the village it is possible to cross on foot the Falls of Bruar, where the water channels through the rocks. Beyond the falls a museum tells the story of Clan Donnachaidh, which was descended from the Celtic earls of Atholl (open: April-Oct 10am-5pm; June-Aug 10am-6pm; tel: (01796) 483264).

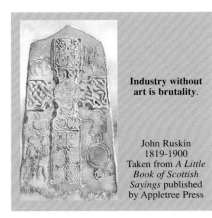

Industry without art is brutality.

John Ruskin
1819-1900
Taken from *A Little Book of Scottish Sayings* published by Appletree Press

© Robert Lees/ The Still Moving Picture Company

Crieff

Blairgowrie Once a centre for flax production, the village of Blairgowrie is now the heart of the soft fruit industry and a skiing centre. The history of flax is exhibited in the **old Keathbank Mill**, now turned into a visitor centre. With the largest water wheel in Scotland, the mill machinery is still operating. The museum contains steam and oil generators, a heraldic carving enterprise and a large model railway (open: April-Sept).

Brechin 10 miles (16 km) west of Montrose. A cathedral founded in 1200 dominates this small market town. It is famous for the town's 10th-century round tower, which was built for the local Culdee monks. The tower is one of only two on mainland Scotland.

Callander 21 miles (34 km) northwest of Stirling. Callander is just on the edge of the Highlands and the gateway to the Trossachs. **The Rob Roy and Trossachs Visitor Centre** housed in the former St Kessog's Church tells the story of the Robin Hood of Scotland (open: Jan-Feb, Sat-Sun 10am-3pm; Mar-May, Oct-Dec, daily 10am-5pm; July-Aug, daily 9am-7pm; tel: (01877) 330342). Only an hour from the centre of Callander is Bracklinn Falls, over whose lip Sir Walter Scott once rode a pony to win a bet. The beautiful journey to the falls travels through pines with open views back to the lowlands. Keen walkers can take the path to Callander Crogs, with views of the Pentlands Hills. Just north of Callander the road and river slip though the mountains at the Pass of Leny, leading to Balquhidder Glen.

The Caterthuns 5 miles (8 km) northwest of Brechin. The builders of the White and Brown Caterthun hill forts (found on either side of the road) lived 2,000 years ago. Today, you can stand in the centre of a great ring of broken stones on the site and look out over the remains of the ramparts.

Ceres 9 miles (14 km) southwest of St Andrews. Ceres' Fife Folk Museum describes life in the area up to the present day and occupies a 17th-century weigh-house and adjoining weavers' cottages (open: Easter, mid-May-Oct, Sat-Thurs 2pm-5pm; tel: (01334) 828250).

Comrie 24 miles (39 km) west of Perth. Comrie stands directly on the Highland Boundary Fault and is known as the earthquake centre of Scotland. Comrie's Earthquake House is a recording station for Scotland's earth tremors. The scenery in the area is spectacular and a good point from which to explore Perthshire's glens.

Crail 10 miles (16 km) south of St Andrews. This East Neuk of Fife fishing village shows a Dutch influence in the crow-stepped gables of its houses. The tolbooth contains the oldest bell in Fife, cast in Holland in 1520. A small local museum, Crail Museum and Heritage Centre, tells the history of the village and its trade with the Dutch (open: Easter week, June-Sept, Mon-Sat 10am-1pm, 2pm-5pm; tel: (01333) 450869).

Crieff 18 miles (29 km) north of Stirling. This hillside town overlooks Strathearn, a very hilly place. It was long a popular centre for the cattle trade and one of the great cattle trysts. Once known as Drummond, it was burned down after the 1715 Jacobite rebellion. The rebuilt village became a popular spa. The Crieff

Cock-a-Leekie

This is probably Scotland's most famous soup and is often found on the menu at a Burns supper or St Andrew's Night dinner. From the humblest crofts to the grandest of royal palaces this was an established favourite. Here is the special recipe of Rosa Mattravers, cook to Theodora Lady Forbes, on Donside in Aberdeenshire.

1 boiling chicken
3 rashers lean bacon, chopped
1 large veal or beef marrow bone (optional)
parsley, thyme and 1 bay leaf
12 leeks, chopped
salt and pepper
4oz/100g/1 cup prunes, cooked

Place chicken, bacon, chopped bone, herbs, and most of the leeks into a large saucepan and cover with water. Put the lid on and let it simmer for 2-3 hours, topping up with more water if necessary, until the bird is cooked.

Season to taste, then strain, picking out the chicken and cutting it into serving pieces and spooning out the marrow bones. Add these to the soup, together with the stoned prunes, and the remaining chopped leeks. Simmer gently for 10-15 minutes.

A recipe from *A Little Scottish Cookbook* published by Appletree Press

Highland Gathering is the home of the Scottish Heavyweight Championship. **The Crieff visitor centre** demonstrates production of Buchan's Thistle pottery and Perthshire paperweights (open: Mon-Fri 9am-6pm; tel: (01764) 654014). **The Glenturret Distillery** offers guided tours and a visitor centre (open: Mar-Dec 9.30am-6pm, Sun 12am-6pm). Two miles (3 km) south of Crieff is **Drummond Castle** (its tower dating from 1491), home to the Drummond Clan. The castle's park comprises a series of terraces and a formal garden in the shape of a St Andrew's cross. The garden (but not the castle) is open to visitors (open: May-Oct 2pm-6pm; tel: (0174) 681257).

Culross 25 miles (40 km) northwest of Edinburgh. Culross once had a monopoly on the manufacture of baking girdles (griddles) and was involved in coal and salt export. When the trade died out the town was all but forgotten and the old merchants' houses of the 17th and 18th centuries were never destroyed. In the 1930s the National Trust for Scotland began restoring them. Most of the buildings are now private residences, but the Palace, Study and Townhouse are open to the public (open: Study and Townhouse, April-Sept 1.30pm-5pm; Oct, Sat-Sun 11am-5pm; Palace, April-Sept 11am-5pm; tel: (01312) 265922).

Cupar 10 miles (16 km) west of St Andrews. Cupar serves as Fife County's administrative centre. The National Trust for Scotland's **Hill of Tarvit House**, a 17th-century Edwardian mansion, has a fine collection of antique furniture, Chinese porcelain, bronzes, tapestries and Dutch paintings (open: house, Easter-May 1.30pm-5.30pm; Oct, Sat-Sun 1.30pm-5.30pm; garden, April-Oct 9.30am-9pm; Nov-Mar, daily 9.30am-4.30pm; tel: (01334) 653127). Just outside Cupar is the **Scottish Deer centre** where you can see red deer up close, take country walks and watch falcons (open: Easter-Oct 10am-6pm; Nov-Easter 10am-5pm; tel: (01337) 810391).

Doune 9 miles (14 km) north of Stirling. History records Doune as the place where prominent gunsmiths made the Doune or Highland pistol for Highland drovers. Today the village is known for its magnificent **Doune Castle**, believed by many to be the finest surviving medieval castle in Scotland. Overlooking the Ardoch Burn and River Teith, the 14th-century castle's most prominent feature is its 95-feet (29 m) keep-gatehouse, which rises four stories (open: April-Sept 9.30am-6.30pm; Oct-Mar, Sat-Wed 9.30am-4.30pm; tel: (01316) 688800).

Dumbarton 36 miles (58 km) west of Stirling. Dumbarton Castle, built on the basalt plug of Dumbarton Rock (240 feet/73 m high), was once the capital of the independent kingdom of Strathclyde. In 1548 the five-year-old Mary Queen of Scots was held at the castle before she was sent to France. From the top of the castle there is a magnificent panoramic view of the Clyde estuary (open: summer, daily; winter, closed Thursday afternoons, Friday; tel: (01389) 732167). Dumbarton's most unusual attraction is the Ship Model Experiment Tank built by William Denny in 1882, the first commercial experimental tank for shipbuilders' scale models. Many of Scotland's famous vessels were designed and tested here (open: Mon-Sat).

Dunblane 7 miles (11 km) north of Stirling. **Dunblane Cathedral** was built in the 13th century on the site of St Blane's tiny 8th-century cell. The seat of the Bishop of the Diocese of Dunblane until the Reformation, the

Tay Bridge, Dundee

cathedral has 15th-century misericords and medieval carvings (open: April-Sept 9.30am-6.30pm; otherwise 9.30am-4.30pm; tel: (01368) 862585).

Dundee 58 miles (93 km) north of Edinburgh. Dundee is Scotland's fourth largest city and an industrial city famed in the past for "jute, jam and journalism". Today, Dundee is described as the City of Discovery, as it is the home of RRS Discovery, the vessel used by Captain Robert Scott on his polar expeditions. The ship was built in Dundee in 1901 and is now permanently

anchored there. A visitor centre and onboard exhibition enable visitors to learn more about the perils of polar voyages (open: April-Oct, Mon-Sat 10am-5pm, Sun 11am-5pm; Nov-Mar, Mon-Sat 10am-4pm, Sun 11am-4pm; tel: (01382) 201245). At nearby Victoria Dock is the frigate **Unicorn**, a 47-gun wooden warship built in 1824. The Unicorn is the oldest British warship still afloat and the fourth oldest in the world (open: mid-Mar-Oct 10am-5pm; Nov-mid-March, Mon-Fri 10am-4pm; tel: (01382) 200900). **Barrack Street Museum** is an excellent natural history museum with exhibits on the wildlife and geology of Angus and the Highlands: the famous Tay Whale eulogised by the notorious William McGonagall is among the exhibits (open: Mon 11am-5pm, Tues-Sat 10am-5pm; tel: (01382) 432067). Dundee's main museum and art gallery is the **McManus Galleries**, which has displays of local history (open: Mon 11am-5pm, Tues-Sat 10am-5pm; tel: (01382) 432020).

Dundee has two castles in its eastern suburbs. **Claypotts Castle** is a 16th-century tower house laid out in a Z-plan (tel: (01316) 688800) and **Broughty Castle** is now a museum on fishing, ferries and whaling, plus displays of arms and armour (open: Oct-June, Mon 11am-1pm, 2pm-5pm, Tues-Thurs, Sat 10am-1pm, 2pm-5pm; July-Sept also Sun 2pm-5pm; tel: (01382) 776121). The jute industry is explained in a multifaceted exhibition in the **Verdant Works**, which includes restored machinery, audiovisuals and tableaux (open: April-Oct, Mon-Sat

© Robert Lees/ The Still Moving Picture Company

10am-5pm, Sun 11am-5pm; Nov-Mar, Mon-Sat 10am-4pm, Sun 11am-4pm; tel: (01382) 225282).

Dunfermline 16 miles (26 km) northwest of Edinburgh. Dunfermline, once the centre of damask linen production, and the birthplace of Andrew Carnegie, was the capital of Scotland during the reign of King Malcolm Canmore in the 11th century. The king married Margaret, was later canonised as a saint and for a time the town became the religious centre of Scotland.
Dunfermline Abbey is connected to the monastery and the royal palace. The complex has many historic connections. Robert the Bruce is buried here, Charles I was born here and the royal court was located here until the end of the 11th century (open: April-Sept, daily, 9.30am-6pm; Oct-Mar, Mon-Wed, Sat 9.30am-4pm, Thurs 9.30am-12am, Sun 2pm-4pm; tel: (01383) 733266). **The Andrew Carnegie Birthplace Museum** honours the town's famous son, who from humble beginnings as a weaver's son, later donated $350 million to good causes. The interesting exhibits include the freedom caskets, which hold the symbolic keys to the town (open: April-May, Sept-Oct, Mon-Sat 11am-5pm, Sun 2pm-5pm; June-Aug, Mon-Sat 10am-5pm, Sun 2pm-5pm; Nov-Mar, daily 2pm-6pm; tel: (01383) 313837).

Dunkeld 14 miles (22 km) north of Perth. Dunkeld is known for its picturesque 18th-century "Little Houses" and Thomas Telford's beautiful bridge, built in 1809. Near Dunkeld is the Scottish Wildlife Trust reserve, Loch of Lowes (with beautiful scenery), best known for the ospreys which visit in the summer (open: April-Sept, daily 10am-5pm; tel: (01350) 727337).

Edzell 6 miles (10 km) north of Brechin. Edzell Castle in the Grampian foothills has a 16th-century red stone tower. Once a stronghold for the Lindsays, it has a magnificent walled sculpture garden (open: April-Sept, daily 9.30am-6pm; Oct-Mar, Mon-Wed, Sat 9.30am-4pm, Thurs 9.30am-12pm, Sun 2pm-6pm; tel: (01316) 688800).

Falkland 8 miles (13 km) north of Kirkcaldy. A royal burgh of twisting streets and handsome little cottages, the village of Falkland is famous for **Falkland Palace**, a Renaissance-style Stuart hunting lodge built in the 1500s whose buttresses and medallions from that era still survive. In its lovely gardens is the oldest tennis court in Britain, which dates from 1539 and is still in use. The palace was a favourite of Mary Queen of Scots; her father King

Ochil Hills and Stirling Castle

James V – who had the palace built – died there (open: April-Oct, Mon-Sat 11am-5.30pm, Sun 1.30pm-5.30pm; tel: (01337) 857397).
Glamis 16 miles (26 km) north of Dundee. Situated in the rich agricultural land of Strathmore, Glamis is home to the National Trust's **Angus Folk Museum**, which consists of attractive 19th-century cottages and an outstanding folk collection depicting the rural life of the past (open: Good Fri-Easter Mon, May-Sept 11am-5pm; tel: (01307) 840288).
Glamis Castle is one of Scotland's best-known castles because of its association with Shakespeare's Macbeth and Britain's present royal family. Built in 1372 it was reconstructed in the 17th century: the keep is all that remains of the original building. The castle has a fine collection of china, tapestries and furniture (open: April-June, late Sept-Oct 10.30am-5.30pm; July-Aug 10am-5.30pm; tel: (01307) 840393).

Kirriemuir 20 miles (32 km) southwest of Edzell. In the heart of Angus's redstone countryside is Kirriemuir, the birthplace of writer and dramatist Sir James Barrie, the author of Peter Pan. The National Trust of Scotland operates Barrie House furnished as it would have been

during the writer's lifetime. A number of manuscripts and personal items are on display. Barrie's first theatre was the washhouse outside (open: Easter & May-Sept, Mon-Sat 11am-5.30pm, Sunday 1.30pm-5.30pm; Oct, Sat 11am-5.30pm, Sun 1.30pm-5.30pm; tel: (01575) 572646). Next door can be found an exhibit entitled "The Genius of J.M. Barrie", giving the literary and theatrical background.

Kirkcaldy 30 miles (48 km) north of Edinburgh. A combination of holiday resort and industrial town, Kirkcaldy in the 19th century was the centre of the linoleum industry in Scotland. The ruins of Kirkcaldy Castle stand on a rocky hill overlooking Kirkcaldy Bay. Built in 1460, the castle is an important example of early artillery fortification. Nearby is Dysart, where the National Trust for Scotland has restored properties around a tiny harbour.

Loch Lomond 20 miles (32 km) from Glasgow. Known as the Queen of the Scottish Lochs, Loch Lomond has the largest surface area of all Scotland's lochs. The loch is 23 miles (37 km) long and 5 miles (8 km) wide at its widest, with a maximum depth of 653 feet (199 m). The

© Paul Tomkins/STB/ The Still Moving Picture Company

world-famous loch is celebrated in the well-known song The Banks of Loch Lomond, written after the 1745 rebellion. The south of the loch has a pastoral setting, while in the north it is surrounded by rugged mountains. Ben Lomond rises 3,192 feet (973 m) on the eastern shore of the loch and is the most southerly of the Munros. It is wise to avoid visiting the loch on weekends because of traffic congestion. The best way to appreciate the loch is to take the boat tour that leaves from Balloch Bridge and stops at Luss, Rowardennan, Tarbet and Inversnaid (tours from Mar-April, apply at Tourist Centre, Balloch; tel: (0139) 753533).

Montrose 40 miles (64 km) south of Aberdeen. Montrose acts as a base for those who wish to explore the beautiful coastline. The River Esk forms the Montrose Basin, a superb area for bird watching. The Scottish Wildlife Trust has a reserve here for all sorts of wildfowl (open: April-Sept, daily 10.30am-6pm; Oct-Mar, Mon, Sat, Sun 10.30am-6pm; tel: (0164) 676336). A National Trust for Scotland property called the **House of Dun** overlooks the Montrose Basin. Designed by William Adam, this 1730 mansion is noted for its spectacular plasterwork. In the courtyard Angus weavers weave linen on traditional looms (open: Easter, May-Sept 1.30pm-5.30pm; tel: (0174) 810264).

Ochil Hills 10 miles (16 km) east of Stirling. The Ochil area is defined by the long, humpbacked hills of an old faultline in hard volcanic rock. The fault provides the elevation for the waterfalls which powered the second largest textile manufacturing area in

Scotland. High open pastures feed the sheep whose wool was used to make the textiles. The Ochil Hills Woodland Park between Alva and Tillicoultry has a large selection of walks and provides access to beautiful Silver Glen.

In the village of Dollar on a high mound above the glen is **Castle Campbell**, once owned by the 1st Earl of Argyll, Chancellor of Scotland to King James IV. John Knox, the fiery religious reformer, preached at the castle. A basic 15th-century tower house with later additions, it rises impressively above the trees at the head of a valley (open: April-Sept, daily 9.30am-6pm; Oct-Mar, Mon-Wed, Sat 9.30am-12am, Sun 2pm-4pm; tel: (01259) 42408).

Perth 43 miles (69 km) north of Edinburgh. A centre for rural life, Perth has a long history. It gave birth to the Scottish Reformation when John Knox's sermon in St John's Kirk began the upheaval in 1559. St John's Kirk, which dates from the 15th century, escaped extensive damage during the conflict, and is now restored (open: Mon-Fri 10am-2pm; tel: (01738) 626159). On the North Inch of Perth is **Balhousie Castle** with the Regimental Museum of Black Watch (open: May-Sept, Mon-Sat 10am-4.30pm; Oct-April, Mon-Fri 10am-3.30pm; tel: (01313) 108530). **Caithness Glass** has an outlet in Perth and a small museum and gallery with demonstrations of glassmaking (open: factory, Mon-Fri 9am-4.30pm; shop, Easter-mid-Oct, Mon-Sat 9am-5pm, Sun 10am-5pm).
There are many castles a short distance from Perth. **Huntingtower Castle** has a novel double tower dating back to the 15th century (open: April-Sept 9.30am-

Sower's Song

Now hands to seedsheet, boys!
We step and we cast; old Time's on wing,
And would ye partake of Harvest's joys,
The corn must be sown in Spring.

Fall gently and still, good corn,
Lie warm in thy earthy bed;
And stand in yellow some morn,
For beast and man must be fed.

Now steady and sure again,
And measure of stroke and step we keep;
Thus up and thus down we cast our
grain, Sow well, and ye gladly reap.

Fall gently and still, good corn
Lie warm in thy earthy bed,
And stand in yellow some morn,
For beast and man must be fed.

Thomas Carlyle (1795-1881)
Taken from *A Little Book of Scottish Verse*
published by Appletree Press

6pm; Oct-Mar, Mon-Wed, Sat 9.30am-4pm, Thurs 9am-12am, Sun 2pm-4pm; tel: (01738) 627231). **Elcho Castle** – once the seat of the earls of Wemyss – is an abandoned fortified mansion on the east side of Perth (tel: (01316) 688800).

© David Robertson/The Still Moving Picture Company

Loch Lomond

Scone Palace is the present home of the Earl of Mansfield and is open to visitors. It was the traditional crowning place of Scottish kings: a mausoleum marks the long-gone Abbey on Moot Hill where coronations took place as the kings sat on the Stone of Scone. The present castle dates from the early 19th century and has a magnificent collection of porcelain, furniture, 18th-century clocks, ivories and 16th-century needlework (open: Easter-Oct 9.30am-5.15pm; tel: (01738) 552308).

Pitlochry 29 miles (47 km) north of Perth. Claimed as the geographic centre of Scotland, Pitlochry is a popular holiday village. Just behind the main street is the Hydroelectric Visitor Centre, which overlooks Loch Faskally and has a fish ladder where you can see fish jumping through a glass pipe. In the area there are two lovely lochs, Tummel and Rannoch, the latter connected to the famous Rannoch moor. The Linn of Tummel is a series of marked walks north of the village. Just north of the Linn is the Pass of Killiecrankie where a famous battle was fought during the Jacobite rebellion in 1689. The National Trust for Scotland operates a visitor centre, which explains the battle and its significance (open: April-Oct 10am-5.30pm; tel: (01796) 473233). A short walk to the west is Queen's View – named after Queen Victoria's visit in 1866 – with magnificent vistas over Loch Tummel.

Pittenweem 10 miles (16 km) southwest of St Andrews. Pittenweem is a picturesque village with a working harbour. Up a close (alleyway) from the waterfront is St Fillan's Cave, which contains the shrine of St Fillan, a 6th–century hermit who lived there (pen: Tues-Sat 10am-5pm, Sun 12am-5pm; tel: (01333) 311495). A short distance inland is 16th-century Kellie Castle, which was restored in Victorian times. It has a peaceful walled garden and extensive grounds (open: Easter, May-Sept 1.30pm-5.30pm; Oct, Sat-Sun 1.30pm-5.30pm; tel: (01333) 720271).

St Andrews 52 miles (84 km) northeast of Edinburgh. The Mecca of golf and the second most visited place in Scotland, St Andrews has a major university and many historic monuments. Legend says the city was founded by St Regulus or St Rule, who was shipwrecked and established a church. St Rule's Tower, built in 1126, is the oldest surviving building in the town (open: April-Sept 9.30am-6.30pm; otherwise 9.30am-4.30pm). **St Andrews Cathedral** was founded in 1160 and is a fragmented ruin today. Near the ocean's edge are the ruins of St Andrews Castle, where a rare

Cathedral ruins, St Andrews

example of a cold and dark bottle dungeon has survived. Linked to the castle is a tunnel dug by castle defenders in order to meet tunnelling besiegers and wage battle underground (open: April-Sept 9.30am-6pm; Oct-Mar, Mon-Sat 9.30am-4pm, Sun 2pm-4pm; tel: (01334) 477196). A visit to St Andrews would not be complete without seeing the **Royal & Ancient Golf Club**, the ruling house of golf worldwide. The clubhouse on the dunes and adjoining the Old Course is only open to members. Just opposite the Royal & Ancient Golf Club is the **British Golf Museum** (open: April-mid-Oct 9.30am-5.30pm; mid-Oct-mid-April, Thurs-Mon 11am-3pm; tel: (01334) 478880). **St Andrews University** is the oldest university in Scotland and now consists of two stately old colleges in the middle of town. It is possible to be given a tour of the building by students robed in their scarlet gowns (tours twice daily, July-early Sept; tel: (01334) 462158).

Stirling 26 miles (42 km) northeast of Glasgow. Stirling has a rich history mainly because of its strategic location on the Forth at its tidal limit and with passage north between the Ochils and Gragunnock Hills. **Stirling Castle** dominates the city from its high stronghold on a crag in the centre of town, the views from which are breathtaking. The castle was home to many of Scotland's royal family, beginning with James III in the 15th century, but after James VI left Scotland

to become King of England it fell into disrepair. The National Trust for Scotland has restored much of James V's palace, including the Chapel Royal of 1594, the great hall and royal apartments (open: April-Sept 9.30am-6pm; otherwise 9.30am-5pm; tel: (01786) 450000). A short distance southeast of Stirling the **Bannockburn Heritage Centre** tells the story of Robert the Bruce's victory over the English (site open all year; visitor centre, April-Oct 10am-5.30pm; Mar, Nov, Dec 11am-3pm; tel: (01786) 812664). **The National Wallace Monument** honours Scotland's first freedom fighter, William Wallace. The view from the top of the spire is worth the 246-step climb up the spiral staircase (open: July-Aug 9.30am-6.30pm; June, Sept 10am-6pm; Mar-May 10am-5pm; Jan, Feb, Nov, Dec, Sat-Sun 10am-4pm; tel: (01786) 472140).

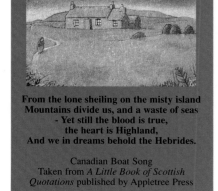

From the lone sheiling on the misty island
Mountains divide us, and a waste of seas
- Yet still the blood is true,
the heart is Highland,
And we in dreams behold the Hebrides.

Canadian Boat Song
Taken from *A Little Book of Scottish Quotations* published by Appletree Press

© STB/ The Still Moving Picture Company

Facing page: Pittenweem, Fife
© Bob West/ The Still Moving Picture Company

HEBRIDEAN ISLANDS

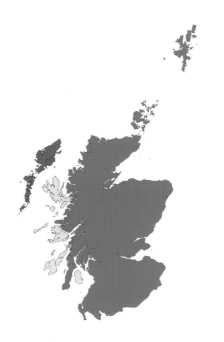

THE INNER HEBRIDES

ARRAN

Arran is 29 miles (47 km) west of Glasgow. It has an area of 165 square miles (265 sq km), is 25 miles (40 km) long and 10 miles (16 km) wide. Sheltered by the Kintyre Peninsula, the island has an extremely mild climate. Access to Arran is by ferry; most people use the one-hour ferry from **Ardrossan**, but there is a short summer ferry from Claonaig (tel: (01475) 650100). Arran is often described as "Scotland in miniature" because it is divided by the Highland Boundary Fault, just like mainland Scotland. The "string road" (A841) runs around the entire island, so bus and car journeys to places of interest are very straightforward. The mountains of Arran are beautiful, the most famous of which is Goat Fell which rises 2,866 feet (873 m) to its conical top: the windswept summit means Goat Fell is also known as the Mountain of the Winds. The mountains conceal some beautiful glens, the most famous of which are Glen Sannox in the northeast and Glen Rosa directly north of Brodick. Glen Rosa has some gentle hill walks and excellent views of the wild mountains.

Brodick The main town on the island, Brodick also has the island's main tourist attraction: **Brodick Castle**. The former seat of the dukes of Hamilton – now owned by the National Trust for Scotland – the 13th-century castle has several of its rooms open to the public, with paintings, silver and sporting trophies on display.

Facing page: Sgurr na Stri, Skye
© David Robertson/ The Still Moving Picture Company

The two castle gardens are world famous: the walled garden dates from 1710, while the large woodland garden has one of the finest rhododendron displays of its kind (late spring and early summer are the best times to visit to enjoy the blossoms). (Open: castle, Mar-Oct 11.30am-4.30pm; gardens, 11.30am-sunset; tel: (01770) 302202.) Also in Brodick, the **Isle of Arran Heritage Museum** documents the life of the island from ancient times to the present. The museum's buildings with period furnishings include a cottage, a smiddy (blacksmiths) and a milk house. It has a good introduction to the island's prehistoric sites (open: April-Oct, Mon-Sat 10am-5pm, Sun 11am-4pm; tel: (01770) 202636).

Corrie 11 miles (18 km) north of Brodick. An arts and crafts centre with all kinds of local craft items for sale.

Lagg 10 miles (16 km) southwest of Lamlash. A small village on the Kilmory Water, with excellent views of Ailsa Craig. If you are a lover of cheese the creamery at Torrylinn makes the world famous Arran Cheddar.

Lamlash 4 miles (6 km) south of Brodick. This seaside resort on Lamlash Bay is supposed to have been the anchorage for King Haakon and his Vikings before the Battle of Largs in 1263. Across the bay are the steep banks of Holy Island with its two lighthouses. From Lamlash visitors can also reach the highest point accessible by car on Arran.

Lochranza 6 miles (10 km) north of Sannox. Lochranza Castle, situated on a low sand spit, is believed to be where Robert the Bruce landed in 1307 to begin his campaign for independence (open: Mon-Fri 9am-5pm; tel: (01316) 888800). A little farther on at Catacol are the Twelve Apostles, a row of fishermen's houses all identical except for the shape of the windows, so that individual homes could be identified from offshore.

Machrie 11 miles (18 km) south of Lochranza. A short walk along a smooth track ends at the eerie Machrie Moor stone circles. The site comprises a small circle of granite boulders with much taller, red sandstone monoliths. The entire area of the Machrie is dotted with Bronze Age monuments such as chambered cairns, hut circles and standing stones.

Sannox 2 miles (3 km) north of Corrie. The bay at Sannox has a sandy beach of ground granite washed down from the mountains. From here there are spectacular views of the rugged mountains of the island interior, particularly Cir Mhor.

Whiting Bay 8 miles (13 km) east of Lagg. A popular seaside resort.

COLL

A three-hour ferry ride from Oban, Coll is a rocky island of acid moorland, 3 miles (5 km) wide and 13 miles (21 km) long, with a population of 130. A restored castle, Breacachadh, was a stronghold of the Macleans since the 15th century and is sometimes open to the public. At Totronald on the west of the island are two standing stones called Na Sgeulachan ("the teller of tales"). Thought to record the movement of the sun, the stones pre-date the Druids and could once have been part of a temple. At Killunaig, near Sorisdale, are the ruins of a medieval church and burial ground. Sorisdale was once the inhabited centre of the island, but all that is left are the ruins of crofts abandoned either because of the potato famine or the Clearances.

COLONSAY

Some 15 miles (24 km) south of the Isle of Mull and a two-hour ferry trip from Oban, Colonsay is just 20 square miles (32 km) of sheep and cattle farms, rabbit-grazed coastal strips, and woods of oak, hazel and willow. It faces the open Atlantic in the west, with a lighthouse the only thing between the island and Canada. All of the island can be explored on good single-track roads. Lord Strathcona's family owns the island and their home, Colonsay House, has a beautiful garden, Kiloran Garden, with rare rhododendrons, magnolias, eucalyptus and even palm trees. The garden is open all year round but the house is not open to the public. A strand that can be walked across at low tide connects Colonsay to the little island of Oronsay, which has the ruins of a 6th-century monastery founded by St Columba. Carved stone tombstones near the ruins include the famous Great Cross of Prior Colin, dating from the early 16th century.

IONA

A five-minute ferry ride from Fionnphort on the Isle of Mull, Iona is a tiny, low-lying and treeless island of just three square miles (5 sq km), but it is also one of the most venerated places in Scotland. In 563 the fiery and argumentative Irish monk Columba chose Iona for his monastery (Iona was the first place from which Columba could not see Ireland). Columba was not the first Christian missionary to Scotland, for he was preceded by St Ninian, who brought Christianity to Galloway in 397. However, the founding of the church on Iona led to the spread of Christianity to the rest of Scotland, including the Picts. Iona was later ravaged by the Norsemen, but today the buildings and the restored abbey are a spiritual centre under the jurisdiction of the Church of Scotland. A curious mixture of the ancient and the devout, the island sometimes has to cope with 1,000 visitors a week but still maintains its peaceful atmosphere. At the 13th-century abbey the Iona Community conducts workshops on Christianity, sponsors a youth camp, offers tours, and on Wednesday leads a seven-mile (11 km) hike to the important sites on the island. Between March and October the community leads seminars, when participants study and stay at the abbey for a week. All guests are expected to spend part of the day on some household chore. The MacLeod Centre provides facilities for youth and persons with disabilities and their families. It accommodates up to 50 guests (tel: (01681) 700404). The nunnery and St Ronan's Church were built about the same time as the abbey. The famous 15th-century Maclean's Cross – with a Crucifixion scene on one side and intricately carved patterns on the other – is alongside the path to the abbey. Iona was the burial place of the kings of Scotland until the 11th century. The "Graves of the Kings" or Reilig Odhrain in front of the abbey contain 48 Scottish kings from Kenneth MacAlpine to Malcolm III, and include Macbeth and Duncan as well as four Irish and eight Norwegian kings. The oldest building on Iona is the restored 12th-century St Oran's Chapel. Of the three standing

© Ken Paterson/ The Still Moving Picture Company

Bowmore, Islay

© Ken Paterson/ The Still Moving Picture Company

Glen Rosa, Arran

high crosses only St Martin's is complete and original, with scenes on its west face. The shaft is all that remains of St Matthew's Cross, while the third is a replica of St John's Cross. The most precious items are found in the Infirmary Museum, with its collection of early Christian and medieval stones and the original 8th-century St John's Cross (open: 9am-5pm; tel: (01681) 700404).

ISLAY

Access to the southernmost Inner Hebridean Islands is by Calmac ferry from West Tarbet on the Kintyre Peninsula, sailing to Port Askaig or Port Ellen (tel: (01475) 650100). Islay Tourist Information Centre is at Bowmore (tel: (01496) 810254).

Bowmore 11 miles (18 km) north of Port Ellen. The most famous landmark in Bowmore (the island's capital) is the round parish church, which was built that way in 1767 so as to deny the devil a corner in which to hide. The town is also well known because of the whisky that bears its name. **Bowmore Distillery** was established in 1779 and its single malt is exported all over the world (open: Mon-Fri 10.30am-3pm, plus summer Saturdays; tel: (01496) 810441).

Bridgend 3 miles (5 km) north of Bowmore. **The Islay Woollen Mill** has been in business for more than a century and has a wide range of country tweeds (it also made most of the tartans for Braveheart). There is a large range of items for sale (open: Mon-Sat 10am-5pm; tel: (01496) 810563).

Bruichladdich West from Bowmore. On the shore of Loch Indaal across from Bowmore, Bruichladdich is another village that gives its name to a famous malt whisky.

Loch Finlaggan 7 miles (11 km) northeast of Bridgend. The small island in the middle of the loch was the former council seat of the Lord of the Isles and the Clan Donald was a mighty force when it ruled here. There are some traces of buildings on the island and an interpretative centre located in a small cottage tells the story of the area and the continuing excavations of the island's ruins (open: April-Sept, Sun, Tues, Thurs 2.30pm-5pm; tel: (01496) 840644).

Loch Gruinart 7 miles (11 km) northeast of Port Charlotte. Pale beaches flank the sea outlet at Loch Gruinart. On the western shore is the ruined Chapel of Kilnave. It was here in 1598 that a group of wounded Maclean clansmen seeking shelter were burned to death by the Macdonalds when they set fire to their roof. The graveyard contains an 8th-century carved cross. From the eastern shore of the loch you can view Colonsay and Oronsay.

Port Askaig 3 miles (5 km) northeast of Loch Finlaggan. Jura's ferry port comprises a few cottages by a pier. **Bunnahabhain Distillery** is on a side road uphill from the village and offers tours by appointment only (tel: (01496) 840207). Caol Ila Distillery is also in Port Askaig (open: Easter-Sept, Mon-Fri morning and afternoon tours; Wed, mornings only; tel: (01496) 840207).

Port Charlotte 11 miles (18 km) west of Bowmore. The Museum of Islay Life located in a converted kirk presents information on the history of Islay (open: April-Oct, Mon-Sat 10am-5pm, Sun 2pm-5pm; tel: (01496) 850358). Eight miles (13 km) from Port Charlotte is a memorial tower on the Mull of Oa for the US seamen and army troops who lost their lives when the Tuscania and the Otranto were torpedoed offshore.

Port Ellen 11 miles (18 km) south of Bowmore. Founded in 1820, Port Ellen on the south coast is Islay's principal port and relatively modern by Islay standards. Two of Islay's most famous distilleries, **Laphroaig and Lagavulin**, are located in Port Ellen. **Lagavulin Distillery** with its gift shop is a popular tour (open: Mon-Fri 10.30am-2.30pm; tel: (01496) 302418). **Laphroaig whisky** on the Ardbeg road has a tangy, peaty, seaweed/iodine flavour very popular the world over (tours by appointment morning and afternoon; tel: (01496) 302418). Further along the Ardbeg road there is a ruined chapel, the churchyard of which has the finest carved cross anywhere in Scotland. Carved from a single slab of epidotic rock, the Kildalton Cross is covered on both sides with elaborate designs in the style of the Iona School. The graveyard also has many gravestones dating from the 12th and 13th centuries. **Port Ellen Pottery** sells distinctive goblets, jugs and mugs, among other items (open: 10am-5pm; tel: (01496) 302345). Three miles (5 km) from Port Ellen is the 18-hole Machrie Golf Course, a challenging course because of the ocean winds coming from all directions.

ISLE OF SKYE

The largest of the islands of the Inner Hebrides, the mystical Isle of Skye is 48 miles (77 km) long and 3-25 miles (5-40 km) wide. Only a small stretch of water separates Skye from the mainland, spanned by a toll bridge. Skye is one of the most beautiful islands in the world and a visit here can provide a memory to cherish for life. The island is dominated by the Cuillin Hills, a range of jagged mountains popular with climbers. **Skye Tourist Information Centre** is at Bayfield House in Portree (tel: (01478) 612137).

Dunvegan
The biggest attraction in the northern part of Skye is **Dunvegan Castle**, the principal seat of the chiefs of Clan Macleod, who have resided here for 750 years. Dunvegan is believed to be the oldest inhabited castle in Britain. Its many interesting relics include the "fairy flag", once believed to have the power to ward-off danger to the clan and twice used for that very purpose. (Open: late March-Oct 10am-5.30pm; tel: (01470) 521206.) Nearby are MacLeod's Tables, two flat-topped mountains where a chief entertaining a king at a torch-lit banquet is reputed to have said, "No one can set a table like this". **The Colbost Folk Museum** is a typical black house with family quarters and byre for the animals under one roof, plus its own

© David Robertson/The Still Moving Picture Company

Elgol, Skye

illicit whisky still (sadly no longer working) (open: Easter-Oct 10am-6pm; tel: (01470) 521296).

Portree
Skye's capital has a population of 2,000 and a picturesque harbour surrounded by high hills. Shops in the village are good: **Skye Original Prints of Portree** (tel: (01478) 612544) stocks artist Tom Mackenzie's etchings, prints, aquatints and greetings cards inspired by the daily life of the island. **The Skye Heritage Centre**, **Aros**, is a good place to begin your visit to Skye. Its walk-through exhibition includes audio commentary and its gift shop has an excellent selection of Celtic music and books about the area. The restaurant provides a good lunch and its outside tables enjoy spectacular views (open: daily, all year; tel: (01478) 613649).

Sligachan Centre of Skye
This remote and beautiful village at the head of a sea loch and at the foot of the Red Cuillins is a popular base for touring the entire island. Paths from here lead to the higher areas of the Cuillins and the nearby fishing is excellent, with plenty of sea trout, brown trout and salmon.

Trotternish Peninsula
This 20-mile (32 km) peninsula is known for its

unusual rock formations. Views of Raasay and Loch Sinzort can be had from the coast road. North of Portree there is a ten-mile (16 km) ridge rising to 3,000 feet (914 m). This area is called the Storr and consists of a succession of jagged rock outcrops, the most famous of which is the rock pinnacle known as the Old Man of Storr. Also north of Portree is a great ridge with numerous rocky bastions called the Quiraing. The ruins of an ancient MacDonald stronghold, Duntulm, stand on a cliff top commanding the sea route to the Outer Hebrides. **The Skye Museum of Island Life** consists of a crofter's house, a weaver's house, a smithy and a ceilidh house. **The ceilidh house** has an interesting display of photographs and documents relating to crofting (open: April-mid-Oct, Mon-Sat 9.30am-5.30pm; tel: (01470) 552206). The main village on the peninsula is Uig, which is the ferry port for Harris and Uist in the Outer Hebrides. **Monkstadt House**, north of Uig, is where Flora MacDonald brought Bonnie Prince Charlie after their escape from Benbecula. At Kilmuir churchyard there is a Celtic cross monument to Flora MacDonald.

Sleat Peninsula The peninsula is known as the Garden of Skye because the warming effects of the Gulf Stream encourage lush vegetation. **Knock Castle**, a ruined MacDonald stronghold, can be visited free throughout the day. Another MacDonald stronghold, **Dunsgiath Castle**, has some well-preserved ruins. The story of Clan MacDonald and their proud title, Lords of the Isle, is told at the Clan Centre in the restored part of **Armadale Castle**. **Armadale Gardens** have extensive plantings and nature trails (open: castle, April-Oct 9.30am-6pm; gardens, all year; tel: (01471) 844305). Just up the road Lord and Lady MacDonald run the Kinloch Lodge.

JURA

The fourth largest of the Inner Hebridean Islands, Jura is a five-minute ferry ride from Port Askaig (tel: (01413) 329766). Some 27 miles (43 km) long and 2-8 miles (3-13 km) wide, the island has only one road. Its population is around 250 people, who live mostly on the east coast. The island's name comes from the Norse word "Jute", which means "deer island": an apt name as there are about 20 deer to every person on Jura. The island is a wonderful retreat, because it is relatively unknown and unexplored by tourists. The Lord of the Isles built **Claig Castle**, on an island in the sound. **Jura House** is in the woods, with sheltered garden walks and magnificent views (open: for tea, June-Aug, Mon-Fri 10am-2pm; garden, daily 9am-5pm; tel: (01496) 820315). North of Jura House in **Craighouse** is Jura's only malt distillery (tel: (01496) 820240). Near the end of the road at Kinuachdrach is a footpath which leads to Corryvreckan, the powerful whirlpool, and Barnhill, where George Orwell lived while he was writing 1984.

MULL

Mull is a 45-minute ferry ride from Oban to Craignure (tel: (01631) 562285). Mull Tourist Centre is on Main Street in Tobermory (tel: (01688) 302182). Mull rivals Skye for beauty, but part of Mull's distinct appeal is its waterfalls. The island also has two nine-hole golf courses: the Western Isle Golf Course in Tobermory and a newer course in Craignure. Mull's whisky distillery is Tobermory Malt Whisky.

Ardmeanach 20 miles (32 km) west of Craignure. The Burg, a National Trust for Scotland property, has its own fossil tree, and is located near the tip of the beautiful Ardmeanachcliffs. The fossil tree andthe dramatic views are well worth the difficult walk.

Carsaig 20 miles (32 km) east of Fionnphort. A demanding hike from this small town leads to the lava cliffs of the Carsaig Arches.

Craignure From the Old Pier Station in Craignure excursions can be taken on the Mull Railway, the only passenger rail service in the Hebrides (open: late April-mid-Oct; tel: (01680) 300389). The train runs on a narrow-gauge track for a mile and a half (2.4 km) to Torosay Castle and its famous gardens. In the 20-minute ride views can be had of unspoiled mountains, glens and coastal areas, and sometimes otters, deer and eagles can be spotted. Caledonian MacBrayne offers "The Mull Experience", where visitors can ferry from Oban, take the train to Torosay then on to Duart Castle and return to Oban by ferry (open: May-Sept, Sun-Fri; tel: (01680) 812421). David Bryce, a famous Scottish architect, designed Torosay Castle and the lovely gardens were designed by Sir. Robert Lorimer: both castle and gardens are typically Victorian in style, and there is even a family portrait by S argent. The grounds feature an Italian-style terrace garden with statuary, a water garden (with tender shrubs which

are only able to grow because of the warming effects of the Gulf Stream) and a Japanese garden with life-size figures by Antonio Bonazza. Torosay is the only privately occupied castle open to the public in the western Highlands (open: castle, Easter-mid-Oct 10.30am-5.30pm; gardens, Easter-mid-Oct 9am-7pm; mid-Oct-Easter dawn-dusk; tel: (01680) 812421).

Three miles (5 km) from Craignure is the ancient seat of the Macleans, **Duart Castle**. It was destroyed by the Campbells in 1691 but restored by Sir Fitzroy Maclean, 26th chief of the clan, in 1911. The chief of the Clan Maclean currently occupies the castle but some rooms are open for viewing, including the banqueting hall and the great tower. The castle has an interesting exhibition on the excavation of the wreck of the Swan, a Cromwellian vessel sunk offshore in the mid-17th century (open: May-mid-Oct 10.30am-6pm; tel: (01680) 812309).

Dervaig 27 miles (43 km) northwest of Craignure. An audiovisual presentation on the history of Mull is available at the **Old Byre Heritage Centre** just before the

© Ken Paterson/ The Still Moving Picture Company

Tobermory, Mull

Rum from Laig Bay, Eigg

village of Dervaig. The centre also has a craft shop and a restaurant known for its thick homemade soups (open: Easter-Oct 10.30am-6.30pm; tel: (01688) 400229).

Fionnphort 36 miles (58 km) west of Craignure. A small village that is really just a giant car park for visitors to Iona.

Tobermory A 35-minute ferry ride from Kilchoan (tel: (01475) 650100), this beautiful fishing town has a brightly painted crescent of 18th-century buildings around its harbour. Tobermory is home to the Western Isle Golf Course (built in 1930), which is reputed to have the best views of any course in the world. A good history of Mull is provided at the **Mull Museum** located in an old bakery (open: Easter-mid-Oct, Mon-Fri 10.30am-4.30pm, Sat 10.30am-1.30pm; tel: (01688) 302208). **Tobermory Malt Whisky Distillery** has been in and out of business through the years but recently began again serving wee drams (open: 10.15am-4.45pm; tel: (01688) 302647). This is the collective name for Muck,

SMALL ISLES

Eigg, Rum and Canna. They can be reached by boat from Arisaig (tel: (01687) 450224). Most people take a day to visit the islands, since accommodationis strictly limited. Rum is the most spectacular of the islands and is overseen by the Natural Trust for

Scotland: the island's red deer and breeding burrow-nesting shearwaters are of particular interest.

STAFFA

Some six miles (10 km) north of Iona by private boat (tel: (01681) 700358), Staffa is well worth a visit to see Fingal's Cave, believed to be the only cave in the world that has basalt columns.
The sea has carved a huge hole in the basalt leaving massive hexagonal columns. The Gaelic name for the cave is Uamh Ehinn, which means "musical cave". The magnificent crash of the waves inspired Mendelssohn to write his Fingal's Cave Overture. Turner painted the cave, and Keats, Wordsworth and Tennyson all praised in poetry. The boat to Staffa runs from March to October, departing from Iona at 10am and 2pm, with a brief stop at Fionnphort. Tours last

60 to 75 minutes depending on the weather. Rubber-soled shoes and warm clothing are essential.

TIREE

A four-hour ferry ride from Oban (tel: (01475) 650100), Tiree has a population of 800, most of whom farm the extremely fertile land of the flat island. Scarinish is the main centre of population in Tiree.
Two exceptional bird-watching areas are Loch Bhasapholl (for wildfowl) and Kenavara, a cave where seabirds can be watched.

The Royal Air Force has a base on the island's reef. A gigantic granite boulder 30 feet (9 m) in diameter stands on the northern rim of the island. It is called the Ringing Stone because it gives off a metallic sound when struck.

It is perhaps a more fortunate destiny to have a taste for collecting shells than to be born a millionaire.

Robert Louis Stevenson 1850-94
An extract from *A Little Book of Scottish Sayings* published by Appletree Press

© Niall Benvie/ The Still Moving Picture Company

THE OUTER HEBRIDES

BARRA

Barra is a five-hour ferry ride from Oban to Castlebay (tel: (01475) 650100) or a 35-minute ride from Lochboisdale to Castlebay by private ferry (tel: (01878) 810223). Castlebay Tourist Information Centre is in Main Street.

Barra lies at the southern end of the Outer Hebrides and is referred to as the garden of the Hebrides because of its abundant wild flowers. Heather-covered hills, beaches, sandy grasslands, rocky bays and lofty headlands all make Barra beautiful. The island is known for its very popular Gaelic Festival (held each year in July) and its association with Clan MacNeil.

Allasdale North of Castlebay. A well-preserved Iron Age fort, Dun Duier, is located here. There are also great opportunities for seal watching in Seal Bay opposite the village.

Borve Northwest of Castlebay. This is the location of Borve standing stones and a chambered cairn. A church dedicated to St Brendan, the Irish navigator who may have voyaged to America before Columbus, is in the hamlet of Craigston. Other ruins in the area are Tigh Talamhanta (a ruined wheelhouse) and a series of standing stones called Dun Bharpa.

Castlebay Barra's capital is home to most of the island's 1300 inhabitants. In the 19th century it was a herring port, but its most important attraction today is the bay from which it gets its name. **Kismul Castle** is the ancient home of Clan MacNeil and dates from 1120. A great deal of the castle was destroyed by fire in 1795, but it was restored from 1938-70 by the 45th chieftain of the clan (open: May-Sept, Mon, Wed, Sat afternoons; tel: (01871) 810336).

Cockle Strand North of Castlebay. The island's airport is a beach of white sand and is the only runway in Britain washed twice daily by sea tides.

Eoligarry North of Castlebay. This town – with its many beautiful beaches and wild flowers – is also the port for ferries to South Uist. St Find barr of Cork, reputed to have converted the islanders to Christianity, is commemorated by St Barr's Church. Novelist Compton MacKenzie and the MacNeil chieftains are buried here. The Celtic stones in the

churchyard are called Crusader Stones. Dun Scurrival, another ruined fort, is on the summit of a small hill near Eliogarry.

Kinloch West of Castlebay. Loch St Clair is reached by a primitive road and has an islet with the ruins of St Clair Castle, called MacLeod's Fort. Also in the area is St Columba's Well, named after the saint.

BENBECULA

Benbecula joins North and South Uist with bridges and causeways. It is the headquarters for the Uist Army Rocket Range in the west and the administrative centre for the southern isles. It has large beaches on its Atlantic coast.

HARRIS

The ferry to Tarbert in Harris from Urg on the Isle of Skye (tel: (01475) 650100) takes 1 hour 45 minutes. Harris is the most mountainous of the western isles and is dominated by one mountain, Clisham, at 2,600 feet (792 m) the highest peak in the Outer Hebrides. The island is reminiscent of Norway with its sea lochs cutting deep into the land. The island's population is 3,000 (inhabitants of Harris are called Hearachs). Harris is world famous for its hand-woven Harris Tweed, even though in recent years the centre of the trade has actually moved to Stornoway on the Isle of Lewis.

Amhuinnsuidlhe Estate North of Tarbert. A Scottish baronial castle built in 1868 for the earl of Dunmore. Sir James

Barrie's Mary Rose was partially written here. A river near the estate has one of the best salmon leaps in Scotland.

Bunavoneadar Northwest of Tarbert. A whaling station set up by the Norwegians in the early 20th century was abandoned in 1930. The slipways and a chimney can still be seen.

Hushinish Point West of Tarbert. A good area for a view of Scarp, now uninhabited.

Leverburgh Southwest of Tarbert. A town named after Lord Leverhulme, the soap manufacturer, who encouraged people to come to the island in the 20th century. The ferry to North Uist and Berneray leaves from here (tel: (01475) 650100).

Rodel South of Tarbert. The route to Rodel passes the Clach Mhicleoid standing stone, located above Nisabost Sands on an impressive site with a good view across the Sound of Taransay to the Isle of Taransay (named after St Tarran). The isle was once populated but now all that remains are some grazing sheep and the remnants of St Tarran's Chapel. Scarista standing stone is on the shore of the Sound of Taransay. The cruciform St Clement's Church was built around 1500 by the eighth chief of the Macleods, Alasdair Crotach. His is one of the three tombs inside, one of which is regarded as the finest on the island and another is decorated with the MacLeod coat–of–arms.

Tarbert The main town of Harris. Anyone visiting the island should purchase necessary supplies here. Bus tours of the island start from here in the summer and a ferry to the scenic little fishing village of Scalpay can be arranged at the visitor centre.

Toe Head Southwest of Tarbert. A peninsula which juts into the Atlantic. One of many prehistoric sites uncovered on its machair surface is Rudh'an Teampull, an ancient chapel.

Traigh Sgarasta / Losgaintir / Taobh Tuath According to the Western Isles Tourist Board, "three of the most superb beaches to be found anywhere in the world".

LEWIS

The ferry to Lewis from Ullapool (tel: (01475) 650100) takes three hours and there is a good air service daily from Glasgow and Inverness (tel: (01345) 222111). The largest of the Outer Hebrides, Lewis is the most northerly of the islands. It is 60 miles (96 km) long and never more than 28 miles (45 km) wide. Its landscape is treeless with marshy peat bogs and can seem rather stark. The islanders are still strict about observing the Sabbath and most things are closed on Sundays.

Arnol 15 miles (24 km) northwest of Stornoway. **The Lewis Black House** is a typical black house with its byre under the same roof as the living accommodation. Many of the original furnishings are still in the home. (Open: April-Sept, Mon-Sat 9.30am-6pm; Oct-Mar 9.30am-4pm; tel: (01851) 710501.)

Callanish 16 miles (26 km) west of Stornoway. The major attraction on Lewis is the Neolithic Temple of Callanish. This famous prehistoric site comprises the Callanish standing stones dating from around 3,000 BC and is referred to as the Stonehenge of Scotland. The cruciform design has 19 monoliths which form a road from north to south through a circle of 13 standing stones. The pleasant visitor centre sells local crafts and serves meals.

Dun Carloway Broch 20 miles (32 km) northwest of Stornoway. North of Callanish is the well-preserved Dun Carloway Broch, with walls standing to a height of 30 feet (9 m) in places.

Ness Ness is on the northern tip of the island at the Butt of Lewis, a wild and magnificent place known as the windiest spot in Britain. Its major attractions are the Butt of Lewis Lighthouse, St Moluag's Church founded by Olav the Black during the Norse occupation in the 12th century, and wildlife such as gannets, skuas and occasional dolphins and whales.

Stornoway Stornoway is the ferry port and the main administrative centre for the western isles, and a bustling town of 5,000 people. Lewis Castle, built in 1818, stands west of the harbour and serves as the college for the area (its garden can be visited). Two miles (3 km) east of Stornoway on the Eye Peninsula is Ui Church, the burial ground for the MacLeods of Lewis, whose carved gravestones can still be seen.

Tolsta 12 miles (19 km) north of Stornoway. The finest beach on Lewis, Tràigh Mhór, meaning big beach, is located at Tolsta.

NORTH AND SOUTH UIST

The ferry from Oban to Lochboisdale on South Uist takes anywhere between five and seven hours; the ferry from Uig to North Uist takes an hour and a half (tel: (01475) 650100). The two islands are joined by road through Benbecula.

NORTH UIST

Known for its fishing, North Uist has excellent bird watching, archeological sites and great walks; it is also one of the least visited islands in the Hebrides. The population of about 2,000 shares an island 35 miles (56 km) long and 12 miles (19 km) wide. The tourist centre is at Lochmaddy (tel: (01876) 500321).

© Ken Paterson/ The Still Moving Picture Company

Isle of Harris

Barpa Langass On the slopes of a hill near here is a chambered cairn thought to be at least 3,000 years old. It is believed that a warrior chief is buried there.

Bayhead Bayhead is the location of the **Balranald Nature Reserve**, at the reception cottage of which visitors can learn more about the birds of the Outer Hebrides (open: all hours; guided tours Tues, Fri 2pm).

Blashaval 2 miles (3 km) northwest of Lochmaddy. Legend has it that the three standing stones known as False Men were once three men who deserted their wives, whereupon a witch turned them all to stone.

Carinish South of Lochmaddy. The Carinish Stone Circle and the Barpa

© Ken Paterson/ The Still Moving Picture Company

Callanish Stones, Lewis

Scottish Cheeses

Caboc has been made in the Highlands for more than 400 years and is the most distinctive. It is a rich, creamy cheese of soft consistency shaped like a croquette and rolled in oatmeal, which gives it a very special nutty taste.

Orkney is produced in the islands to the north of the mainland. Made from skimmed milk, it is like a mild Cheddar, and is available in red or white. Smoked varieties have the best flavour.

Dunlop is similar to Cheddar, available in red or white and is soft with a mellow flavour. It is named after a village in Ayrshire. A local woman who fled to Ireland to avoid religious persecution in the late seventeenth century, Barbara Gilmour, brought the recipe back with her.

Stewart Cheeses are Scottish versions of Stilton. There are white and blue varieties which are slightly milder than Stilton. The blue cheese is generally more popular, the white is rather salty.

Crowdie is a very old type of cheese traditionally made in the crofts of the Highlands. It is now available commercially, usually in cartons as it is a very soft cheese. It is made with milk fresh from the cow and is only semi–cooked. Excellent with salads, and on oatcakes and bannocks.

Taken from *A Little Scottish Cookbook* published by Appletree Press

Facing page: The Cuillin from Gesto Bay
© David Robertson/ The Still Moving Picture Company

Carinish, the site of Trinity Temple, are the major attractions on the island. The 13th-century monastery was founded by Beathag, the first prioress of Iona, daughter of Somerled, founding father of the MacDonalds. Franciscan scholar Duns Scotus, one of the most influential medieval philosophers and theologians, attended classes here when it was a great college. Nearby is the Teampull Clan A'Phlocair, the Chapel of the MacVicars, where visitors can see ancient cup and ring markings. The MacLeods of Harris and the MacDonalds of Uist met near her in 1601 and the site is called the "Field of Blood."

SOUTH UIST

Part bog, South Uist is 20 miles (32 km) long and 6 miles (10 km) wide. There are many archeological sites on the island and Clan Ranald left many ruins and fortresses called "duns".

Airidh Mhuilinn A cairn at the top of a small hill marks the spot where Flora MacDonald was born in 1722.

Askernish Askernish is the site of a nine-hole golf course.

Drimsdale Clan Ranald's large dun – a fortification in a loch where villagers retreated when under attack – was their stronghold in this area until the early 1500s.

Garrnamonie North of Pollachar. The Church of Our Lady of Sorrows was consecrated in 1964 and has a famous mosaic of St Mary. It can be visited at any time during the day.

Loch an Duin 6 miles (10 km) northwest of Lochmaddy. An island in the loch has a fine example of a broch, Dun Torcuill, that provided defence for villagers. It can only be reached on foot at low tide.

Loch Bee A large loch populated with mute swans nearly bisects the northern part of South Uist.

Loch Druidibeg National Nature Reserve Britain's most important breeding ground for the native greylag goose.

Lochboisdale South Uist's biggest village stands at the head of a deep sea loch and was settled in the 19th century by people who had been evicted from their homelands during the Clearances.

Lochmaddy The main town and ferry port of North Uist.

Ormiclete The ruins of Ormiclete Castle, which was constructed by the Clan Ranald chieftains in the early 18th century.

Pollachar 6 miles (10 km) from Lochboisdale. This village shares its name with the famous Pollachar standing stones.

Rueval Hill A 30-feet (9 m) statue of the Virgin and Child was erected in 1957 on the side of this hill, which is now called the mountain of miracles. It is the largest religious statue in Britain.

Solas South of Lochmaddy. Many of the cairns and standing stones on both sides of the road date from around 2,000 BC.

ABERDEEN AND THE NORTHEAST

Aberdeen is the Granite City, the gateway to the great North Sea oil fields. An interesting mix of modern buildings and older structures, the city is surrounded by gentle landscape rising from the coast to the Grampian Mountains (among the highest in Scotland). The wild coastline takes in the Moray Firth and North Sea shore, with sandy beaches and steep cliffs. The roads are signposted with an extensive Castle Trail. Aberdeen is at the heart of the mainland distilling industry, with most distilleries centred on the River Spey and its tributaries.

ABERDEEN

Built between the rivers Dee and Don, Aberdeen was established in 1124 as the United Kingdom's most northerly city. Its first major industry was the exportation of silver-grey granite, when Aberdeen was known as the Silver City. The discovery of North Sea oil in the 1970s revitalized Aberdeen's economy.

Most of the city's places of interest are within easy walking distance. You can begin at Union Street, which leads to the old town. A castle once stood here, but all that remains is a castle gate. On the north side of Castle Street is the 17th-century **Tolbooth**, from which Aberdeen was governed for 200 years. The museum tells much of the city's history (open: Tue-Sat 10am-5pm, Sun 2pm-5pm; tel: (01224) 621167). Just beyond King Street stands the Mercat Cross, on the parapet of which are 12 portraits of Stuart monarchs. Dominating Broad Street is the granite **Marischal College**, founded in 1593 as a Protestant alternative to the Catholic King's College. The two colleges

combined in 1860 to form Aberdeen University. A museum exhibits photographs and artefacts of the northeast (open: weekdays 10am- 5pm, Sun 2pm-5pm; tel: (01224) 273131). Across the street from the college is the 1545 Provost Skene's House, one of the city's steeply gabled rubble-built townhouses, now a museum of civic life (open: Mon-Sat 10am-5pm; tel: (01224) 641086).

Robert Gordon's University in the Schoolhill area of Aberdeen was built in 1731 as Robert Gordon's Hospital for the education of poor boys. It became a university in 1993. Next door is **Aberdeen Art Gallery**, which has an excellent collection of 18th-20th-century works (open: Mon-Sat 10am-5pm, Sun 2pm-5pm; tel: (01224) 646333). Nearby is St Nicholas Kirk, known as the Mither Kirk because it is the original burgh church. Its pillars and clerestory windows date from the 12th century. In Ship Row, one of the oldest streets in town, is the **Provost Ross's House**, built in 1593 and now housing the Aberdeen Maritime Museum, which tells the story of the city's involvement with the sea, from clippers to oil rigs (open: Mon-Sat 10am-5pm, Sun 11am-5pm; tel: (01224) 337700).

© Harvey Wood/ The Still Moving Picture Company

Drum Castle, Aberdeenshire

Old Aberdeen, once a separate community near the River Don, lies north of the city centre. Here, Kings College was founded in 1494. It has a famous chapel dating from 1500 with a crown spire, wooden ceilings and intricate wooden carvings. Old Aberdeen has some fine restored Georgian homes, including the 1720 Old Aberdeen Townhouse on High Street. Northward is **St Machar's Cathedral**, originally built in 580. Nothing remains of the original

building, but most of the existing structure dates from the 15th and 16th centuries. The cathedral was badly damaged during the Reformation but was restored in the 19th century (open: daily 9am-5pm; tel: (01224) 485988). Nearby is one of Aberdeen's most beautiful parks, Seaton Park, especially so in the spring when the daffodils bloom.

Alford 28 miles (45 km) west of Aberdeen. Alford's Grampian Transport Museum specialises in road transportation. One of its more unusual exhibits is a steam-driven creation once used by the local postman to deliver mail more efficiently. Adjoining the museum is a narrow-gauge railway (open: April-Oct 10am-5pm; tel: (01975) 562292).

Ballater 43 miles (69 km) west of Aberdeen. Ballater has more "By royal appointment" shop signs than any other Scottish town because **Balmoral Castle** is just west of town. Balmoral was rebuilt and modified for Queen Victoria by Prince Albert in 1855. The castle is open partially but visiting hours are dependent on royal visits. Twelve miles (19 km) southwest at Glen Muick the red deer are abundant and easy to see.

Banchory 19 miles (30 km) west of Aberdeen. The castle is the main attraction in this village. Near an ancient forest of oak and pine is the 13th-century Drum Castle with its foursquare tower (open: Easter, May-Sept 1.30pm-5.30pm, Oct weekends 1.30pm-5.30pm, gardens daily 9.30am-dusk).

Banff 47 miles (76 km) north of Aberdeen. At the mouth of the River Deveron on the Moray Firth, Banff is an attractive town of Georgian houses. Its main attraction is the Baroque Duff **House** – the most sophisticated country house in northeast Scotland – designed by William Adam in 1735 for William Duff, MP (open: April-Sept 10am-5pm, Oct-Mar, Thurs-Sun 10am-5pm; tel: (01261) 818181). Three miles (5 km) east of Banchory is **Crathes Castle**, a 16th-century L-shaped tower house built by the Burnett family, Keepers of the Forest Drum. The castle comes with its own ghost of a green lady, plus magnificent painted ceilings and fine furniture. The castle also has grand symmetrical gardens of clipped yew (open: April-Oct 11am-5.30pm, gardens and grounds 9am-dusk).

Braemar 60 miles (96 km) west of Aberdeen. The village of Braemar is known for Braemar Castle, built in the 17th century with a defensive wall plan in the shape of a pointed star. The rebel flag was first raised here in 1715 to start the Jacobite rebellion. Thirty years later it was a garrison for Hanoverian troops (open: Easter-Oct, Sat-Thurs 10am-6pm; tel: (01339) 741219). The community is also famous for its Highland Gathering held in September. **The Highland Heritage Centre** has information on the Gathering and the relationship of the town to Balmoral (open: 9am-5pm, extended hours in summer; tel: (01339) 741944). The spectacular views around the River Dee and over the Linn of Dee should not be missed.

Burghead 12 miles (19 km) northwest of Elgin. Set on a head overlooking Burghead Bay is Scotland's most important Pictish centre, famous for its six 7th-8th-century stone carvings known as the Burghead Bulls.

Corgarff Castle 23 miles (37 km) northeast of Braemar. Corgarff, a lonely tower house with a star-shaped defensive wall, was built as a hunting seat for the earls of Mar in the 16th century. It became a garrison for Hanoverian troops whose duties included preventing illegal whisky distilling in the area (open: April-Sept 9.30am-6pm, Oct-Mar 9.30am-4pm, Sun 2pm-4pm).

Craigellachie 4 miles (6 km) northwest of Dufftown. Known for its great fishing on the Spey, as you enter Craigellachie you will see the large Speyside Cooperage with its visitor centre. Here you can see displays of centuries-old barrel-making skills (open: Mon-Sat, closed Sat in winter; tel: (01340) 871108). The town also has a handsome suspension bridge built in 1814, which is bypassed by the modern road.

Glenfiddich Distillery

© Paul Tomkins/ STB/ The Still Moving Picture Company

Dufftown 54 miles (87 km) from Aberdeen. Built in 1817, the planned village of Dufftown surrounds a central square with a landmark clock tower used to hang the famous freebooter Macpherson and a former jail, now the local museum (open: April-Oct, Mon-Sat 10am-5pm; tel: (01309) 673701). Not far away is **Mortlach Church**, set in a hollow by the Dullan Water, believed to be one of the oldest religious spots in Scotland. In the churchyard is a weathered Pictish cross. Inside is the "leper's squint", a hole where lepers could watch church services separated from everyone else (open: Easter-Oct 10am-4pm). Dufftown's main industry is malt whisky. North of Dufftown is the famous **Glenfiddich Distillery**, offering one of the best audiovisual presentations and tours (open: Mon-Fri 9.30am-4.30pm, Easter-mid Oct also Sat 9.30am-4.30pm, Sun 12am-4.30pm; tel: (01340) 820373). On a hill just behind Glenfiddich is the grim, grey and square curtain-wall of the 13th-century **Balvenie Castle** with its moat (open: April-Sept, Mon-Sat 9.30am-6.30pm, Sun 2pm-6.30pm).

Elgin 16 miles (26 km) north of Aberlour. The heart of the Moray area, Elgin became an important religious centre in the 13th century, and the town grew up around the cathedral. **Elgin Cathedral** (known as the Lantern of the North) was founded in 1224 and was burned in 1390, but was still used throughout the Reformation (open: April-Oct 9.30am-6pm, Nov-Mar, Wed and Sat 9.30am-4pm, Thurs 9.30am-noon, Sun 2pm-4pm; tel: (01343) 542666). **Elgin Museum** is one of the finest museums in the north and includes the remains of the oldest dinosaurs found in Britain (open: Easter-Oct, Mon-Fri 10am-5pm, Sat 11am-4pm, Sun 2pm-5pm; tel: (01343) 543675). At the top of Lady Hill at the town's West End is the ruin of a castle occupied by King Edward I of England.

Nearby is Duffus Castle, the remains of a moat and bailey castle with a 14th-century tower (unusually, the moat is still filled with water). A former bishop's mansion, Spynie Palace affords good views of the town from its six-storey keep and 9-feet- (3 m) thick walls. The fishing town of Lossiemouth is the former port for Elgin and has the **Lossiemouth Fisheries and Community Museum** (open: Easter-Sept, Mon-Sat 10am-5pm; tel: (01343) 813772). The coastline is beautiful around Elgin but often disturbed by a busy airbase nearby. The 13th-century **Pluscarden Abbey** (still occupied by an order of monks) is within easy reach of Elgin (open: 5pm-8.30pm).

Fettercairn 6 miles (10 km) north of Edzell. This small red sandstone village on the southern edge of the Grampian Hills has a Gothic arch commemorating the visit of Queen Victoria. Near Fettercairn is Fasque House, the Gladstone family home for six generations. Built in 1809 it is a castellated mansion in the Georgian Gothic style with a beautiful oval staircase. The scenic hill road to Banchory leads past the Cairn of the Mount. The road reaches it highest point of 1,488 feet (453 m) at a cairn dating from the second millennium BC. This historic pass was used by drovers, whisky smugglers, royalty and marching armies and has magnificent views south over Angus and the Howe of Mearns to the sea.

directly opposite the museum to see the Earth pillars – curious eroded sandstone pillars framed by tall pines. At the mouth of the River Spey is the **Tugnet Ice House,** once the centre of the salmon industry. The fish were stored in the house using ice gathered in the winter (open: May-Sept 11am-4pm; tel: (01309) 673701). Eight miles east of Fochabers is the fishing village of Buckie, where an unusual museum designed like a fishing drifter tells the story of the herring industry (open: April-Oct, Mon-Sat 10am-5pm, Sun 12am-5pm; tel: (01542) 834646). **The Peter Anson Gallery** in Buckie has a

event like a battle. South of Forres the picturesque **Dallas Dhu Distillery** is built of stone and slate. No longer an active distillery, it is a complete museum of the distilling process (open: April-Sept 9.30am-6.30pm, Oct-March, Mon-Wed, Sat 9.30am-4.30pm, Thurs 9.30am-12.30pm, Sun 2pm-4.30pm; tel: (01309) 676548). Eight miles (13 km) west of Forres, **Brodie Castle** has been the home of the Brodies since 1567. A Z-plan tower house with many later additions, it houses a fine collection of furniture, porcelain and paintings (open: early April-Sept, Mon-Sat 11am-5.30pm, Oct

Forres, Moray

Fochabers 9 miles (14 km) east of Elgin. Just outside Fochabers is the home of Baxter's of Fochabers, a food company known all over the world. **The Baxter's Visitors Centre** has video presentations, a model of Baxter's first grocery shop, and many of Baxter's own goods, plus two restaurants (guided tours Mon-Fri 10am-11.30am, 12.30pm-4.30pm; tel: (01343) 820666). **Fochabers Folk Museum** is housed in a converted church filled with a fine display of rural items, ranging from carts and carriages to farm implements (open: winter 9.30am-1pm, 2pm-5pm; summer 9.30am-1pm, 2pm-6pm; tel: (01343) 821204). For an excellent view of the River Spey take the road south

display of watercolours related to the fishing industry (open: Mon-Fri 10am-8pm, Sat 10am-12am; tel: (01542) 832121).

Forres 11 miles (18 km) east of Nairn. The town of Forres has a medieval street plan with mostly Victorian houses and award-winning floral displays. The **Falconer Museum** explores local history, including man traps for poachers (open: daily, April-Oct 10am-5pm, otherwise Mon-Fri 10am-5pm; tel: (01309) 673701). On the outskirts of town is a 20-feet (6 m) high sandstone cross slab, superbly carved on all sides by the Picts sometime in the 900s. This remarkable monument probably commemorates some historic

weekends only; grounds open all year daily 9.30am-sunset; tel: (01309) 641371). A beautiful view of the Moray Firth stretching east to meet the Highlands can be seen at Califer Braes viewpoint.

Fraserburgh 47 miles (77 km) north of Aberdeen. Fraserburgh is a fishing port with a beautiful sandy beach backed by wind-swept sand dunes. On the most northeastern point of Scotland is **Kinnaird Head Lighthouse**, a 16th-century castle which was converted by the Northern Lighthouse Board into its first lighthouse in the 1780s. The museum contains beautiful Fresnel lenses and a guided tour all the way to the top of this

working lighthouse (open: April-Oct, Mon-Sat 10am-6pm, Sun 12.30pm-6pm, Nov-Mar, Mon-Sat 10am-4pm, Sun 12.30am-4pm; tel: (01346) 511022).

Fyvie Castle 20 miles (32km) northwest of Ellon. Fyvie is a complex castle of five great towers and an opulent Edwardian house. The magnificent interiors have fine furniture and a superior painting collection, including 12 Raeburns (open: April-June, Sept 1pm-5.30pm, July-Aug 11am-5.30pm, Oct weekends 1.30pm-5.30pm; grounds daily 9.30am-dusk; tel: (01651) 891266).

Glenshee Between Braemar and Bridge of Cally. The highest main road in the United Kingdom, surrounded on both sides by mountains over 3,000 feet (914 m) high. A spectacular drive with great views.

Haddo House Northwest of Ellon. Designed by William Adam and built in 1732, Haddo House is elegant with light and graceful designs, and curving wings on both sides of a harmonious facade. The chapel has beautiful stained-glass windows designed by Sir Edward Burne-Jones (open: Easter weekend, May-Sept 1.30pm-5.30pm; Oct weekends 1.30pm-5.30pm; garden and country park all year daily 9.30am-sunset; tel: (01651) 881440).

Huntly 48 miles (77 km) northwest of Aberdeen. A busy market town which has been the seat of the house of Gordon, whose ancestral home stands at the confluence of the Bogie and Deveron rivers. The 15th-century **Huntly Castle** is known for its elaborate heraldic carvings (open: April-Sept 9.30am-6.30pm, otherwise daily 9.30am-4pm, closed Thursday afternoons, Fridays in Oct-March; tel: (01466) 793191).

Inverurie 15 miles (24 km) northwest of Aberdeen. Inverurie is the chief town of the Garioch region, an agricultural basin east of the Grampian hills. The area is covered with relics from the ancient Picts. Bennachie overlooks the town with its vitrified Pictish fort. Five miles (8 km) away is the 9th-century Maiden Stone, an impressive red granite monolith with the "Pictish elephant", one of the most mysterious of the Picts' designs. Eight miles (13 km) northwest is a large prehistory park, which includes the Iron Age **Berry Hill Fort**. A gallery features interactive exhibits exploring myths and legends (open: Mar-Oct 9.30am-5pm, Nov-Feb 11am-4pm; tel: (01464) 851500). A short walk north of Inverurie is Loanhead Recumbent Stone Circle, with a recumbent figure common to the area.

Facing page: Insh Marshes
© *W S Paton/ The Still Moving Picture Company*

A low ring cairn used for funerals at a later date is in the middle of the circle.

Keith 17 miles (27 km) southeast of Elgin. The home of John Ogilvie, Scotland's recently canonised saint (1976), is the beginning of the Whisky Trail, which leads to seven malt whisky distilleries. Keith is home to the first, **Strathisla Distillery**, the oldest working Highland distillery, founded in 1786 (open: Mon-Sat 9:.30am-4pm, Sun 12.30pm-4pm; tel: (01542) 783044).

Kildrummy 23 miles (37 km) north of Ballater. Kildrummy Castle was built in the 13th century and looks a great deal like many European medieval castles. A rebel headquarters during the 1715 Jacobite uprising, it was destroyed after Culloden (open: April-Sept 9.30am-6pm; tel: (01975) 571203). Behind the castle is **Kildrummy Castle Gardens** with their own entrance. The gardens occupy the quarry from which the stone for the castle was taken and feature shrubs, alpines and water plants (open: April-Oct 10am-5pm; tel: (01975) 571203).

Leith Hall 7 miles (11 km) south of Huntly. Leith Hall is the home of the Leith family and has been expanded with each generation, beginning in 1650. The house is full of family possessions, including a prized shagreen writing case given by Prince Charles Edward Stuart on the eve of Culloden (open: Good Friday-Sept 1.30pm-5.30pm; gardens and grounds open all year 9.30am-sunset; tel: (01464) 831216).

Mintlaw 13 miles (21 km) from Fraserburgh. In the vast Aden Country Park the North East Agricultural Heritage Centre tells the story of the struggle of the people of the northeast to turn a

wilderness into productive fields. Housed in a courtyard of a handsome farm, with displays, implements and buildings, it is a delightful place to visit (open: May-Sept 11am-4.30pm, April-Oct and early November weekends 12am-4.30pm; tel: (01771) 622857).

Stonehaven 18 miles (29 km) south of Aberdeen. Stonehaven, once a fishing village, is located on a bay sheltered by two rock headlands, Downie Point to the south and Garron Point to the north. It is now a popular port for pleasure craft. In the old town a 16th-century Tolbooth serves as the local museum, which has displays on fishing and coopering (open: June-Sept, Mon, Thurs, Sat 10am-12pm, 2pm-5pm, Wed and Sun 2pm-5pm; tel (01771) 622906). The coast road south reaches **Dunnottar Castle**, a 14th-century fortress, which was the stronghold of the Earls Marischal of Scotland. The crown jewels of Scotland were hidden here from Cromwell's army (open: daily except for winter weekends). Under the floors of Kinneff Old Church, one mile off of the A92, the Scottish Regalia, the Honours of Scotland, were hidden. Lewis Grassic Gibbon, the famous author of the trilogy A Scots Quair, was born in Arbuthnott a few miles farther south. His birthplace is celebrated with a memorial stone and the small **Grassic Gibbon Centre** (open: April-Oct 10am-4.30pm; tel: (01651) 361668).

Tomintoul 14 miles (22 km) east of Grantown-on-Spey. Founded by the Duke of Gordon in 1779, Tomintoul stands on a flat plateau at the foot of the Cairngorm Mountains. The southern tip of the whisky trail, the Glenlivet Estate, is nearby, with its beautiful forests and high moors.

© *STB/ The Still Moving Picture Company*

Kildrummy Castle Gardens

THE GREAT GLEN &
THE WESTERN HIGHLANDS

The Great Glen surrounds the fault line that splits the Highlands and takes in Loch Lochy, Loch Oich and Loch Ness. The Caledonian Canal links these lochs with the River Ness and the Moray Firth. Most of the terrain is rugged, except for around Nairn by the Moray Firth and the beautiful Kintyre Peninsula. The mountains of the region are wonderfully open and expansive compared with other Scottish mountains. The highest mountain in Britain, Ben Nevis at 4,406 feet (1,343 m), is at the southern end of the Glen. Inverness, the capital of the Highlands, is at the edge of the Moray Firth and has become famous for its monster "Nessie", reputed to reside in Loch Ness. The southern side of the Moray Firth, eastward from Inverness, has spectacular sand dunes and many famous and exciting golf courses. Many of the courses can be found in the golf tours outlined in this guide. The area around Inverness played a prominent part in the Jacobite rebellion and includes the site of the famous Battle of Culloden. Fort William - on the Road to the Isles – is the last major town before the coastal areas, which look out over the Hebrides. West of the Great Glen are the big Glens of Cannich and Affric with their extraordinary scenery. The Spey River gives its name to the Speyside area with its pine trees and Cairngorm Mountains. With its abundant wildlife this area is a good place for hill walking, especially as many of the best spots are away from the road. The Western Highlands around Argyll present one magnificent view after another of mountains and lochs. These areas are remote and even in the height of the tourist season are not crowded.

Aviemore and Strathspey 29 miles
(47 km) southeast of Inverness. Aviemore,

in the heart of the Highlands and the Strathspey, is a bustling ski resort. From the train station in the centre of Aviemore the **Strathspey Railway** steam locomotive departs to follow the valley of the River Spey for five miles (8 km): tickets and boarding are at Aviemore or Boat of Garten (open: late Mar-late Oct 9.30am-5pm; tel: (01479) 810725). A favourite stop is the **Aviemore Mountain Resort,** an all-purpose cultural, sports and entertainment complex that includes ice skating, a dry ski slope, snooker, discos and much more (open: 10am-1pm, 2pm-5pm, 6pm-9pm; tel: (01479) 810624). A perfect place to gain a general overview of the area is the **Landmark Visitor Centre** at Carrbridge, which provides audiovisual displays, plus outdoor attractions such as a maze, nature trail and adventure playground (open: April-Oct 9.30am-6pm; July-Aug 9.30am-8pm; Nov-Mar 9.30am-5pm; tel: (01479) 841613). **Rothiemurchus Estate** is a superb place to observe and learn about the Speyside countryside. It offers fly-fishing for salmon and trout, guided walks, safari tours, off-road driving and clay pigeon shooting (open: all year; tel: (01479) 810858). Nearby is the **Highland Wildlife Park**, where all kinds of animals can be seen (open: April-Oct 10am-4pm, otherwise by appointment; tel: (01540) 651270). An interesting speciality nursery, **Inshriach Nursery**, is for rock garden enthusiasts (open: Mon-Sat).

Boat of Garten and Loch Garten A typical Speyside village, Boat of Garten has an excellent golf course, a choice of hill walks among the pines and great views of the Cairngorms from the Strathspey Railway. Nearby on Loch Garten there is a unique opportunity to observe osprey from the hide provided by the Royal Society for the Protection of Birds: ospreys were absent from Scotland for over 40 years, until they returned in 1959 (open: late April-Aug, 10am-6pm; tel: (01479) 810725).

Cairngorms 30 miles (48 km) south of
Inverness. This magnificent mountain range contains four of the five highest peaks in Britain: Ben Macdhui at 4,296 feet (1,309 m), Braeriach at 4,084 feet (1,245 m), Cairn Toul at 4,241 feet (1,293 m) and Cairn Gorm at 4,084 feet (1,245 m). There are fine hill passes and rock climbing, and skiing has become popular although it is damaging the natural beauty of the area. The mountain range has important examples of Arctic-Alpine flowers. The Cairngorm National Nature Reserve is a vast protected area of open wilderness. One legend of the mountains is of a famous ghost, the GreatGrey Man of Ben Macdhui, who has been seen wandering in the hills.

Caledonian Canal From Corran to
Inverness. Thomas Telford engineered the Caledonian Canal, which linked the east and west coasts of Scotland in 1822. It connects the lochs of Lochy, Oich and Ness through a series of 29 locks. Fort August is a good place to watch the comings and goings on the canal. For a waterborne view of the countryside, boats can be rented by the week to cruise the canal (open: Mar-April; tel: (01463) 236328).

Cowal and Kyle of Bute 30 miles
(48 km) west of Glasgow. One of the most beautiful waterways in the world is only 30 miles from Glasgow and can be enjoyed from the Cowal Peninsula. Access is easy via a 20-minute ferry ride from Gourock to Dunoon (open: all year; tel: (01475) 650100). Another spectacular way to reach the peninsula is to drive south over the Arrochar Alps and the breathtakingly scenic "Rest and Be Thankful", 860 feet (262 m) above Loch Fyne west of Arrochar. The Argyll Forest Park covers most of the area between Loch Fyne and Long. The enormous forest – established in 1935 as the first of its kind – is perfect for hill walking and pony trekking. At Benmore the **Younger Botanical Garden**, an outstation of the Royal Botanical Garden of Edinburgh, is a woodland garden in a mountain setting with some of the largest trees in Scotland, plus rhododendrons and azaleas (open: mid-Mar-Oct 9.30am-6pm; tel: (01369) 706261). Two fingers of the peninsula reach out on either side of Bute. They are called the Kyles of Bute and are unequalled in their beautiful coastal scenery.

Crarae Garden 10 miles (16 km)
southwest of Inveraray. Believed by many to be Argyll's most beautiful garden because of its magnificent hillside setting around a trickling burn, Crarae has extensive displays of tender shrubs, eucryphia, a range of Himalayan species, and large-leafed rhododendrons. To see the best range of colours visit in the spring or autumn (open: 9am-6pm; tel: (0156) 886614).

Fort William 63 miles (101 km) south
of Inverness. On the shores of Loch Linnhe, Fort William stands on the site of a fort built by General Monk in 1690 and named after William, Prince of Orange. It was torn down in 1864 to make way for the railway. During the Highland Clearances many of the starving and evicted people were shipped from here to America. In the centre of town, next to the tourist office, is the **West Highland Museum**, which tells of the local history and way of life, especially the 1745 Jacobite rebellion (open: July-Aug, Mon-

Sat 10am-5pm, Sun 2pm-5pm; Sept-June, Mon-Sat 10am-5pm; tel: (01397) 702169). The town is dominated by Ben Nevis, Britain's highest mountain. North of town are the ruins of Old Inverlochy Castle, the scene of the famous battle of 1645, and a little further on one of the most beautiful glens in Scotland, Glen Nevis, with spectacular hill scenery. Two parallel lines, known as the Parallel Roads of Glen Roy, are etched on the side of the glen. Millions of years ago they were the shorelines of an Ice Age loch. Three miles (5 km) northwest is a series of nine locks on the Caledonian Canal known as Neptune's Staircase: it raises boats 64 feet (19 m) up the canal. Fort William is a good starting point for touring the Highlands.

Glen Affric 32 miles (51 km) southwest of Inverness. The moody splendour of Glen Affric is often

Loch Achtriochtan, Glencoe

considered one of the most beautiful glens in Scotland, even after its hydroelectric dam was built. Many quiet, serene walks can be taken here, the most famous of which is to Dog Falls. The lower areas of the glen have oak woods combined with hay fields, while higher up there are wild lochs and pine forests, great views and wildlife.

Glen Coe 94 miles (151 km) north of Glasgow. This is probably the most famous glen in Scotland and is easily accessible by car. The main road winds between Buchaille Etive Mor guarding the east end of the Glen and the "Three Sisters", the three long spurs running off Bidean nam Bian, the highest peak in Argyll. This is also the site of the

infamous massacre of 1692 when the Campbell clan, acting as government militia, broke clan tradition by slaughtering their hosts, the MacDonalds, committing murder "under trust". The National Trust for Scotland tells the story of the massacre at its visitor centre (open: April-mid-May, Sept-Oct 10am-5pm; mid-May-Aug 9.30am-5.30pm; tel: (01855) 811307).

Glenfinnan 10 miles (16 km) west of Fort William. Bonnie Prince Charlie raised the flag of rebellion in August of 1745 in this magnificent area of lochs and mountains: the Glen Finnan monument with its Highlander atop was placed here to mark the event. A National Trust for Scotland visitor centre tells the story of the campaign (open: April-mid-May, Sept-Oct 10am-1pm, 2pm-5pm; mid-May-Aug 9.30am-6pm; tel: (01397) 722250). Nearby, there is a beautiful viaduct carrying the Mallaig extension of the West Highland line, where steam trains run in the summer months.

Grantown-on-Spey 24 miles (39 km) south of Nairn. Among tall pines flanking the River Spey, James Grant of Castle Grant's new town (planned in 1776) has some handsome buildings constructed from the local silver granite. It has some interesting shops and is otherwise tranquil. **The Speyside Heather Garden Centre** has over 300 varieties of heather in a beautiful setting (open: April-Oct, Mon-Sat 9am-6pm, Sun 10am-6pm; tel: (01479) 851359).

Inveraray 57 miles (92 km) northwest of Glasgow. Inveraray, a small resort and a royal burgh, enjoys a splendid setting on the shores of Loch Fyne. The town was planned by Archibald, 3rd Duke of Argyll, in 1743 to be near his castle. Inveraray receives more rain than anywhere else in the Highlands. The parish church and its tower occupy a prominent place in this community. The 10th Duke of Argyll conceived the idea of building a bell tower as a memorial to all the Campbells. Its ten bells are each named after a Celtic saint and they all ring out on a daily basis. The 176-step climb to the top gives a good view of Loch Fyne and the countryside (open: mid-May-Sept 10am-1pm, 2pm-5pm; tel: (01499) 302259). In the town itself there is a recreation of a 19th-century county prison, complete with courtrooms and cells with live prisoners and jailer (open: April-Oct 9.30am-6pm; Nov-Mar 10am-5pm; tel: (01449) 302381). In the harbour there is a 1911 lightship and a rare example of a riveted iron vessel. The maritime history of the River Clyde and Scotland's west coast is told in the exhibition on board the Arctic Penguin

(open: April-Oct 10am-6pm; Nov-Mar 10am-5pm; tel: (01499) 302213). **Inveraray Castle** is east of the town, across some beautiful bridges built by Robert Mylne. The hereditary seat of the dukes of Argyll, the castle has been home to the Clan Campbell since the 15th century. Built during the Gothic revival by Roger Morris, it contains many historic furnishings and pictures, and a famous armour hall with over 1,300 pieces (open: April-June, Sept-Oct, Sat-Thurs 10am-1pm, 2pm-5.45pm; July-Aug, Mon-Sat 10am-5.30pm, Sun 1pm-5.45pm; tel: (01499) 302203). In the castle grounds is the only example of a **Combined Operations Museum** in Britain. On display are scale models, newspapers, campaign maps and many other documents which explain the role of the centre during the Second World War.

Six miles (10 km) southwest of Inveraray is **Auchindrain**, the last communal tenancy farm township to have survived on its original site. Many of the buildings have been restored and the open-air museum presents a unique glimpse into rural life in this 1,000-year-old town (open: April-Sept 10am-5pm; tel: (01499) 500235).

Inverness 156 miles (251 km) north of Edinburgh. Lying at the northern end of the Great Glen on both sides of the Ness River, Inverness is the capital of the Highlands, a royal burgh and seaport. It is the best base for touring the north, with a bustling city centre. Tolbooth Steeple dates from 1791; its spire can be seen on High Street. **Inverness Castle** was built in 1834-47, but just east of the building King David I built the first stone castle in 1141. Nearby is a statue of Flora MacDonald, who helped Bonnie Prince Charlie escape from his pursuers. Fraser Street near the river at the foot of the castle has many beautiful residences, the oldest of which is Abertarff House on the corner of Church Street. This is the headquarters of **An Comunn Gaidhealach – the Highland Association** – whose aims are to preserve Gaelic language and culture. If you continue down Church Street you will pass Bow Court, which dates from 1700. Near the end of the street is the restored **Dunbar hospital**. Old Mercat Cross, which is said to be the stone on which women rested their wash tubs as they climbed up from the river, is opposite the Town House. The Town House itself was the scene in 1921 of the first Cabinet Meeting outside of London. The Victorian **St Andrew's Cathedral**, the northernmost diocese of the Scottish Episcopal Church, is on Ardross Street (open: 8.30am-6pm; tel: (01463) 233535). The **Inverness Museum and Art Gallery**

© Angus Johnston / The Still Moving Picture Company

is dedicated to the social and natural history of the Scottish Highlands, including its archeology, art and culture (open: Mon-Sat 9am-5pm; tel: (01463) 237114). **Balnain House** on Huntly Street is a five-bay Georgian house that has been adapted to give visitors a taste of genteel life in the Highlands. Audiovisual displays also describe the history of the unique musical tradition of the area and visitors can try their skill at the bagpipes and the clarsach, a type of harp (open: summer, daily 10am-5pm; winter, Tues-Sat 10am-5pm; tel: (01463) 715757). Shopping is very good in Inverness, since it serves most of the more remote Highland areas. For an excellent view of the city and its magnificent setting – including the river, the Moray Firth and various bridges – go west of the river to the wooded hill known as Tomnahurich, "the hill of the fairies", with its cemetery.

Six miles (10 km) to the southeast of Inverness is **Culloden Battlefield** on Culloden Moor. Bonnie Prince Charlie and the Jacobite army were crushed here on 16 April 1746. **Leanach Cottage**, around which the battle took place, still stands. A path from the visitor centre leads to the **Field of the English** where they are buried. Other areas of particular interest at Culloden are the **Graves of the Clans**, a communal burial place where a simple stone bears the name of each clan, and where there is a memorial cairn erected in 1881, the Well of the Dean and a huge stone from which Cumberland viewed the 40-minute battle which killed 1,300 of the Prince's army and 300 of his own. A visit to the battlefield should begin at the visitor centre (open: Nov-Dec 10am-4pm; Feb-Oct 9am-6pm; Jan closed; tel: (01463) 790607). Near the Cumberland Stone is the impressive Clava Cairns, three cairns surrounded by stone circles and a small ring of boulders. Built in late Neolithic times (4,400-2,000 BC), each cairn and stone formed a single design.

The small town of Beauly 12 miles (19 km) west of Inverness is a delightful little place that takes it name from a 13th-century priory. The red sandstone priory now has no roof but retains its elegant west front, unusual trefoil windows in the nave and beautiful windows in the chancel (to enter, apply to key-keeper). The Black Isle across the Kessock Bridge from Inverness is a magnificent green peninsula formed by the Beauly, Moray and Cromarty Firths. It is a peaceful place with many large farms. Chanonry Point – with its magnificent lighthouse – looks over towards Fort George. A monument commemorates the Brahan Seer, who was put to death for prophesying (many Highlanders have believed the Brahan Seer's prophecies because so many of

Glen Affric

them have appeared to come true).Northwest of Inverness is **Strathpeffer**, a Victorian spa town with monkey-puzzles and other exotic conifers. Most of its spas are closed but a small pump room and spa pavilion survive. The railway station with a glazed canopy and ornate cast-iron columns is now the charming **Highland Museum of Childhood** (open: mid-Mar-Oct 10am-5pm; July-Aug also 7pm-9pm; Nov-Feb by appointment; tel: (01997) 421031), with displays on everything related to children, from birth to toys and games.

Fort George, 11 miles (18 km) northeast of Inverness, is Europe's finest surviving example of 18th-century military architecture. Built between 1748 and 1769 for George II's troops after the Jacobite rebellion, it stands on a peninsula jutting out into the Moray Firth. Although it is still an army barracks, visits can be made to the guardroom, historic barracks rooms, the grand magazine and the chapel. The governor's house and the fort major's house are now a museum for the Queen's Own Highlander's Regiment. (Open: April-Sept, daily 9.30-6.45; Oct, Mon-Sat; Mar, Mon-Sat 9am-4.30pm, Sun 2pm-4.30pm; tel: (01664) 462777.)

Kilmartin and Dunadd 30 miles (48 km) southwest of Inveraray. Kilmartin is a small village whose churchyard is dotted with finely carved medieval grave stones and crosses from the **Loch Awe school of carving**, dating from the 14th and 15th centuries. Inside the church, cross number three is famous for its faces of Christ (open: April-Sept 9.30am-6pm, otherwise apply at house). A number of ancient monuments are located between Kilmartin and Dunadd. Of special interest are the 3,000-year-old cairns at **Nether Largie**, the **Templewood Stone Circles**, and five cairns in a straight line named **Ri Cruin Cairn**. **Dunadd Fort** was

a stronghold or capital of the first kingdom of the Scots, Dalriada, when they arrived from Ireland, it lasted between 498 and 843. The hilltop fort contains carvings of a boar, an outline of a footprint and a hollowed-out basin, along with some inscriptions written in the Ogham script (believed to have originated in Ireland), which comprises a group of strokes scored at various angles to a baseline. From its hilltop location the fort commands tremendous views toward the Crinan canal.

Kingussie 13 miles (21 km) southwest of Aviemore. Kingussie is a typical Speyside tourist town. Occupying what was once an 18th-century shooting lodge, the **Highland Folk Museum** displays 18th-century furniture, clothing and tools. Outside are recreations of some Highland buildings, and local weavers and other artisans show Highland crafts (open: April-Oct, Mon-Sat 10am-6pm, Sun 2pm-6pm; Nov-Mar, Mon-Fri 10am-3pm; tel: (01540) 661307). Nearby is Ruthven Barracks, the ruins of one of the four English infantry barracks built to keep law and order after the 1715 Jacobite rising. The barracks were burned in the 1746 Jacobite rebellion. On the road beyond the barracks is Insh Marshes, Scotland's largest inland marsh, which is a reserve of the Royal Society for the Protection of Birds. In the winter 10 per cent of the United Kingdom's whooper swans are found here; in the summer, sandpipers mass and all year long huge numbers of hen harriers and buzzards are in residence. North of Kingussie are the Monadhliath Mountains, which separate Speyside from the Great Glen. These mountains have good hill walking and are less crowded than the Cairngorms.

Kintyre Peninsula South of Lochgilphead. Some 60 miles (97 km) long, Kintyre is the longest peninsula in Scotland and has beautiful scenery, quaint villages and miles of sandy

Mull of Kintyre

© Paul Tomkins / STB/ The Still Moving Picture Company

beaches. Kintyre was part of the first Kingdom of the Scots and its largest town is Campbeltown on the southeastern coast. The tip of the peninsula is only 12 miles (19 km) from Ireland. Tarbert is on the narrow stretch of land that forms the northern boundary of the peninsula and has been called the world's prettiest fishing port. Tarbert means *isthmus*, or "portage place", in Gaelic and refers to places where the boats could be pulled across the land on rollers. Robert the Bruce dragged his boats across here to attack Castle Sween in 1315. The ruins of 13th-century **Bruce Castle** are above the village on the south side of the bay. At Skipness, 10 miles (16 km) south of Tarbert, are the remains of **Skipness Castle and Chapel**, which include a 5-feet (1.5 m) tower. Built in the 13th century, its function was to control shipping on Loch Fyne. Panoramic views are available of the Sounds of Kibrannan and Bute from the castle. Carradale on the eastern shore of Kintyre is a small town with a popular beach. The harbour is still an active fishing port. Also on the eastern shore is **Saddell Abbey**, a 12th-century Cistercian foundation established by Reginald, the son of Somerled, Lord

of the Isles. It is believed that Reginald is buried at the castle. The courtyard has many 14th-16th-century grave slabs depicting an unusual selection of subjects like warriors, galleys and interlacing. The walls of the original building still remain.

Campbeltown, the peninsula's largest town, is known as the "wee toon". Fishing is the main industry in the area but the malt whisky industry is not far behind. On the quayside in the middle of town is the Campbeltown Cross, which dates from the 14th century and is the finest ancient carving in the peninsula. At low tide it is possible to walk to Davaar Island in Campbeltown Loch, otherwise boat trips are available. The island has an 1887 crucifixion cave painting, rock gardens and a lighthouse. At the southern tip of the peninsula stands the village of Southend, across from the Mull of Kintyre. It has sandy beaches, golf courses and views of the Island of Sanda (with its unique lighthouse) and of Ireland. Dunaverty Rock, once a MacDonald stronghold, was the scene in 1647 of a great massacre, when 300 MacDonalds lost their lives. A narrow winding road leads to a high

mountain plateau called "the gap", from which it is possible to walk to the Mull of Kintyre lighthouse: the views are spectacular and well worth the trip. Near the road to the lighthouse are Columba's steps, two footprint-shaped impressions on a flat-topped rock near an ancient chapel site. On the west side of the peninsula Machrihanish is known for its 18-hole golf course, but also has a beautiful sandy beach. Further north on the west side are the ferry ports of Tayinloan (with a ferry to Gigha Island) and Kennacraig (with boats to Islay and Jura).

Knapdale 6 miles (10 km) southwest of Lochgilphead. This area stretches from the Crinan Canal to the northern end of the Kintyre peninsula. The landscape is one of hills, forest and water surrounded by two sea lochs, Sween and Caolisport. Crinan Canal, a nine-mile (14 km) canal built to avoid sailing around the Mull of Kintyre, was built in 1817. Using 15 lochs it links the Sound of Jura with Loch Fyne. Once used by the large herring fleet, most of its traffic now consists of private yachts. A great place to watch the boats is from the coffee shop in the Crinan Hotel. On the east shore of Loch Sween stands the ruin of Somerled's foursquare castle, built in the 12th century. It is thought to be one of the mainland's first castles. The ruined chapel at Kilmory Knap has a good collection of West Highland sculptured monuments. **Macmillan's Cross** commemorates Alasdair Macmillan, a powerful member of the clan which ruled Knapdale; it depicts the figure of Christ crucified accompanied by John and Mary, with interlacing and a claymore on one side. On the other side is a hunting scene.

Loch Awe 18 miles (29 km) east of Oban. Over 25 miles (40 km) in length, Loch Awe is Scotland's longest loch. Today the loch is used to generate hydroelectric power and the **Cruachan Dam Visitor Centre** tells how 400 MW of electricity is provided by running water from the dam on Ben Cruachan down into the loch, from where it is pumped back at off-peak times. A short minibus ride takes visitors to see the turbines (open: Easter-Oct 9am-4.30pm, minibus tour by appointment; tel: (018662) 822673). **Kilchurn Castle**, a 15th-century stronghold built by Sir Colin Campbell, is just a short walk across the flats of Loch Awe. The castle can only be viewed from the outside and is in a beautiful location. The road behind Dalmally affords one of the best views in the Highlands.

West of the castle are the **Ardanaiseig Gardens** (well worth a visit) as well as the Bonawe Furnace, a 1753 charcoal furnace used for smelting iron. The furnace with its water wheel and the vast charcoal and iron ore sheds are still visible on the site. (Open: April-Sept 9.30am-6.30pm, Sun 2pm-6.30pm; tel: (01886) 822432.)

Loch Ness
10 miles (16 km) southwest of Inverness. Loch Ness is 24 miles (39 km) long, a mile (1.6 km) wide and 755 feet (230 m) deep, and has the largest volume of water of any of the Scottish lochs. It is said never to freeze. The Loch Ness monster ("Nessie") story began in 565 when the first alleged sighting was made public. Since then the story has refused to go away and many alleged sightings have been reported. All types of high-tech underwater contraptions have been used to search for the monster and a university from the United States maintains a year-round watch with sonar-triggered cameras and strobe lights suspended from a raft at Urquhart Bay. The road on the west bank goes through Drumnadrochit with its " **Official Loch Ness Monster Visitor Centre**". The exhibition has a scale replica of Nessie, with the story presented in audio and video. It is the most visited place in the Highlands of Scotland, with more than 200,000 people annually (open: Mar-June, Sept-Oct 9.30am-5.30pm; July-Aug 9am-7.30pm; Nov-Feb 10am-3pm; tel: (01456) 450573). Nearby **Urquhart Castle** was once one of the largest castles in Scotland and belonged to the Clan Grant. The Grants blew the castle up during the Jacobite rebellion in 1692 to keep it from falling into the wrong hands. It has magnificent views but is very busy with lots of bus tours. The east side of the loch is more peaceful and has superb views and hill walking along the old military road completed by General Wade in 1726.

Mallaig
46 miles (74 km) west of Fort William. The views of Eigg, Muck and Rum over the Sound of Arisaig are magnificent from this little village at the end of the road sheltered by two large headlands. The harbour is busy and the last ferry to the Isle of Skye, a 30-minute trip from Mallaig to Armadale, leaves from here. (There are up to five ferries daily, which from November to Easter are for pedestrians only; tel: (01457) 650100.)

Nairn
16 miles (26 km) east of Inverness. Located on the sheltered Moray Firth, Nairn has been a popular seaside resort ever since 1855, when the Inverness-Nairn railway was completed. The former fishing town on the harbour is separated from the main shopping area by the road. A small local museum tells

how Thomas Telford built the harbour in the 1820s and how a hundred years later the herring fishing declined (open: June-Sept, Mon-Sat 2.30pm-4.30pm, also Wed, Fri 6.30pm-8.30pm;. tel: (01667) 453331). **Cawdor Castl**e is southwest of Nairn. Its tower dates originally from 1370 and was added to in the 15th, 16th and 17th centuries. The Thanes of Cawdor built the castle and have lived in it ever since, except for the century after the Jacobite uprising, when the castle stood empty. Its interior contains a large collection of historic artefacts accumulated by the family over the years. Outside the castle walls are sheltered gardens and peaceful walks. The castle has a famous literary association: in Shakespeare's Macbeth, Macbeth becomes Thane of Cawdor as prophesied by the witches. (Open: May-mid Oct 10am-5pm; tel: (01664) 404615.)

Newtonmore
16 miles (26 km) southwest of Aviemore. **The Clan Macpherson Museum** in Newtonmore displays many artefacts relating to the 1745 rebellion, as well as older exhibits connected with the clan (open: April-Oct, Mon-Sat 10am-5pm, Sun 2pm-5pm; tel: (01540) 673332). General Wade, the British officer charged with improving Scotland's roads in the 17th century, completed two significant projects in the area. At Garvamore a dual-arched b ridge was built in 1735 and on the western shore of Loch Laggan the road hugs the loch as it follows the route Wade chose in order to avoid the

Corrieyairack Pass. The mountain-covered heartland to the north and the silvery pine-clad hills of the Grey Corries to the south offer superb views from the road. There is a track from the road to the Pass but it is deteriorating due to excessive use.

Oban
85 miles (137 km) northwest of Glasgow. One of the most popular coastal resorts, Oban's harbour is sheltered by the island of Kerrera and was a busy fishing port in the 1800s. From Pulpit Hill there are magnificent views across the Firth of Lorn and Sound of Mull. McCaig's Folly stands on Pulpit Hill. John Stuart McCaig built it as a memorial to his family and to create jobs for the locals. Shaped like the Colosseum of Rome, its walls are 2 feet (.6 m) thick and 37-70 feet (11-21 m) high. It is floodlit at night and is in a spectacular position overlooking the town and the harbour. **Dunollie Castle**, the 13th-century home of the lords of Lorn, who once owned a third of Scotland, lies one mile (1.6 km) north, at the end of the bay. **Gylen Castle**, home to the MacDougalls since 1578, stands on the island of Kerrera. **Dunstaffnage Castle** is only three miles (5 km) north of Oban and was also an old MacDougall stronghold. The present castle was built around 1263 and once controlled all the sea routes to Argyll. The views from the castle towards Ben Cruachan are magnificent (open: April-Sept 9.30am-6.30pm; tel: (01631) 562465).

© David Robertson / The Still Moving Picture Company

Argyll and Bute, Oban

THE NORTHERN HIGHLANDS

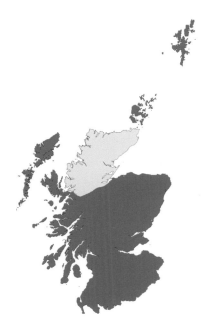

The northern region of Sutherland and Caithness is sparsely populated and less visited by tourists due to its distance from Scotland's main cities and other more frequented areas. Many of the region's roads are winding and hilly, but it is easy to travel to the northern Highlands, and visitors are rewarded with some of Scotland's most beautiful scenery. Caithness consists of green farmland rolling down to the sea, while Sutherland is predominantly wet moorland and rocky mountains.

Achiltibuie and the Summer Isles
25 miles (40 km) northwest of Ullapool. Magnificent views of Stac Polly and the Summer Isles can be had from the single-track road through Coigach beyond Ullapool to Achiltibuie. The Summer Isles is a group of beautiful uninhabited islands, the largest of which is Tanera More. There is abundant bird life here, and boat trips to the Isles are available in the summer months (contact the Tourist Information Office; tel: (01854) 612135).

Applecross
24 miles (29 km) southwest of Shieldaig. Until a few years ago access to remote Applecross was mainly by sea, but has been made easier since the construction of a road from Shieldaig. The views across the water to Raasay, Rona and Skye are splendid. St Maelrubha established a monastery in the area in 673, but all that remains are some portions of old crosses.

Bettyhill
43 miles (69 km) west of Thurso. Refugees from the Clearances built this small village on the east side of Torrisdale Bay. Bettyhill is named after Elizabeth, Countess of Sutherland, whose husband removed more than 1,000 people from the area. In Farr Church is the **Strathnaver Museum**, which tells the story of the Clearances (open: April-Oct, Mon-Sat 10am-1pm, 2pm-5pm; tel: (01641) 521330). West of Bettyhill there are some spectacular views of the great sea loch Kyle of Tongue, with the Rabbit Islands in its centre. To the south is a breathtaking view of Ben Loyal.

Cromarty
23 miles (37 km) north of Inverness. On the tip of the Black Isle, a pleasant mix of woods and farmland, Cromarty's gentle character is made up of cottages, Georgian mansions and townhouses. The 1773 **Cromarty Courthouse** with its octagonal clock tower and five-bay structure is now a visitor centre telling the story of the area and the town (open: April-Oct 10am-5pm; tel: (01381) 600418). Its self-guided walking tour of the town is excellent. Cromarty's most famous son is **Hugh Miller**; a mason turned writer and geologist. His thatched-cottage birthplace dates from 1711 and is now a museum with geological exhibits and information on his career (open: May-Sept, Mon-Sat 10am-1pm, 2pm-5.30pm, Sun 2pm-5.30pm; tel: (01381) 600245). A beautiful lighthouse stands on Cromarty Point and offers views across the Cromarty Firth to the Hills of Nigg.

Dingwall
15 miles (24 km) northwest of Inverness. One of the major livestock markets for the Highlands, Dingwall was an important settlement in the 11th century. A short distance from the town at Evanton the River Glass runs through the mountains and has cut Black Rock Gorge, which is as much as 98 feet (30 m) deep and 13 feet (4 m) wide; the gorge is so named because of the black rocks that form its walls. The Brahan Estate near Dingwall is associated with the Brahan Seer – a famous Highland prophet – believed to have been Coinneach Odhar ("Brown Kenneth"), who came to work at the estate in the 17th century. Despite his ability to see into the future he was not able to save himself from being burned in a tar barrel by Lady Seaforth. Some have claimed that many of his unsettling prophecies have come to pass, especially in the form of the Clearances.

Dornoch
63 miles (101 km) northwest of Inverness. The ancient cathedral city of Dornoch is Sutherland's major town. Known as the St Andrews of the north, it is famous for its popular golf club, first established in 1616 (tel: (01862) 810219). The site of the 13th-century cathedral in the town centre was occupied by Celts from the 6th century. The cathedral has some fine examples of stone carving, but its modern stained-glass windows are what attract most visitors. The hotel across the street from the cathedral occupies the 16th-century bishop's palace, which retains its original tower. Between Dornoch and Golspie, and standing high on Beinn a Bhragaidh, is a large statue of the first Duke of Sutherland, one of those lords most committed to the Clearances.

Dounreay
8 miles (13 km) west of Thurso. For four decades Sandside Bay has been home to the world's first fast breeder nuclear reactor and fuel reprocessing centre. The plant has been extremely controversial and is in the process of being decommissioned. The visitor centre tells the story (open: June-Sept 10am-4pm).

Dunnet
8 miles (13 km) east of Thurso. Dunnet Head is the most northerly point in Scotland. From Dunnet Head lighthouse there are excellent views of the Orkneys and Stroma. On the northern edge of the village of Dunnet there is the former home of **Mary-Ann Calder**. A typical crofting cottage with outbuildings, it illustrates what farm life in the area was like (open: Tues-Sun 2pm-4.30pm; tel: (01593) 721325).

Durness
55 miles (88 km) north of Lochinver. Once a crofting community, Durness has become a tourist-oriented town at the northwest corner of Scotland. The town is built on limestone and the sea has cut caverns into the rock, the most famous of which is **Smoo Cave**. Boat rides to the cave (tel: (01971) 511259) show visitors where the Allt Smoo plunges down a sinkhole to reappear at the mouth of the outer cave (only the outer cave is open to the public). A mile west of town is a former radar station that has been turned into a workshop craft centre, with ceramics, jewellery, weaving, bookbinding and leatherwork on display and for purchase (open: April-Sept 10am-6pm; tel: (01971) 511277). A journey to Cape Wrath lighthouse begins with a ferry across the Kyle of Durness, followed by a 40-minute minibus ride through 11 miles (18 km) of bleak and eerie moorland owned by the Ministry of Defence. The highest mainland cliffs in Scotland lie between Kyle and Cape Wrath; the best known is Cleit Dubh, which reaches 800 feet (244 m) in height. This exposed cliff provides outstanding views of churning seas and the superb coastline, plus lots of puffins during the summer.

Fortrose
30 miles (48 km) north of Inverness. The principal town of the Black Isle, Fortrose's main attraction is its 13th-century cathedral dedicated to St Peter and St Boniface. The ruin is beautifully set between green lawns and red sandstone houses. Fine architectural

Coffee with Drambuie

Drambuie is the liqueur of Scotland and has an ancient and honourable pedigree. Fleeing from the English forces, Bonnie Prince Charlie took refuge with the Mackinnons of Strathaird on Skye. As a gift for their hospitality, he gave them the recipe for his own liqueur. It is still made to this day from that secret recipe based upon whisky. Coffee with Drambuie is delicious served at the end of a meal.

1 measure Drambuie
1-2 tsp soft brown sugar
pot of strong coffee
double cream

To make each serving, take a stemmed glass and warm. Add Drambuie, stir in the brown sugar and fill with coffee to just an inch below the rim. Stir until the sugar is fully dissolved then pour on the cream over the back of a teaspoon so that it floats on the surface.

A recipe from *A Little Scottish Cookbook* published by Appletree Press

detail from the 14th century is still preserved in the remains of the building. Adjoining Fortrose is Rosemarkie, inhabited since the Bronze Age and with its own beautiful beach. The area was a centre for Pictish culture and it is believed that St Moluag founded a monastery here in the 6th century. **Groam House Museum** has an excellent Pictish stone with elaborate interlaced designs (open: May-Oct, Mon-Sat 10am-4pm; Nov-April, Sat-Sun 2pm-4pm; tel: (01463) 790607).

Gairloch 114 miles (183 km) northwest of Inverness. Situated at the head of Loch Gairloch, this small fishing port bustles with tourists, for the Torridon Mountains are not far away and there are sandy beaches on the coastline. One of the few golf courses on the northwestern coast of Scotland, the **Gairloch Golf Club** is a nine-hole course (tel: (01445) 712407). The story of life in the area from prehistoric times to the present is told in the **Gairloch Heritage Museum** (open: April-Oct, Mon-Sat 10am-5pm; tel: (01445) 712287). Nature trails and an information centre run by Scottish Natural Heritage are situated southeast of Gairloch on beautiful Loch Maree,

which is 12 miles (19 km) long and 3 miles (5 km) wide. It was on Isle Maree, a tiny island in the Loch, that St Maelrubha lived in his cell in the 7th century. Also in the area are the magnificent two-stage Victoria Falls, named after Queen Victoria who came to see them.

Inverewe Gardens, six miles (10 km) northeast of Gairloch, lies as far north as Labrador in Canada, but the North Atlantic Drift gives the area its temperate climate. Plants bloom later here than elsewhere, and the contrast between the colours of the formal garden and those of the bleak coastland headlands and moor is very striking. The view toward Poolewe with the Torridon Mountains in the background is worth

the trip alone (open: mid-Mar-Oct 9.30am-9pm; Nov-mid-Mar 9.30am-5pm; guided walks April-Sept, Mon-Fri 1pm; tel: (01445) 781200).

Golspie 12 miles (19 km) north of Dornoch. **Dunrobin Castle**, the largest house in the northern Highlands, was built in the 13th century. The castle is the home of the earls and dukes of Sutherland, who once owned vast areas of Scotland (the 3rd Duke of Sutherland was western Europe's largest landowner in 1892). The current countess has an apartment at Dunrobin but many of the 180 rooms are empty. Those open to the public include a furnished dining room, a billiard room and Queen Victoria's room, where she slept in the gilded four-poster

© Ken Paterson / The Still Moving Picture Company

Dunrobin Castle

bed. The summerhouse is now a museum, which contains many relics of the Sutherland history, including trophies and the regimental colours of the 93rd Sutherland Highlanders (open: April, May, Oct, Mon-Sat 10.30am-4.30pm, Sun 1pm-4.30pm; June-Sept, Mon-Sat 10.30am-5.30pm, Sun 12.30pm-5.30pm; tel: (01408) 6633177).

Helmsdale 36 miles (58 km) south of Wick. In the 16th century Helmsdale's harbour held 300 ships as part of an attempt to turn the crofters evicted by the Sutherlands into fishermen. The former tolhouse which guarded the elegant twin-arched bridge over the River Helmsdale is now the **Timespan visitor centre**, with displays, relics and audiovisual presentations of the story of the area from the Stone Age to the 1869 gold rush in the Strath of Kildonan (open: April-June, Sept-Oct, Mon-Sat 9.30am-5pm, Sun 2pm-5pm; July-Aug, Mon-Sat 9.30am-6pm, Sun 2pm-6pm; tel: (01431) 821327). It is still possible to pan for gold on the Strath using equipment available at the craft shop in Helmsdale. The vast **Forsinard Nature Reserve** provides good walking and a visitor centre in Forsinard Station, Scotland's most remote railway stop (open: April-Oct 9am-6pm; tel: (01641) 571225). Some 17 miles (27 km) northeast of Helmsdale is the small village of Dunbeath, whose Heritage Centre focuses on the landscape and how it helped to inspire the work of the famous Scottish writer Neil Gunn (open: Easter-Sept, Mon-Sat 10am-5pm, Sun 11am-6pm; tel: (01593) 731233).

John o' Groats 21 miles (34 km) east of Thurso. Claimed as the most northerly point of mainland Britain, John o' Groats' many visitors invariably have their photographs taken at "The Last House". However, John o' Groats is not the most northerly point in Britain; that honour belongs to Dunnet Head a few miles to the west. John o' Groats' biggest attraction is Duncansby Head and its lighthouse, which has panoramic views toward the Orkney Islands and Stroma Island. A short walk from the lighthouse are the famous pointed Stacks of Duncansby. In the summer puffins can be seen here. Some of the stores in John o' Groats sell Groatie Buckies – small Arctic cowrie shells once used as decoration by the first settlers in Caithness. During the summer a daily passenger ferry sails for 45 minutes across the Pentland Firth to the Orkney Islands. The trip includes a bus tour of the main island (tel: (01955) 611353).

Kintail 45 miles (72 km) west of Invergarry. The Kintail Mountains and Forrest lie north of the A87 going west

Puffins

© David Robertson / The Still Moving Picture Company

towards the Isle of Skye. The National Trust for Scotland cares for most of the area, which includes the beautiful Five Sisters of Kintail (all of which are Munros). The magnificent Fall of Glomach drops 377 feet (115 m) into the remote Glen Elchaig and is only accessible after a taxing hill walk. The best known and definitely the most photographed castle in Scotland is Eilean Donan, on an islet in Loch Duich. Built in 1214 as a defence against the Danes, it lay in ruins for over 200 years but was restored as a **MacRae Clan memorial and museum** in 1932. The museum has many artefacts from the Jacobite wars and a shop sells kilts and woollens (open: April-Oct 10am-5.30pm; tel: (01599) 555202). One of the best-preserved brochs

on the Scottish mainland, Dun Telve, stands at the top of a dead-end road from Glen Shiel to Glenelg. Nearby are the ruins of the Bernera Barracks, originally built around 1722 to control the Jacobite rebellion.

Lochcarron 23 miles (37 km) southwest of Achnasheen. This small village of 200 people on the banks of the loch has no real centre as such, but somewhat surprisingly it does have its own golf course. There are also very good views of the wilderness of the Applecross Hills and the Torridons on the opposite bank of the loch.

Lochinver 38 miles (61 km) north of Ullapool. This busy little fishing village

Loch Torridon

lies in the shadow of Suilven, a "sugarloaf" mountain. Drumbeg Loop to the north has incredible views (plus some heart-stopping curves on a single-track road). Beside Loch Assynt east of town is the 15th-century ruin of a Clan Macleod stronghold, **Ardvreck Castle**. There are some good cliff walks to the west of Stoer Point lighthouses. The Old Man of Stoer is a red sandstone sea stack. At Tarbet a boat is needed to reach the Stack of Handa, a Royal Society for the Protection of Birds nature reserve with thousands of birds nesting in the cliffs. Nearby, Inverpolly National Nature Reserve is known for its wild cats and golden eagles.

Melvich 19 miles (30 km) west of Thurso. This crofting community marks the dividing line between the gentler landscape to the east and the rugged, isolated areas of the Sutherland Mountains. From the war memorial behind the hotel there are splendid views over the large sand bar in Melvich Bay to the Orkney Islands and the Island of Hoy.

Plockton 6 miles (10 km) north of Kyleakin. This almost too-neat-to-be-true village has a main street lined with palm

trees which looks out over the sheltered bay of Loch Carron. Plockton started as a refugee village after the Clearances, but is now a popular tourist destination. Also on the Lochalsh peninsula, Lochalsh Garden has beautiful sheltered walks along the bay. Some of the trees in the garden are over a hundred years old.

Strathy Point 27 miles (43 km) west of Thurso. This lighthouse-dominated peninsula surrounded by dunes and coastal grasslands is home to many rare plants, including the tiny, spring-blooming Scots primrose. There are excellent views of the Orkney Islands and Sandside Bay.

Tain 11 miles (18 km) south of Dornoch. St Duthac's Chapel (built from 1065 to 1256) marks the birthplace of St Duthac, an early missionary to the Picts. The chapel was once the most popular place of pilgrimage for Scottish kings. The 14th-century St Duthus Church also served many pilgrims. **The Tain and District Museum**, a centre for Clan Ross, stands in the grounds of the church and provides an innovative self-guided audio tour that takes visitors through the

town's history, taking in the museum, St Duthus and the pilgrimages (open: April-Oct 10am-6pm; Mar-Nov, Dec 12pm-5.30pm; tel: (01862) 894089).

Torridon Mountains 66 miles (106 km) west of Inverness. Wild and desolate, the Torridon Mountains were for many years very difficult to reach from the centre of Scotland. However, the roads have since been improved to a good single-track in some stretches and the mountains are in sight within an hour from Inverness. The best way to view the Torridons is to leave your car in a car park and walk. A good path leaves the waterfall car park and leads to spectacular views of the northern slopes. The shore path by Diabaig and the route to the headland at Shieldaig are easier to walk and also have good views. Rassal Ash Wood nature reserve provides a glimpse of Scotland at it once must have been before sheep and deer were kept in such large numbers that they destroyed the tree cover. Glen Torridon is located east of Shieldaig and is among the best mountain scenery in Scotland. Liathach ("Grey One"), rising to 3,456 feet (1,053 m) with its

© Doug Corrance / The Still Moving Picture Company

Ullapool 59 miles (95 km) northwest of Inverness. Founded in 1788 on the shores of Loch Broom by the British Fisheries Society to exploit the herring fishing, Ullapool is the ferry port for the boat to the Isle of Lewis. Eleven miles (18 km) south of town on the northern shore of Loch Broom, in a peaceful mountain setting, are the **Falls of Measach**. In a wooded cleft of the mile-long Corrieshalloch Gorge, the **River Droma falls** 150 feet (46 m).there is a bridge over the chasm and a viewing platform. On the edge of Inverpolly Nature Reserve is the Knockan Cliff with exposed geological stratification. A nature trail along the cliff reveals some interesting geology and plant life.

Wick 22 miles (35 km) southwest of Thurso. The town of Wick was one of the first to be developed for fishing the "silver darlings" (herring) and at one time there were 1,000 boats working out of the harbour. The Wick Heritage Centre tells the story of the fishing industry (open: May-Oct, Mon-Sat 10am-5pm; tel: (01955) 605393). Today's flourishing industry is Caithness Glass, based in Wick. Demonstrations of glass blowing are held at its factory (open: Mon-Fri 9am-5pm; tel: (01955) 602286). South of Wick are some impressive megaliths: Grey Cairn and Round Cairn, the latter with a low 20-feet (6 m) long entrance way, through which intrepid visitors have to crawl. The much larger Long Cairn is 195 feet (59 m) long and 33 feet (10 m) wide. Two beehive cairns form part of the complex. North of Wick, overlooking sandy Sinclair's Bay, are the rugged ruins of Girnigoe and Sinclair Castles. Castle Girnigoe has an evil dungeon, still visible. Both castles were the seats of the Sinclair earls of Caithness. Farther south is the Northlands Viking Centre at Auckengill, focused on the

seven tops, overlooks the lower part of the glen. Beinn Eighe, at 3,309 feet (1,008 m), is Scotland's oldest nature reserve. The National Trust for Scotland operates the **Torridon Countryside Centre** at the end of the glen (open: May-Sept, Mon-Sat 10am-5pm, Sun 2pm-5pm; tel: (01445) 791221).

© Doug Corrance/ The Still Moving Picture Company

Shepherd

finds from excavations of local brochs. On display are models of Viking settlements at Freswick, a Viking long ship and some coins (open: June-Sept 10am-4pm; tel: (01955) 603942).

An Invocation

Bless, O Chief of generous Chiefs,
Myself and all that is near to me,
Bless me in all my actions,
Make me safe for ever,
Make me safe for ever.

From every brownie and banshee,
From every sprite and water-wraith,
From every fairy-mouse and grass-mouse,
From every fairy-mouse and grass-mouse.

From every troll among the hills,
From every spirit hard-pressing me,
From every ghoul that haunts the glens,
O, save me till the end of my day,
O, save me till the end of my day.

Taken from *A Little Book of Celtic Verse* published by Appletree Press

© STB/ The Still Moving Picture Company

Summer Isles

NORTHERN ISLANDS

ORKNEY ISLANDS

The Orkney archipelago comprises 67 islands, but the 19,000 people who live in the Orkneys inhabit less than 30 of them. The many Norse-sounding place names point to the influence of the Vikings on the islands. The ancient Orkneyinga Saga tells of the Viking occupation of Orkney. The islands have the greatest concentration of prehistoric relics of anywhere in western Europe. Farming is extensive and many visitors are surprised by the pastoral landscape of green fields in summer and the golden fields of autumn. The islands' cliffs are home to thousands of sea birds and it is common to see seals and otters among the rocks on the shore.

WEST MAINLAND

Stenness contains the Stones of Stenness, the Ring of Brodgar and Maeshowe, as well as parts of Stenness and Harray Lochs. At Houton, the departure point for the ferry to Hoy, King Hakon beached his ship in 1263. Houton's Round Kirk, the remains of Scotland's only circular medieval church, stands next to the Earl's Bu, a Viking drinking hall mentioned in the Orkneyinga Saga. Sandwick lies north of Stromness, embracing Skara Brae, the spectacular beach of the Bay of Skaill and the dramatic cliffs of Row Head and Yesnaby.

Birsay, the northwest corner of the Mainland, is the garden of Orkney, famed for its oats and barley. The Brough of

Birsay, a tidal islet, was a Christian settlement before the Norsemen arrived. Evie lies east of Birsay, facing Eynhallow Sound. The view of the sound from the well-preserved 100 BC Broch of Gurness is breathtaking. At nearby Binscarth, the trees were planted 100 years ago.

EAST MAINLAND

Holm, the parish on the edge of Scapa Flow, is mentioned in the Orkneyinga Saga. At Paplay is **Castle Howe**, thought to be the remains of a large Norse stronghold. The beaches of St Andrews make up the northern half of the east Mainland; **Mill Sands** is a good place to see waders and seals. **Deerness**, the most easterly part of the Mainland, rises to 154 feet (47 m) at Mull Head, where kittiwakes, guillemots and razorbills breed on the cliffs. To the south lies the Brough of Deerness, site of a simple ancient monastery. A short distance away the Gloup forms a dramatic archway over the sea.

Burray and South Ronaldsay

The Churchill Barriers link Burray and South Ronaldsay to the Mainland. South Ronaldsay's most distinctive point of interest is the Italian Chapel below St Marys (see Scapa Flow). South Ronaldsay has many beautiful spots, including the village of Herston, Hoxa Head and the magnificent Sands o' Right, where the tranquillity is disturbed once a year by the horseplay of the August Boys' Ploughing Match. In **Burwick** the passenger ferry leaves for John o' Groats, and here also is the astonishing Tomb of the Eagles, named after the claws found in the 5,000-year-old burial chamber.

Burray's east side has a tranquil sandy beach called the Bu. At Viewforth the Orkney Fossil and Vintage Centre overlooks Echnaloch and Scapa Flow. It has a good display of fossils and relics of the island's past life (open: April-Oct 10am-6pm; tel: (01856) 731255).

Stromness Nearly two hours north by ferry from Scrabster, the town of Stromness is situated on the west coast of Orkney in a sheltered bay protected by a hill from the prevailing westerly winds. Its narrow streets and lanes lend it much character and make it popular with visitors. Hudson Bay skippers came here for provisions and recruits for Canada, and whaling ships stopped here en route to Greenland. **The Pier Arts Centre**, a former merchant's house, holds a permanent collection of 20th-century painting and sculpture (open: Tues-Sat 10.30am-5pm; tel: (01856) 850209).

Stromness Museum is a natural history museum with vivid displays of the islands' maritime heritage, including preserved birds, shells, exhibits on fishing, shipping and whaling and on the Hudson Bay Company (open: May-Sept 10am-5pm; Oct-April, Mon-Sat 10.30am-12.30pm, 1.30pm-5pm; tel: (01856) 873191).

Five miles (8 km) northeast of Stromness is the **Ring of Brogar**. This circle of 37 stones originally comprised 60 stones surrounded by a deep ditch. The stones stand between the Loch of Harray and the Loch of Stenness (open: all times; tel: (01316) 688800). One mile (1.6 km) farther on the A965 from the Ring of Brogar is Maes Howe, a huge burial chamber dating back to 2,500 BC, its workmanship unsurpassed in western Europe. When the Vikings found the chamber it was already 3,500 years old (open: April-Sept, Mon-Sat 9.30am-6.30pm, Sun 2pm-6.30pm; Oct-Mar, closed Thurs pm, Fri). Eight miles (13 km) north of Stromness is the Neolithic village of Skara Brae, with houses with cupboards, stone beds and fireplaces that have survived since 3,000 BC (before the pyramids were built). The site remained concealed in stone until it was uncovered in 1850. Skaill House is a 17th-century mansion situated beside Skara Brae (tel: (01856) 841501). North of Skara Brae on the B9056 is the Marwick Head Nature Reserve, where thousands of birds live in the cliffs. The Kitchener Memorial commemorates the sinking in 1916 of HMS Hampshire, and stands on a cliff top (open: all times; tel: (01856) 791298).

Kirkwall Located on the northern tip of the Kirkwall-Scapa isthmus, where it divides the mainland into east and west, the burgh of Kirkwall is the capital of Orkney. The **Tankerness House Museum,** located in a fine 16th-century mansion house, tells the story of almost 6,000 years of known human habitation of Orkney. The islands have one of the richest concentrations of archeological remains in Europe, to which the displays at Tankerness House Museum provide a vivid introduction (open: Mon-Sat 10.30am-12.30pm, 1.30pm-5pm, Sun 2pm-5pm; tel. (01856) 87319). The remains of the 16th-century bishop's palace also include a round tower added in the 1600s (open: April-Sept, Mon-Sat 9.30am-6pm, Sun 2pm-6pm; tel: (01856) 875461). **Earl Patrick's Palace** was built in 1607 and is the best surviving example of Renaissance architecture in Scotland. Kirkwall's most famous landmark is **St Magnus Cathedral,** built between 1137 and 1200 by Jarl Rognvald and dedicated to his uncle, **St Magnus**. The building is still in use today (open: Mon-Sat 9am-

Facing page: Eshaness, Shetland Islands
© *David Robertson/ The Still Moving Picture Company*

Skara Brae, Orkney Islands © Richard Welsby/ The Still Moving Picture Company

1pm, 2pm-5pm, Sun for services at 2pm, 6pm). The Orkney Wireless Museum tells the more recent story of wartime communications at Scapa Flow during the Second World War (open: April-Sept; tel: (01856) 874272). Highland Park, Scotland's northernmost whisky distillery, is just out of town and a great place to finish a visit to Kirkwall (open: April-Oct, Mon-Fri 10am-5pm; July-Aug, Mon-Fri 10am-5pm, Sat-Sun 12pm-5pm; Nov-Mar, Mon-Fri 10am-2pm).

ISLANDS

Birsay 12 miles (19 km) north of Stromness, 25 miles (40 km) northwest of Kirkwall. **The Brough of Birsay**, the remains of a Romanesque church and a Norse settlement are on an island just off of Birsay, which can only be reached at low tide (open: daily, subject to tides; tel: (01316) 688800). Eight miles (13 km) from Birsay is a 10 feet (3 m) Iron Age tower called the **Gurness Broch** (open: April-Sept 9.30am-6pm; tel: (01316) 68800). Kirbister in Birsay is the last surviving "firehoose", with a central hearth that formed the heart of every home. **The Kirbister and Corrigall Farm Museums** display traditional crafts, such as heather and straw work(open: Mar-Oct; tel: (01856) 873191).

North Ronaldsay Access by Orkney Ferries from Kirkwall (tel: (01856) 872044; fax: (01856) 872921). North Ronaldsay is the most northerly island, low-lying and about 17 miles (27 km) long and 7 miles (11 km) wide, with a

population of just under 100.
Island life in some ways differs from that of the other islands in that old traditions still prevail, such as the communal grazing of sheep on the seashore: the sheep live on seaweed and are kept off the island's agricultural land by a 13-mile (21-km) dry-stone sheep dyke.

Papa Westray Access by Orkney Ferries from Kirkwall (tel: (01856) 872044; fax: (01856) 872921). Papa Westray is just over 4 miles (6 km) long and 1 mile (1.6 km) wide. There are nearly 50 archeological sites on the island, an astonishing testimony to 5,500 years of habitation. Howar, a farmstead by the west shore, was built before the time of the pyramids and is the oldest standing house in Europe. St Boniface Kirk is one of the oldest churches in the north of Scotland. Pictish brochs have been identified at several sites across the island, notably at Munkerhouse.Westray Island Access by Orkney Ferries from Kirkwall (tel: (01856) 872044; fax: (01856) 872921). Westray's attractions include two medieval churches, St Mary's and the well-preserved Crosskirk Church at Tuquoy. At the point of Cott there is a long stalled cairn dating from about 3,000 BC. Noltland Castle, built in the 16th century by Gilbert Balfour – who held high office under Mary Queen of Scots – is a fine example of a Scottish fortified Z-plan house. Noup Head cliffs provide excellent birdwatching; huge numbers of nesting seabirds can be seen here between April and July.

Sanday Island Access by Orkney Ferries from Kirkwall (tel: (01856) 872044;

fax: (01856) 872921). Sanday is an attractive island with white sandy beaches. Around 4,000 BC, farmers were settled here, attracted by the light sandy soils which were easy to cultivate. Great stone tombs were erected, that at Quoyness among the finest. Hundreds of prehistoric mounds at Tofts Ness provide one of the most important funerary landscapes in Britain.

Eday Island Access by Orkney Ferries from Kirkwall (tel: (01856) 872044; fax: (01856) 872921). Situated centrally among the North Isles of Orkney, 14 miles (22 km) northeast of Kirkwall, Eday is an isthmus isle, eight miles (13 km) long and "pinched" in the middle. The quality of Eday red sandstone has long been recognized; much of the stone used to build St Magnus Cathedral and Earl Patrick's Palace in Kirkwall was quarried on Eday. The first settlers arrived in Eday some 5,000 years ago and a reminder of their presence is the mysterious standing stone of Setter, often compared to a giant's hand and probably the finest stone of its type in Orkney. There are also several burnt mounds dating from the Bronze Age which were used for cooking.

Stronsay Island Access by Orkney Ferries from Kirkwall (tel: (01856) 872044; fax: (01856) 872921). Stronsay's gentle green landscape has some of the best farms in Orkney. Hillock of Baywest is a long mound containing a stalled cairn burial chamber built around 3,000 BC. In the north of the island is a mound that contains a broch tower and the ruins of an Iron Age village. There are also other standing stones and several Bronze Age house remains. The island's fine lochs and marshes support a variety of ducks and waders.

Rousay Island

Rousay Island Access by Orkney Ferries from Kirkwall (tel: (01856) 872044; fax: (01856) 872921). Rousay, a hilly and fertile island, contains some of the richest and best-preserved monuments in the north of Scotland. There are four well-preserved prehistoric burial cairns. The **Taversoe Tuick** is an unusual two-storied cairn with two separate entrances and a "mini tomb" at one entrance. **Blackhammar** is a stalled cairn, which contained only two burials.

The **Knowe of Yarso**, another stalled cairn, contained the remains of 21 people. **Midhowe Cairn** is the largest and longest cairn in Orkney. The circular Midhowe Broch overlooks Eynhallow Sound and has some great views. Many species of birds can be seen at the Trumland RSPB reserve, as well as on the cliffs on the island's west coast. Offshore from Rousay is Egilsay, a small island dominated by **St Magnus Church**, which is one of only two distinctive round-towered churches built by the Vikings. Wyre is the site of **Cubbie Roo's Castle**, one of the oldest and best-preserved castles in Scotland, built by Kolbein Hruga around 1150.

Shapinsay Island

Shapinsay Island Access by Orkney Ferries from Kirkwall (tel: (01856) 872044; fax: (01856) 872921). Agriculture is an important industry in Shapinsay. There are several broch sites situated at Howe, Ness of Ork and Steiro. **Balfour Castle** is an intriguing and elegant building which started as "Cliffdale" in 1674 but was burned by the Hanoverians in 1746. The new house built by John Balfour has remained unchanged since 1796. There are special tours of the castle and gardens, and visitors can enjoy a farmhouse tea in the servants' hall. It is possible to book accommodation in the castle (tel: (01856) 711282).

Hoy, Graemsay, and Flotta

Access by ferry from Houton, Orphir to Lyness in Hoy, calling at Flotta (tel: (01856) 811397) A pedestrian-only ferry sails from Stromness pier to Moaness, North Hoy, calling at Graemsay (tel: (01856) 872044). Hoy, the second largest island in the Orkney chain, contains one of Orkney's most famous landmarks, the **Old Man of Hoy**, a sea-stack standing 450 feet (137 m) on a lava flow in the sea.

In the beautiful valley of Rackwick lies the only prehistoric rock-cut chambered tomb in Britain. Known as the **Dwarfie Stane**, it is an isolated block of red sandstone, some 28 feet (2.5 m) long, which dates from about 3,000 BC.

The tomb consists of a passage and two cells. **The Lyness Naval Base and Interpretation Centre** in one of the oil storage facilities left over from the Second World War tells the story of Lyness during both world wars and contains many interesting displays. **Melsetter House and Rysa House**, designed by William Lethaby for the Middlemore family, have some of the oldest and finest gardens in Orkney. The RSPB's North Hoy Nature Reserve is a haven for a large variety of birds, including Red Grouse. A beautiful Stevenson-designed lighthouse, Cantick Head, is a good place to begin a walk on the shoreline and to examine the various wild flowers.

Graemsay is a small island between Hoy and Stromness with two lighthouses built in 1840, Hoy High and Hoy Low. Flotta, meaning "flat island", was used by the navy in both world wars. Scapa Flow Visitor Centre tells the story of the Royal Navy's northern base and its role in the wars (open: May-Sept, Mon-Fri 9am-4pm, Sat 9am-3.30pm, Sun 9am-6pm; Oct-April, Mon-Fri 9am-4pm; tel: (01856) 791300). Flotta has one of the most spectacular 360-degree panoramas in the United Kingdom, from the sweep of the Hills of Hoy, the great expanse of Scapa Flow and the hills of Mainland Orkney beyond, to east Burray and South Ronaldsay, completing the circle by looking out across the Pentland Firth to the Scottish mainland. Flotta is thought to be the only place in Orkney where you can see Kirkwall and Stromness at the same time.

Scapa Flow The causeways that leads to the south islands were made for protection, not connection. At the start of the Second World War, HMS Royal Oak was sunk by German submarine U47 with the loss of 833 lives (today, the vessel is an official war grave, lying below Gaitnip cliffs). Winston Churchill ordered more blockships to be sunk and causeways to be constructed. The Churchill Barriers, as they are called, were designed to be impregnable.

At the end of the First World War the German Grand Fleet, consisting of 74 battleships, cruisers and destroyers, was interned in Scapa Flow. Their crews scuttled them all. Though most wrecks have been salvaged, seven large warships and four destroyers remain on the bottom.

The Italian Chapel at Lamb Holm has been called the "Miracle of Camp 60" and you can easily see why. Italian prisoners of war lined the corrugated iron with plasterboard and cast an altar and altar rail in concrete. Domenico Chioccetti painted a Madonna and child and a fresco of a white dove. The whole of the hut was lined, the top painted to look like brick, the bottom to look like marble.

SHETLAND ISLANDS

The northernmost outpost of Scotland – closer to Norway than to Scotland – the Shetlands is a group of 100 islands, only 20 of which are inhabited. Nowhere in the Shetlands is more than 5 miles (8 km) from the sea, due to the "voes" and smaller "geos", the long fingers of sea that reach far inland. The Shetlands have 900 miles of coastline, with crofts and small fields making up most of the treeless landscape. The islands have a wild beauty, solitude and emptiness, whose total population is little more than 27,000. In spite of the islands' location, winters are only slightly colder here than on the mainland because of the North Atlantic Drift (an extension of the Gulf Stream). Summers are cool, when the gloaming is filled with days that never seem to end. Winds can be strong but rainfall is less than that of many areas in mainland Britain.

MAINLAND

Brae 24 miles (39 km) north of Scalloway. Beyond Brae the sea cuts into the landmass of the main Shetland Island so far that at Mavis Grand you can throw a stone from the Atlantic to the North Sea across the narrow strip of land.

Eshaness North end of Mainland Shetland. Many beautiful rock formations and sea sculptures are at Eshaness: Hols a'Scraada, a blowhole up though a cliff; Da Grind o da Navis, a gateway in the cliff from the shore to the sea; and Dore Holm, a formation offshore which looks like a huge stone dinosaur drinking from the sea. The house of John Williamson – who administered the first known inoculations for smallpox – is available for an overnight stay. There is also a beautiful Stevenson-designed lighthouse.

Lerwick 14 hours by ferry from Aberdeen. The port capital Lerwick, with a population of 8,000 (one third of the Shetland population), stands on a hill overlooking a natural harbour sheltered by Bressay Island. The name comes from the Norse leir vik, meaning "mud bay". The older buildings on the waterfront still have "lodberries" built out over the water. Lerwick's main street, with an excellent selection of shops, is flagged and part of it has been made a pedestrian-only area. A good place to begin your visit is the **Shetland Museum**, which covers 5,000 years of archeology, maritime, social and folk life, and contemporary art (open: Mon, Wed, Fri 10am-7pm; Tues Thurs, Sat 10am-5pm; tel: (01595) 695057). **Clickhimin Broch**, a broch within an Iron Age fort, is on the edge of Lerwick surrounded by new buildings (open: April-Sept 9.30am-6pm; Oct-Mar, Mon-Sat 9.30am-4pm; Sun 2pm-4pm; tel: (01595) 693434). The **Böd**, a simple building which housed fishermen and their gear during the season, is represented by the Böd of Gremista Museum, an 18th-century Böd famous as the birthplace of Arthur Anderson, founder of P&0 ferries (open: June-mid-Sept, Wed-Sun 10am-1pm, 2pm-5pm; tel: (01595) 695057). Arts and crafts are featured at the **Islesburgh Exhibition** on King Harald Street, which includes locally produced knitwear, arts and crafts, old photographs of the Shetlands, and performances by local fiddle and dance groups (open: late May-mid-Sept; tel: (01595) 692114). The third week in January, **"Up Helly AA "** (Viking Fire Festival) takes place in Lerwick with thousands attending. The Up Helly AA Exhibition on Sunniva Street has a galley shed with a permanent display of a replica galley, costumes, shields, paintings, photographs and videos (open: mid-May-mid-Sept; tel: (01595) 693434).

Sandwick 14 miles (22 km) north of Lerwick. Sandwick is the departure point for boat trips to the famous Broch of Mouse, the best preserved of all the broch towers. It dates from the Iron Age and is 43 feet (13 m) high; the stairs between the broch's double walls lead upward to six galleries (open: April-Sept, daily 9.30am-6pm; Oct-Mar, Mon-Sat 9.30am-4pm, Sun 2pm-4pm; tel: (01950) 431367).

Scalloway 6 miles (10 km) west of Lerwick. Scalloway is the second largest settlement on the island and older than Lerwick. The town is dominated by **Scalloway Castle**, begun in 1600 by Earl Patrick who coerced the locals to build it for him. He was later executed for his cruelty and the castle was never used again (open: April-Sept, daily 9.30am-6pm; Oct-Mar, Sat 9.30am-4pm, Sun 2pm-4pm; tel: (01595) 693434). **Scalloway Museum** displays maritime exhibits, including information on the Shetland Bus, the name given to the small craft which went between Norway and Shetland during the Second World War ferrying saboteurs and refugees.

Sumburgh 4 miles (6 km) south of Voe. Sumburgh, the most southerly town on the mainland of Shetland, is the location

of **Jarlshof**, a centuries-old Norse site. Many layers of prehistoric civilisation have been uncovered and visitors can walk through the tunnels and walls (open: April-Sept 9.30am-6pm; tel: (01590) 460112). Sumburgh also has Shetland's airport and one of the largest puffin colonies on the island, with puffins by the thousands. In the south of the town is **Old Scatness Broch Excavation,** one of the world's best preserved Iron Age villages, once hidden for centuries (open: July-Aug; tel: (01595) 694688).

Voe 7 miles (11 km) south of Sandwick. The **Shetland Croft House** is a 19th-century thatched house with a broad range of artefacts illustrating the old Shetland way of life (open: May-Sept 10am-1pm, 2pm-5pm; tel: (01950) 431367).

ISLANDS

Bressay Island Ferry from Lerwick (tel: (01806) 566226). Bressay shelters Lerwick and provides it with an excellent harbour. The small island of Noss (accessible by small boat) has spectacular coastal scenery, including cliffs of narrow horizontal bands of sandstone carved into ledges. This is a perfect home for sea birds such as gannets, guillemots, puffins, skuas and terns (open: May-Aug; tel: (01595) 693345). The sea caves at the south end of the island are called the Ord and the Bard. There are also the remains of many brochs, an ancient ruin of a cruciform church and the Bressay Lighthouse.

Fair Isle Ferry from Grutness, Sumburgh (tel: (01595) 760222). Famous for its sweater designs, Fair Isle is a remote and beautiful island. **The George Waterson Memorial Centre and Museum** provides a glimpse into Fair Isle's varied and fascinating history (open: May-mid-Sept; tel: (02595) 760244).

Foula Ferry from Walls and sometimes West Burrafirth (tel: (01595) 753232 , (01426) 986763). The most isolated inhabited island in Scotland and the most westerly of the Shetland group lies 14 miles (23 km) out from mainland Shetland. The strong sense of community in this isolated place is one of its most striking features. There are some interesting stacks and cliffs.

Out Skerries: Housay, Grunary and Bruray Islands
Ferry from Lerwick (tel: (01806) 566226). A close fishing community living in neat, trim and colourful cottages on very little arable land. Only Housay and Grunary are inhabited and a bridge

links the two islands. Grunary has Old Man's Stack and Lamba Stack. A small island, Bound Skerry, has a Stevenson lighthouse.

Papa Stour Ferry from West Burrafirth. A beautiful island with some of the finest sea caves in Scotland. The best example is Kirstan's Hole in the southwest: at the head of narrow burn a columnar stack guards the entrance of the cave, the glistening walls of which are 230 feet (70 m) high.

St Ninian's Isle Western shore of South Mainland. St Ninian's is a tombolo - a spit of sand that connects an island to the mainland. It has an ancient chapel site and was the location of an archeological find of 28 silver objects from the 8th century.

Unst Island Ferry from Gutcher, Yell (tel: (01957) 722259). **The Hermaness Bird Reserve** is one of the most important in Britain. Its gigantic cliffs are filled with kittiwakes, razorbills, guillemots and puffins. Unst is also a good place to see small herds of Shetland ponies.

Muness Castle, Scotland's most northerly stone castle, is a desolate ruin of a building constructed in 1598 with a circular tower (open: April-Sept, daily 9.30am-6pm; Oct-Mar, Mon-Sat 9.30am-4pm, Sun 2pm-4pm; tel: (01595) 693434). **Bordastubble**, Shetland's largest standing stone, is also on Unst. The summit of Saxa Vord has views of Out Stack and Muckle Flugga Lighthouse, some of Shetland's most spectacular cliff scenery and the magnificent cleft of Burra Firth. The Unst Heritage Centre and Boat Haven covers all aspects of island life and history (open: May-Sept; tel: (01595) 693434).

Whalsay Island
Ferry from Laxo (tel: (01806) 566259). Whalsay, often called the Bonny Isle, has green pastures with an attractive rolling landscape. The economy revolves around fishing, which is diverse, because the offshore rocks, reefs and skerries give good protection to lobsters, prawns and white fish. Worth a visit is Bunzie Hoose and Yoxie Biggins, 3,000 BC Neolithic farmhouses.

Yell Island Ferry from mainland (tel: (01957) 722259). Yell Island has brochs, including the important broch at Ness of Burness. **The old Haa** (hall) of Burravoe, the oldest building on the island and formerly a merchant house, has an upstairs museum about the history of the island (open: late April-Sept, Tues-Thurs 10am-4pm, Sun 2pm-5pm; tel: (01957) 22339).

GAZETTEER INDEX

Guide & Key To Atlas

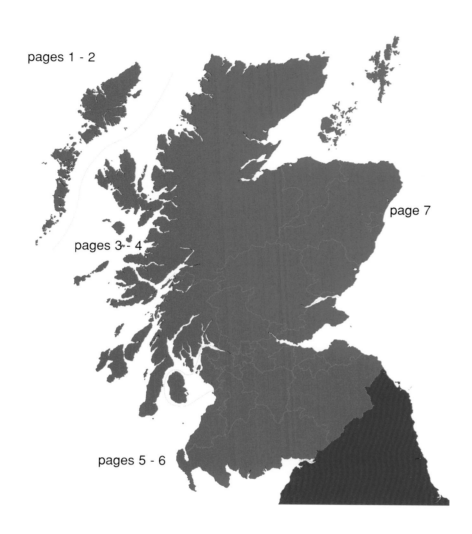

pages 1 - 2
page 7
pages 3 - 4
pages 5 - 6

MAP KEY - SYMBOLS

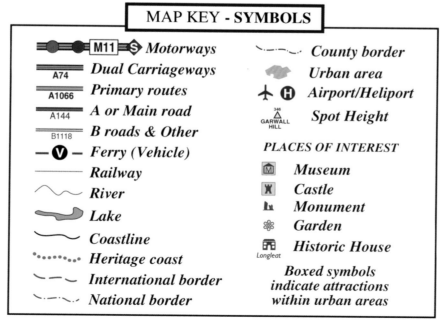

- M11 *Motorways*
- A74 *Dual Carriageways*
- A1066 *Primary routes*
- A144 *A or Main road*
- B1118 *B roads & Other*
- V *Ferry (Vehicle)*
- *Railway*
- *River*
- *Lake*
- *Coastline*
- *Heritage coast*
- *International border*
- *National border*
- *County border*
- *Urban area*
- *Airport/Heliport*
- 346 GARWALL HILL *Spot Height*

PLACES OF INTEREST

- *Museum*
- *Castle*
- *Monument*
- *Garden*
- Longleat *Historic House*

Boxed symbols indicate attractions within urban areas

1 CM = 7.98KM   1 INCH = 12.60 MILES

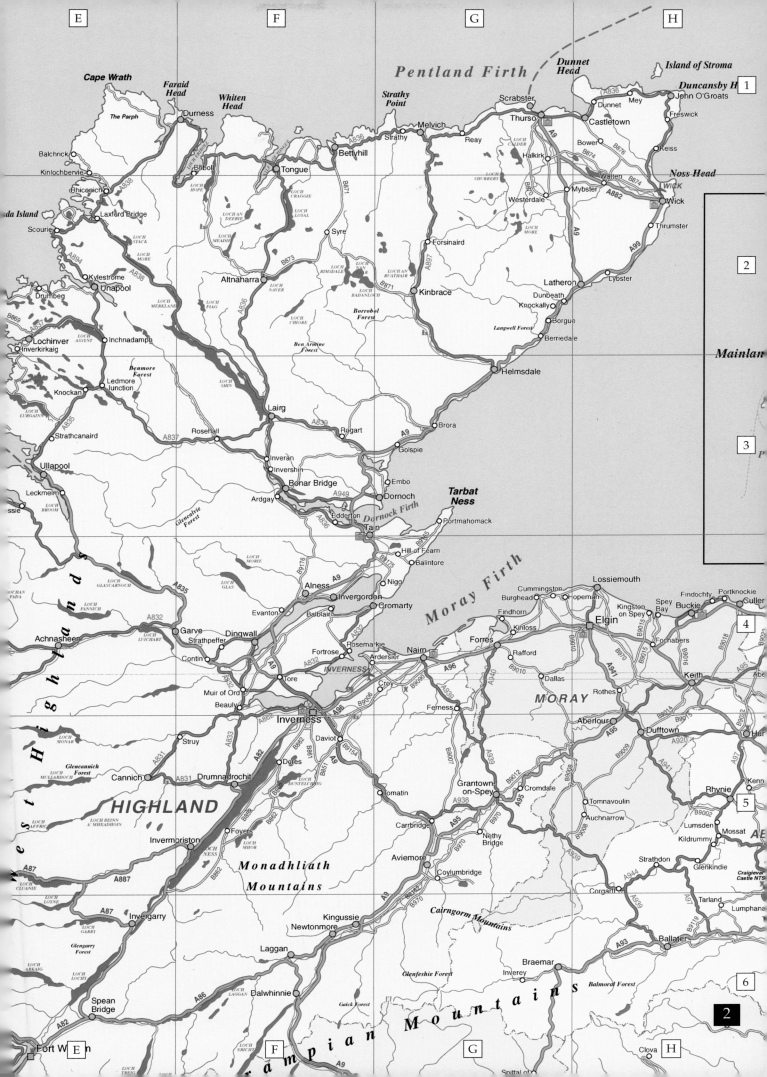

Grid References

A **B** **C** **D**

1

2

3

4

5

6

7

Map Labels

Dunnet Head
Island of Stroma
Duncansby Head
John O'Groats
Mey
Dunnet
Freswick
Castletown
Bower
Keiss
Watten
Noss Head
WICK
Mybster
Wick
Thrumster
Latheron
Lybster
Dunbeath
Knockally
Borgue
erriedale
LOCH MORE

Unst
Fetlar
Yell Sound
Yell
St Magnus Bay
Muckle Row
Whalsay
Papa Stour
Mainland
ABERDEEN
Foula
The Deeps
Lerwick
Bressay
Sumburgh Head
STROMNESS

Papa Westray
North Ronaldsay
LERWICK
Westray
North Sound
Sanday
Rousay
Sanday Sound
Eday
Stronsay
Mainland
Shapinsay
Kirkwall
Scapa Flow
Hoy
Burray
South Ronaldsay
Pentland Firth
Island of Stroma
ABERDEEN

Cummingston
Lossiemouth
Hopeman
Findochty
Portknockie
Spey Bay
Buckie
Cullen
Portsoy
Whitehills
Macduff
Rosehearty
Sandhaven
Fraserburgh
Kingston on Spey
Elgin
Fochabers
Banff
B9031
New Aberdour
Memsie
Inverallochy
St. Combs
MORAY
Keith
Aberchirder
New Byth
New Pitsligo
Strichen
St. Fergus
Dallas
Rothes
Bride of Marnoch
Turriff
Cuminestown
New Deer
Old Deer
Mintlaw
Peterhead
Aberlour
Dufftown
Auchterless
Methlick
Hatton
Boddam
Fyvie
Haddo House NTS
Cruden Bay
Tomnavoulin
Huntly
Tarves
Ellon
Auchnarrow
Kennethmont
Insch
Old Rayne
Oldmeldrum
Pitmedden
Collieston
Rhynie
Pitcaple
Newburgh
Lumsden
Mossat
ABERDEENSHIRE
Inverurie
Kildrummy
Monymusk
Kemnay
Kintore
Balmedie
Strathdon
Alford
Castle Fraser NTS
ABERDEEN
Glenkindie
Craigievar Castle NTS
Dyce
Corgarff
Tarland
Westhill
ABERDEEN CITY
Lumphanan
Garlogie
Aberdeen
Ballater
Torphins
Echt
Peterculter
Banchory
Portlethen
Cookney

BERGEN SUMMER ONLY
TÓRSHAVN SUMMER ONLY
LERWICK STROMNESS

ATLAS INDEX